SHAKESPEAREAN COMEDIES

Sarbani Putatunda

ATLANTIC
PUBLISHERS & DISTRIBUTORS (P) LTD

Published by
ATLANTIC
PUBLISHERS & DISTRIBUTORS (P) LTD
B-2, Vishal Enclave, Opp. Rajouri Garden,
New Delhi-110027
Phones : 25413460, 25429987, 25466842

Sales Office
7/22, Ansari Road, Darya Ganj,
New Delhi-110002
Phones : 23273880, 23275880, 23280451
Fax : 91-11-23285873
web : www.atlanticbooks.com
e-mail : info@atlanticbooks.com

ISBN 81-269-0684-7

Printed in India
at Nice Printing Press, Delhi

PREFACE

Shakespearean comedies have been the source of technical dispute right from their inception. Both his contemporaries and the writers of the Restoration Age found them to be technically unacceptable since they failed to conform to the Aristotelian strictures. Social commitment, they argued, supposed to be mandatory on the part of a comic playwright was simply sidetracked in comedies like *As You Like It, Twelfth Night, A Midsummer Night's Dream* etc. But what these critics failed to appreciate in these writings was their subterranean depth where the bard manifested an undying anxiety for vices he found permeating every social stratum of his age. To them both the early comedies like *The Comedy of Errors, Merry Wives of Windsor* etc., and the middle comedies like *A Midsummer Night's Dream, Twelfth Night* etc., were mere manifestation of the saturnalia, where only the Lord of Misrule thrived and prospered.

In their persistent efforts to stigmatize the bard as an irresponsible artist, they failed to perceive one basic fact; and that is Shakespeare wrote about a society quite different from theirs and it was not right on their part to always assume a continuity of meanings between his world and theirs. Apparent similarities which they tended to surmise as their own were often masks bridging a gulf between the lived experiences of their world and the playwright's world. Why else did they fail to hear the wailing protests of Hermia in the very opening scene of *A Midsummer Night's Dream* when her father prods her to marry a person whom she rejects downright? The existing society clearly indicates that the poet here, instead of opposing the father sides with him, tries to throttle the wishes of the poor girl. The reason for such absurdity is understandable, an Elizabethan girl was considered to be paternal property; hence it was her father's prerogative to bequeath her to anyone 'he' preferred. Consequently, the girl's preference is completely abstracted and when she goes to the duke to seek justice, the duke instead of acting as an impartial judge advises her to obey her father's wishes and in case of disobedience face dire consequences. The palpable disaster which threatens to upset the comic balance right from the start is however, adeptly managed by Shakespeare by introducing the supernatural and the play proceeds to end in a congenial note.

Deification of the bard, however, began with the romantics who saw in him their icon. Keats, for instance, found in him everything that could be aspired in a poet. So was the case with the others who followed. But significantly, it was not before the middle of the twentieth century that English critics took note of the host of sub-texts in each comedy, which clearly demarcated the playwright's personal views from the central plot. These critics for the first time pointed out the playwright's sympathy with the marginalized characters. And it was only then that Hermia's words were acknowledged as an expression of her woe. While considering a multidimensional play like *A Midsummer Night's Dream* they opined that though fundamentally Shakespeare was a romantic, he never for once remained impervious to his social commitments. Behind the array of romanticism the playwright conscientiously sought to air his protest against the rising malaises of the Elizabethan society and thereby fomenting a change in the social order.

The critics of the 70s, however, went a step ahead. With the commencement of four new parameters in literary criticism—

cultural materialism, psychoanalysis, feminism and new historicism, the critics started re-viewing the comedies from a totally different perspective. The poor poet was then re-valued (for the first time), and recognized as a true and responsible citizen of the Elizabethan age. In their analysis of the opening scene of *A Midsummer Night's Dream,* they carefully chose to point out, how instead of mere subversive misrule, Shakespeare here conscientiously tried to usher in a new wave in Elizabethan thinking. This was indeed a novel way of looking at the play. Consequently, it pioneered a fresh attitude for all the other plays as well. Unlike their predecessors who remained satisfied examining it linearly, they felt the subdued yet perpetual strife between the tragic and comic elements in it. This was the device Shakespeare deliberately used to highlight the vices rampant in the Elizabethan society, and thereby acted as a catalyst, to herald in a new world.

Justifiably, with this new approach during the eighties and the nineties criticism took a fresh turn. Critics influenced by the aforementioned parameters, after a time started scanning the works of the playwright from a radically different viewpoint. Contrary to their forerunners, they further refused to contain themselves within the framework of conventional generic division of each play. And in their efforts to read between the lines of each play they inferred, that the constant juggling of the tragic undertones in a predominantly comic plot essentially implied the playwright's desire to do away with any form of compartmentalization. Their argument if viewed in terms of total human experience is understandable. By fragmenting the plays as either comedy or tragedy there is a possibility of generalising them as a presentation of life, which is either unmitigated sorrow or unadulterated joy (This new approach, however, has a parallel in the ancient Sanskrit plays where this generic segregation is absent). If a play is expected to present a facet of human life, then is it rational to believe that this facet will be totally emerged in either deep tragedy devoid of any comic overtures or can a human being be constantly frolicking in a Bacchanalian manner without any tragic impinge? And would a master playwright like Shakespeare being aware of this fallacious approach present such a lopsided view of human life? Hence, is the constant strife between the tragic and the comic in his comedy and vice versa.

However, before proceeding to analyse the plays themselves, a brief survey of the gradual evolution of different theories of comedy criticism is deemed necessary for a better understanding of the texts. Therefore, the endeavour of the first chapter is to present summarily the gradual evolution of different theories of comedy, both from the standpoint of a genre and Shakespeare's conformity to these regulations.

The book, however, will not restrict itself simply on classification of these literary theories, but will scrutinize at length some of the early comedies and a few middle comedies of Shakespeare in their terms. This has been done with an intention to reveal how in each one of them Shakespeare makes a scrupulous effort to reflect his society and its values within the infrastructure of the plots. All the absurd incongruities, comic situations depicted in them are the inherent vices of the Elizabethan society itself. But Shakespeare's humane approach easily removes their unpleasant savour, thus distinguishing him from all his predecessors.

Sarbani Putatunda

ACKNOWLEDGEMENTS

Acknowledging debts is always a difficult task, particularly when one is as fortunate in the number of friends and well-wishers as I am. I am sincerely grateful to Prof. Lawrence Manley, Chairperson of Renaissance Studies, Yale University, who inspired me to take up this herculean task. I convey my thanks to Amartya Sen, my student, who was of great help in completing this book. Above all, I owe a great debt to Prof. Mohit K. Roy, my teacher at Visva Bharati Santiniketan, West Bengal, who went through my work and guided me to get it published through the renowned publishing house, Atlantic Publishers and Distributors (P) Ltd., New Delhi.

It also gives me great pleasure to record my indebtedness to Prof. Stanley Wells of Shakespeare Institute of Birmingham University, and Prof. G. C. Pandey of Allahabad Museum Society, Allahabad for kindly recommending a few critical works, which proved to be of considerable use in my understanding and appreciation of Shakespearean comedy.

The present book is the outcome of the repeated instigations of my husband Mr. Satya Jyoti Putatunda, my sister Ms. Anuradha Mukherjee and my mother Smt. Sagarika Mukherjee. Throughout the tenure of editing, I faced great difficulty in arranging the work and updating it. The process is assuredly not a pleasant one and the resultant temper tantrums, I must confess, was borne out patiently by my ever smiling husband. I am also indebted to him for his constant words of encouragement, which kept me going right from the outset of the present work.

Then there are numerous friends and well wishers whom I would love to name individually but that would take up more than half of the entire content of this book and hence I desist from it. Nonetheless, I do owe them a lot and without their constant support I would never ever attempt to undertake this task.

Sarbani Putatunda

CONTENTS

THE BEGINNING

Look on this form where Humour quaint and sly,
Dimples the cheek, and points the beaming eyes;
Where gay Invention seems to boast its wiles
In amorous hint, and half-triumphant smiles;
While her light masks or covers Satire's strokes,
All hides the conscious blush her wit provokes.*

Before proceeding to Shakespeare a brief survey of a few pre-Shakespearean comedies should not be judged detraction. It will rather emphasize the master playwright's ingenuity in delineating the society of the Elizabethan period in his alleged romantic comedies.

According to the literary history of England, towards the end of fifteenth century the allegorical morality plays were being gradually replaced by a new set of comic and realistic plays called the Interludes. Structurally these plays were not very different from the medieval plays but while the traditional morality plays dealt with personified abstractions of virtues and vices, the new Interludes being rather secular in approach, dealt with the general moral problems of the Elizabethan society. The trend towards secularisation of the morality plays continued well till the sixteenth century when the Interludes in order to enrich themselves further started including scenes and themes which were far removed from the medieval morality.

* R.B. Sheridan, *The Rivals*, ed. Robert Herring, Macmillan, London, 1929, rep. 1952, p. 4

These new type of Interludes then with pronounced comic and realistic elements in them came to be treated historically as those plays which marked the real transition from medieval drama to Tudor secular drama. An exact documentation of this transition is however, a difficult task as many texts have been lost.

However, it is presumed that Henry Medwall's Secular Interludes with their genial satirical elements actually set the trend of a new type of secular plays called the satirical interludes. His *Fulgens and Lucres*[1] considered to be the first English comedy, in spite of dealing with a commonplace medieval discussion and revealing in the process a sophisticated use of the convivial atmosphere of the prevailing Tudor mansions, actually paved the path for later Elizabethan comedies.[2] As records of the Royal household indicate, the play was specifically designed by the playwright to entertain certain foreign ambassadors (from Flanders and Amba of Spain), who visited England on a friendly mission.[3] The Royal household after treating the guests to a sumptuous banquet had arranged to entertain them through this play of Medwall, and hence it was the playwright's great responsibility, to both please and satisfy the sentiments of the visiting dignitaries. And Medwall seemed quite adept at his job. Disguising the English actors "after the guise (gyse) of Spain (Spayne)" he arranged an elaborate dance sequence in the second half of the play (ll 380-92) thereby pleasing the visiting personages. But the playwright's message of love, peace and harmony blended with the contemporary predilections for human integrity in social codes.

The story of the Interlude consisting of a main plot and a comic subplot is divided into two parts. The first part of the play is separated from the second by course of the Royal Banquet and though the setting of the story is ancient Rome, the stage is designed for performance in the great hall of a Tudor mansion in presence of guests seated at tables with drinks at their side and a blazing fire in the great hearth. Hence the beginning of the play is marked by a conscious effort on the part of the playwright (through the welcome speech of the servant A) to extend a warm welcome to these eminent guests of the Royal household. (ll 8-24) At the conclusion of the aforementioned speech his compatriot B enters to inform the audience that a play is to be enacted very soon. "A: Shall here be a play?/ B: Ye for certain (certayne)" (ll 136-7). After a detailed enquiry about the forthcoming performance, servant A suddenly tantalizes B by saying: "... I thought verily (verely) by your apparel (aparell) / That ye had been a player"(ll 148-9). Unexpectedly the flippant attitude of B is replaced by an uncanny seriousness. Curtly reminding his friend that times have changed he remarks, presently it is indeed difficult to ascertain man's social status by his apparels. B here is actually voicing the playwright's view – reminding the audience of the new spirit of humanism which stressed man's inner potential instead of his acquired legacy or any other foppish display of wealth. B's word therefore appears to strike hard at the sensitivity of A who after profuse apology diverts the attention of his friend by asking him to reveal to the audience the central plot of the play.

The play, informs B, is about the marriage of Lucres, the good-looking daughter of Fulgens, a Roman senator. Lucres narrates B is wooed by two suitors in turn, Flaminius, a wise plebian who has risen high in office through rendering invaluable service to the state, and Cornelius, the idle and dissolute patrician. The choice between the two lies on Lucres's because Fulgens unlike the Elizabethan fathers[4] is reluctant to interfere in this matter as he had complete faith in the discretionary powers of his daughter. Medwall's approach here therefore, appears to be quite in tune with the ideologies preached by Renaissance Humanists.[5] Lucres chooses Flaminius the wise plebian while Greene's Angelica in *Orlando Furioso* chooses Orlando. It will not be wrong to presume here that the choice of these two girls is indicative of the two playwrights' own preferences – valuing human virtues over acquired heritage. Moreover, the Italian sources of both the plays may have contributed in their own way to this humanistic attitude. Medwall's preference for Flaminius is echoed by the senators as well (ll 123-25) thus reflecting the playwright's implicit desire to please John Morton, his sponsor, who due to the generosity of Henry VII had risen to the highest office in the English church, from a very modest beginning. Like Flaminius, Morton too had worked hard to reach the top and had drawn the attention of the king who personally liked to promote men like Morton and create a band of loyal courtiers around him. These men, he foresaw would remain dedicated to him till the end unlike the titular nobility. Fulgens' appearance to express summarily his desire to see his daughter married to the best possible suitor is interrupted by Cornelius. Contrary to Cornelius's expectation Fulgens promises him next to nothing when the young man seeks his daughter's hand. Since Lucres had assured the suitor that she would marry according to the advice of her father Cornelius pleads to the old man to forward his case. Fulgens' lukewarm reception clearly disappoints Cornelius and he departs totally dejected. Next Flaminius arrives to woo Lucres and in contrast to Cornelius his words appear rather brusque and unpolished, which Lucres voluntarily overlooks. Unlike Cornelius she does not distance her second suitor and instead willingly admits that his proposal is worth reflecting upon.

In the second part of the play Medwall further elucidates the arguments of the senators in favour of Flaminius thereby justifying the choice of Lucres. The parameters of judging the eligibility of a suitor in the market of marriage is analyzed in details in this part along with a detailed account of Lucres as an individual. The playwright appears to be rather careful in portraying his heroine as a rational and intelligent human being, whose discretionary powers are at par with the wisest men of the country, the senators. This again reflects the growing popularity of the philosophy of the Renaissance Humanists who preached spiritual equality of women. Everybody in the play appears to appreciate Flaminius, his nobility of soul and his dedication to his vocation (ll 775 -79). The play finally ends with an epilogue of Medwall where explains his purpose in *Fulgens and Lucres* – to edify and to amuse the audience. So the social message is unfailingly registered. According to the playwright, man's righteousness and decency is not an acquired legacy; it is an intrinsic aspect of his personality, which ought to be valued. Lucres's decision to marry Flaminius a wise plebian, an act also endorsed by the erudite senators, helps to enhance the playwright's personal regard for the young man.

John Rastell's *The Nature of the Four Elements*, which followed *Fulgens and Lucres,* contains the traditional allegorical figures, but all the characters markedly aim at instructing humanity in contemporary science and geography. With interesting references to recent geographical discoveries this interlude cannot be strictly called a secular one rather its structures appear to the reader as a Humanist morality play. Similarly, John Redford's *Wit and Science* another Humanist morality play makes ample use of allegorical figures without being able to arouse the interest of the reader.

In contrast, John Heywood's *The Four PP*[6] manifests the playwright's deliberate efforts in edifying the vices of contemporary society. In a rather blunt and stark manner Heywood throws aside his orthodox Christian values and criticises with vigour and enthusiasm all manner of clerical failings of his time. He equates all his characters – the Palmer, the Pardoner, the Pothecary and the Pedlar as the beans of the same stock – avaricious, dishonest and lusty, aspiring only to accumulate wealth at the cost of others. (This attitude also has a historical basis, because the Church at that point of time was considered to be the source of all corruption, and it was with deliberation the playwright chose to highlight this malaise.) But the importance of the play lies in its typicality of utterance of the Pre-Renaissance spirit in England. There is absolutely no trace of foreign influence in the play, and its subject matter is English to its core, with firm and effective character sketches.

The Four PP is often considered to be the chief and most comprehensive work of Heywood which finds the playwright throwing aside his orthodox Christian values and rallying with vigour and enthusiasm against the clerical failings of his time. The Interlude introduces the four stock characters of the medieval society – the Palmer, the Pardoner, the Pothecary, and the Pedlar, conniving against one another.

The play begins with a conversation between the Palmer, a professional pilgrim and the Pardoner, a self-proclaimed saviour of lost souls of the world enjoying the Papal shelter. The Palmer is narrating his experiences to the Pardoner while traversing the world and observing "many a fair and far country."[7] The reason cited for such an undertaking was the urge to save his soul from being hurled into the everlasting bonfire after his death. This travelling to lands far off is clearly a reflection of the historical ventures undertaken by the merchant community of the time for trade related reasons. But the words of the Palmer instead of pacifying the Pardoner infuriates him for he feels that such a perusal is fruitless on his part as it is the Pardoner who has full authority to redeem the human souls from the endless cycles of death. "For at your door myself doth dwell,/Who could have saved your soul as well."[8] While they are busy negotiating each others role the Pothecary enters and addresses the Pardoner "And all other whom thou list to procure./If I took an action, then were they blank."[9] As a medical practitioner it is his prerogative to liberate human souls first from the bondage of their mortal bodies and then on receiving his approval it is the Pardoner's right to bestow upon them the church's blessings. But in reality neither the Pardoner nor the Pothecary is really interested in salvaging men, instead, their due rates received on such occasions are of prior importance. So that is what the church dignitaries actually aspired for in practice while frightening the poor citizens out of their wits. Their arguments continue unabated till the arrival of the Pedlar who interrupts them by forwarding his wares. "I could be merry if that I had catched / Some money for part of the ware in my pack."[10] The forthright and mundane approach of the Pedlar expectedly shocks all the other three characters to ground reality. And abandoning all theologies the Pardoner first professes his curiosity regarding feminine apparels sold by the man: "I pray you tell what causeth this,/That women, after their arising, / Be so long in their appareling?"[11] Only too obliging at the expectation of selling his wares the Pedlar readily patronizes but his ulterior motive of business transaction finds no takers. But they will not let him off either cause they need in him a neutral judge who could settle their dispute amicably. After crossing him for a while and being fully convinced of his capacity to give a verdict they appoint him their arbitrator. Confident of his own competence the Pedlar then lays down certain criteria in assessing their ability to help distraught dying souls. The three cannot but agree. The indication is clear – the Pedlar here represents the rising mercantile class who historically ruled the roost of the country's exchequer and hence enjoyed a position of eminence in the society. And this is what the church had reduced itself to – subjugating itself to the powers of money. Added to it their ready admittance also indicates their unconscious confirmation of the fact that like the Pedlar they too are not above petty corruption in their professional lives.

The three then proceed to narrate their tales of achievements intermixed obviously with a lot of deception and lies. But none of their tales impress the Pedlar and the point to be noted here is that none of the three men are ready to acknowledge the superiority of the other and hence finally the verdict is clearly for the Palmer for his tale proves to be the most ingenious one. The importance of the Interlude however lies in its typicality of utterance of the Pre-Renaissance spirit of England. Unlike the Moral Interludes which confined themselves to mere exhortation against the besetting of sins of youth and to the praise of learning, Heywood's *The Four PP* is clearly a satiric attack on the society of the religious men and the laity alike.

Both the aforementioned dramatists unfailingly manifested in their works the growing discontent of the common men against the Tudor regime. Being over zealous in their orthodoxy the Tudor monarchs Henry VII & VIII employed bishops as their counsellors of state whose moral corruption had tremendous evil impact upon the common citizens. The playwrights realizing this prevailing evil of the society and being both learned and committed writers registered their protests in their works. Thus when Cardinal Wolsey of the Tudor age being a mere instrument of the Papal power started treating nobles and gentlemen like dirt beneath his feet, paving the path for anti-clerical revolution, Heywood's *The Four PP* assumed a far reaching social significance. Heywood's other satirical interludes *Mery Play between Johan and Husbond, Tybe his Wyfe and Syre Jhon the Priest*, and *Mery Play between the Pardoner and the Frere, The Curate and neghbour Pratt* manifest similar social themes.

The five-act structured English comedy first came into vogue with Nicholas Udall's *Ralph Roister Doister*[12] written about the middle of the sixteenth century. Based upon Plautus's *Miles Glorious* this play centers round the amorous activities of Sir Ralph Roister Doister – a typical representative of Elizabethan knight-at-arms. Sir Ralph's unsuccessful attempt to seduce an honest woman, while her betrothed is away at sea, forms the principal action of the comedy. But unlike its source, the play is definitely a product of its age because the playwright repeatedly refers to Sir Ralph's scorn aimed at the merchant community. "But is your love, tell me first in any wise/ In the way of marriage or merchandise?" (I ii). The rising conflict between the nobility and the newly risen merchant community possibly prompts Udall to make his hero utter such statements off and on. Moreover, the knight's braggadocio is perhaps a comic reminder to a certain class of the society who thrived on some assumed values.

The play consists of two staple comic figures of the classical plays, the braggart soldier Sir Ralph Roister Doister and a wily parasite Mathew Merrygreek his servant. But both of them are well adapted by the playwright to the conditions of English life and made the chief actors to the "bourgeois drama"[13] with a natural and well constructed plot. Sir Ralph is in love with a rich widow Christian Custance and he confides his feelings to Merrygreek who being aware of his master's weakness encourages him with all false hopes:

> But in your love, tell me first, in any wise
> In the way of marriage or merchandise?
> If it may other wise than lawful be found.
> Yet get none of my help for an hundred pound (I ii).

The word merchandise is significant in two fold ways – one the dramatist's indication of the merchandise of unscrupulous Merrygreek, who is clearly exploiting his master's sentiments for personal gains. Two, the affection of Sir Ralph is also not free from the typical mercenary motives of the contemporary age in the name of marriage, because the widow was reputedly richly endowed by her former husband.

But Custance does not prove to be a lusty young widow, (as portrayed by Sir Ralph) who enjoys playing with the affections of all eligible bachelors around. She is in no way inclined to befriend Sir Ralph as she is betrothed to one Gawain Goodluck an absent merchant. The concept that she is disposed to marry a merchant is viewed scornfully by Sir Ralph – a typical attitude of the decaying aristocracy against the newly risen merchant community. Custance quite in favour of the current trend readily discards the proposal of the knight by refusing to accept his amorous letters. But finally when such letters do reach the lady due to Merrygreek's manipulations she unleashes her wrath upon her servants. Sir Ralph's effort does remind the reader of Falstaff in Shakespeare's *The Merry Wives of Windsor*. Unexpected return of Goodluck at this juncture complicates matters as the gentleman is roused to jealousy. Finally, the lady's effort does help to settle everything amicably and in her way to celebrate her victory she turns the knight into a butt of ridicule: "Nay as for charming me, come hither if thou dare. / I shall clout thee till thou stink, both thee and thy train / And coil thee mine own hands and send thee home again" (IV viii). So the end product like *The Merry Wives* is again the disarmament of another aristocrat which was plausibly a reflection of the current hostility of the common citizens against this class of men.

Gammer Gurton's Needle, possibly written by William Stevenson, closely followed Udall's *Sir Ralph Roister Doister* in its adaptation of the classical framework of act and scene divisions. But unlike Udall's, the plot of this play basically provides a sketch of low countryside and the general out look of the common people.

English comedy before Shakespeare was improvised in a scholarly fashion largely by a group of talented university men, Lyly, Peele, Greene, Lodge and Nashe. Lyly's court comedies manifested to the Elizabethan audience the superficial courtly manners quite common in the Royal court, while in some of the more important plays he wrote, turned to the politics of both England and the world outside. In *Mother Bombie*[14] for instance, Lyly begins with Dromio's reference "to a pick-staff(e) to take a purse on the high way" (II 5). This indirectly provides an evidence of the current social disorder of England after the War of the Roses. Even the attendant of a powerful lord or knight practised the art of stealing other people's purses, and at times even cutting their throats in order to earn a proper livelihood. And as seen in *The Merry Wives of Windsor*, their masters too had share in the booty. Therefore such criminal activities were often patronised by them for self-sustenance.

The beginning of the play is marked by an interesting conversation between Memphio an avaricious old man and his servant Dromio. Memphio is mortified by three things in life – one "paucity of fund," two "a crust wife, and third a fool(e) to my heir(e)" (I i 2-3). This paucity of fund seems to permeate every stratum of Elizabethan society. And Dromio's instantaneous remedy for these malaises opens the doorway to another sort of misrule that prevailed in fifteenth century England:

> Why then sir, there are three medicines for these three maladies;
> A pike-staff(e) to take a purse on the high way,
> A holy (holly) wand to brush cholar from (fro) my mistress tongue (tong)
> And a young wench for my young (yong) master:
> So that as your Worship being wise begot a fool (e), so he being (beeng)
> A fool(e) may tread out a wise man (I i 4-8).

The use of pike-staff to snatch purses on the high-way was a practice rampant in the 15th century England as indicated earlier. And very often it was the aristocrats who ousted by the rising bourgeoisie[15] were perforce converted into high-way robbers. Likewise, the use of holy wand to brush the choler of the shrewish wife is not mere hypothesis but a social reminder to the Elizabethan male audience of the medieval practice of wife beating which received the divine sanction of the church.[16]

The conversation between Stello and Riscio two neighbours of Memphio presents another interesting insight to existing social order regarding marriage: "I like not solemn (solemne) wooing (woing), it is for/ courtiers; let country (countrie) folks (folks) believe (beleeve) other reports as much as their /own opinions"(I ii 36-37). The concept of wooing a lady and marrying her was not appreciated by Elizabethan parents even though Renaissance Humanism preached spiritual equality to all. The parents therefore preferred the wagging tongues of their neighbourly gossips than abstract concept of wooing. Mockery of a school teacher that found its way even in Shakespeare is found in this play (I iii 5) exemplifying the general contempt of the common citizens of the age.

The most interesting character of the play is Mother Bombie who because of her extraordinary intelligence and intellectual prowess is considered to be a witch (II iii 86) by the patriarchy. After all the intelligence of a lady is always a cause of discomfort for the male folks! Yet Lyly treats the lady differently illustrating how such a talented woman employs her capacities to redeem the society in which she lives. Her role of prophesying the future of the citizens definitely saves some of them from forming an incestuous alliance thereby leading the play towards a happy ending.

In *Endimion* and *Sapho and Phao* Lyly discreetly narrates the romantic tale of Queen Elizabeth and Leicester, which was never publicised. In *Endimion,* the playwright condemns the medieval practice of witchcraft, which won the approval of the common people. "There cannot be(e) a thing more monstrous than (then) to/force attention by sorcery" (I iv 6-7). *The Woman in the Moon(e)* is considered to be the playwright's satiric attack on the vices of women in contemporary society. Pandora epitomizes the spirit of evil and hence throughout the play she is found to be a cunning manipulator who succeeds in disturbing the peace of her country. Combining the sense of reality with allegorical plot to emphasize the real malady of contemporary society the playwright managed to make a successful dramatic career.

Peele who followed Lyly's career quite closely chose the countryside of Elizabethan England. In *The Old Wives' Tale*[17] he makes Madge, a blacksmith's wife the central character, who lives in a remote village. His focus of interest is however, mainly on the menial class. Contemporary social beliefs and customs beautifully blend to make the play interesting and also informative. The mercenary attitude of man towards any relationships with women at large is hinted at (l 214), while the corruption of the clergy is satirically treated in lines like "because he would not make them up a full hundred" an innocent man was being denied a decent burial "they would not bury him" (ll 474-75).

Madge as mentioned above is the wife of old Clunch who narrates a pleasant tale to entertain her three guests, Fantastic, Antic and Frolic. The tale which is enacted in the form of a dream sequence is divided into two parts. The three menials while searching for a night's shelter is provided for by Clunch indicating the hospitality of the rustics. But unlike his three guests he has an independent source of income which prevents him from participating in the general frolic of his guests. The guests on the other hand thriving on the munificence of the nobility have ample time to waste and hence the story-telling session. Enchanters and magic galore in the narrative which otherwise appears to be rather disjointed, increasing its entertaining value. But beneath this fun and hilarity the playwright's satiric attack against the vices existing in the church is quite apparent. Like Heywood's *Four PP* even here we find a corpse being denied official burial "because he would not make them up a full hundred" and consequently "they would not bury him" (ll 474-75). so money seems to be prime mover here as well signifying the changing social values with the rise of the bourgeoisie.

Socially realistic plays were however, given an artistic form in the writings of Greene. *The History of Orlando Furioso*[18] is a striking document of many contemporary social practices. The play begins with the ringing of marriage bells of Angelica (I i 129-139) the princess of Africa. As the princess of Africa and the sole heiress of her father's empire she is considered to be the most desired match by young men universally. Her suitors await her approval in the courtroom[19] but she is determined to marry Orlando, a youth – her father's subject, and hence much below her socially. Two conflicting values of the age have been reflected in this play, one mercenary outlook of men regarding the institution of marriage, two, the evolving new social perception of evaluating a person and assessing his worth, according to his individual achievements and qualities instead of his inherited title. But Angelica's preference for Orlando provokes one of the suitors to seek revenge. He feels insulted and his desire to win the hand of the princess forces him to resort to unfair manipulations. Unlike Orlando, Sacripent is motivated purely for mercenary gains – to get access to the throne of Africa by marrying the sole heiress of the Emperor. So the rising concept of romantic love is desecrated by the act of Sacripent and the playwright has no sympathy for him. His ploy employed for the purpose results into Orlando's insanity and the Emperor disowning his daughter. Though a final reconciliation is reached but not before the playwright has set a few things straight. The rising popularity of the middle class, as indicated by Angelica's preference, the existing corruption in the courts, through Sacripent's villainy and finally the Emperor's insensible decision to disown his daughter[20] are perhaps a few things the playwright had in mind while constructing his plot.

In *The Honorable History of Friar Bacon and Friar Bungay*[21] (written in collaboration with Thomas Lodge) the subplot of love idyll between Lacy and Margaret echoes a similar evaluation along with Greene's own disapproval of the courtly ladies for "their coyness" which were "but foolery"(ii). The medieval practice of magic and witchcraft is discarded when Friar Bacon renounces his magic powers and cordially welcomes the new world of judiciousness. Greene's idealized concept of womanhood receives a tremendous jolt in his last important play written in collaboration with Thomas Lodge, *A Looking Glass(e) for London and England.* It is a ruthlessly satiric record of all the vices rampant in contemporary London society. All the characters of the play are in some way or other a mere carbon copy of what the playwrights saw in their society. The sycophants of Ninevah's court betray all kinds of vices, which ultimately corrupt the morale of the nation. But King Rasni prefers them, as he feels comfortable in their company. All the female characters are also afflicted by perversities like incest, adultery and lust. Both within the court and outside it men appear to be blinded by the corrupting influences of avarice, infidelity, lust and utter selfishness (I ii 160-170). The reality is startlingly bleak and the overall effect of the play is grim, which surely frightens the audience.

Therefore, the trend that began with the Interludes to illustrate to the enlightened audience the existing depression of the society was well perpetrated by Shakespeare too. But the difference was the difference of attitude. Shakespearean comedies never really override their entertaining value because Shakespeare's comic approach is much more generous and liberal. He never tries to undermine the importance of contemporary social values and norms but presents them for the sake of his audience. Moreover, he has the liberalness to accept men with all their failures. He does not shun them; even when he decidedly mocks at the varied human failures his attitude is that of a gentle creator who takes all the pain to carve out a decent figure out of the most incongruous objects.

Notes

1 All textual references to *Fulgens and Lucres* are from *Fulgens and Lucres*, eds. F.S. Boas and A.W. Reed, Oxford University Press, London, 1926 (MCMXXVI) .

2. Regarding his other writings little can be deduced because of the scarcity of materials.

3. Derived from the short story of Bonaccorso the interlude manifests a clear mingling of serious elements with comic scenes, an art that was to be perfected later by Shakespeare.

4. George Page in *The Merry Wives of Windsor* and Egeus *in A Midsummer Night's Dream.*
5. Similar instance of father's liberality can be cited in Greene's *Orlando Furioso* where Angelica the heroine has the sanction of her father the Emperor of Africa to choose the man she likes best, from a court full of kings and princes. And coincidentally both Angelica and Lucres choose men who are socially inferior to them.
6. All textual references to *The Four PP* are from *The Dramatic Writings of John Heywood*, ed. John S. Farmer, Charles W. Traylen, England, 1968.
7. *Ibid.*, p. 29.
8. *Ibid.*, p. 32.
9. *Ibid.*, p. 33.
10. *Ibid.*, p. 35.
11. *Ibid.*, p. 36.
12. All textual reference to *Ralph Roister Doister* are from *The Dramatic Writings of Nicholas Udall*, ed. John S. Farmer, Charles W. Traylen, England, 1966.
13. F.S. Boas, *Shakespeare and his Predecessors*, Mr. John Murry Pub. Ltd., London, 1896 Indian rep. 1963, p. 17.
14. All textual references to *Mother Bombie, Endimion, The Woman in the Moon(e)* are from *The Complete Works of John Lyly* III, ed. R. Warwick Bond, Clarendon Press, London, 1902 rep. 1973.
15. This refers to the social misrule that plagued England since the 15th century war of the Roses. Historically the period is generally considered to be a period of social disorder, when the livery of a powerful lord or knight gave one the immunity for cutting of purses and even of throats when necessary. Dromio's suggestion here though conveyed in light tone actually speaks of such deeper social maladies.
16. The practice however continued and contaminated even the 16th century society of England.
17. All textual references to *The Old Wives' Tale* are from *Elizabethan and Jacobean Comedies*, eds. C.W. Witworth and Brian Gibbon, Ernest Benn Ltd., Gt. Britain, 1984.
18. All textual references to *The History of Orlando Furioso, A Looking Glass(e) for London and England* are from *The Plays and Poems of Robert Greene* I ed. J.C. Collins, Oxford University Press, Oxford, 1905 (MDCCCCV).
19. The scene of the princess choosing her own husband under the vigilance of her father reminds one of the ancient Indian swayamvar sabha. In our epics, the Ramayana and the Mahabharata we find

similar incidents. It is strange non-the-less because nowhere else do we find such a scene. Possibly the source of this scene was its Italian counterpart. The only difference here is while the Indian princesses could not evade the social hierarchy, i.e., they had to choose a prince here Angelica can choose a groom who is socially inferior to her. This again is the result of the newly risen humanistic approach in treating men according to their individual worth and not inherited legacy.

20. A parallel insanity of disowning his daughter can be cited in Shakespeare's *King Lear*.

21. All textual references to *The History of Friar Bacon and Friar Bungay* are from The Fortune Play Books, *Friar Bacon and Friar Bungay* ed. G.B. Harrison, Robert Holden and Co. Ltd., London, 1927.

1

NATURE AND FUNCTION OF COMEDY: SOCIAL PERSPECTIVE

> Comedy assumes that society must be made to work, that creatures must learn to live together.*

Before considering the social realism in the early and middle comedies of Shakespeare it is almost perfunctory to enquire briefly into the comic in general and how far Shakespeare conforms to it in spite of his alleged deviation to a world of fantasy and make-believe. But I have surveyed the history of literary criticism in essentials to explore only the general basis of comedy with a special emphasis on those theories, which categorize comedy as an ideal agent for the rectification of the social evils.

I

Right from its inception comedy as an art form has proved to be the most effective and successful medium for the playwrights to reveal to the masses the evils inherent in their society. Though the treatment of the form has differed from one playwright to another, some preferring the satirical mode to scoff at the social maladies, while some others adopting the milder form to merely laugh at human failings, the basic aim of all comic playwrights down the ages has been to utilize the medium as a literary agent to wipe out the corruptions both entrenched in human nature, and also embedded in the society

---

* E.M. Tillyard, 'The Nature of Comedy and Shakespeare', *Essays Literary and Educational*, Chatto and Windus, London,1962, p. 17.

in which he lives. And Shakespeare when studied from that perspective is in no way different from any other comic playwright in spite of his most original way of handling the traditional plots of his time. Preferring the milder form of comedy, Shakespeare merely sought to laugh at human failings, and not demoralise them psychologically by harshly rebuking them. In most of his plays, therefore, the comic situation arises from a feeling of superiority in the theater-audiences who tend to laugh at a person committing blunders, which they themselves easily avoid. And when a clever man like Falstaff walks easily into the trap laid by the merry wives of Windsor, a sense of superiority is aroused among the conspirators; which is then discharged through laughter both of the audience and characters in the play. Though the reason for such a pleasure is not very clear, the pleasures of a comedy are unmistakably present, establishing Falstaff as a butt of ridicule. And the most important thing in the mind of the dramatist here is the exhilarating sensation of joy that, he is above falling into the error, which becomes the occasion of laughter.

Underlying the comic situation of Falstaff however, there is an intrinsic note of social criticism perceived from the very beginning of the play *The Merry Wives of Windsor*. Falstaff being a representative of the declining aristocracy betrays a totally different and uncomfortable reality. As a person he is unprincipled, and this feature in him is the end result of the growing financial paucity that was plaguing the Elizabethan aristocracy. The nobility, which failed to comply with the whims and interests of the rising bourgeoisie, was on the point of social extermination and Falstaff belongs to that class. With no land to fall back upon for survival the man goes to the extent of seducing the respectable and faithful wives of decent country folks. But he does not suffer from any moral compunction for his action. A brand of rogues whom he calls his assistants aid him initially to achieve his end, vindicating once again the truth of the axiom that a man is known by the company he keeps. The attire of aristocracy also assists him and he utilizes it to cover up his evil designs. Falstaff appears therefore, to be specifically designed by Shakespeare to highlight a few outstanding corruptions prevailing in the society of the Renaissance aristocracy, the moral laxity of the nobility, and the various vices such as adopting an iniquitous means by them to surge over their financial crunch.

Despite all such social undertones the comedies of Shakespeare have often been accused of non-conformity to the comic theories advanced by literary critics. Instead of giving a realistic picture of society he allegedly prefers to take his viewers and readers alike to a world of fantasy and make-believe, where all is fair and happy without a particle of the existing evil of the actual society. Undeniably, Shakespearean comedies do contain certain amount of romanticism in them, but romanticism is not the ultimate message of any of his comedies. Like *The Merry Wives of Windsor,* all of them have an undercurrent of social realism that belonged to sixteenth century England. In fact, on a closer analysis the comedies very often reveal a wonderful and balanced combination of romanticism and realism, where one does not overrule the other and disturb the balance of the play.

Like *The Merry Wives of Windsor*, *As You Like It* too superficially appears to be a mere pastoral comedy, set in the forest of Arden, far away from the mundane everyday reality. But when the play is studied carefully and analyzed in details this make-believe world of Arden clearly starts showing signs of the maladies of the Elizabethan society. Orlando's suffering, bordering on a tragic gambit is hinted by Shakespeare, right from the onset of the play, as the end result of an unfair law of the land 'the law, of primogeniture', whose prey is Falstaff as well. In this law except the eldest son nobody could inherit the ancestral property and the younger sons had to remain content merely with their inherited titles. It was therefore, a curse for an Elizabethan youth to be born as the second or third son of a wealthy father. Orlando's misfortune hence is very logical and must have instantly caught the fancy of the Elizabethan viewers. Similarly, the irrational parental control over the lives of the Elizabethan youths seems to be the plaguing vice in the society of elves and fairies in *A Midsummer Night's Dream.* Parallel to the Fairyland of Oberon and

Titania are the Elizabethans afflicted by all kinds of worldly sufferings. Hermia as referred to in the preface of this book is an innocent young girl who loves Demetrius while her father Egeus opposes her choice for no conclusive or even compelling reasons. Egeus's opposition is entirely arbitrary yet the law of the land is such that his arguments are never questioned – the ruler of the land sides with him and threatens Hermia of unyielding punishment. Neither the girl nor the concerned young man is allowed to marry according to the dictates of their hearts because society does not permit them that much autonomy.

In the early comedies of Shakespeare, however, the romantic element is relatively less obvious, because in these plays (*The Comedy of Errors, The Two Gentlemen of Verona, The Merry Wives of Windsor,* and *Love's Labour's Lost*) social realism in the form of social criticism is emphasized instead of the world of fancy and make-believe. Whereas in the middle comedies the romantic elements seems to be all permeating, giving the critics greater scope to allege Shakespeare of inculcating romanticism in his comedies.

II

Like all other art forms comedy too has inspired a large number of critics down the ages to formulate different theories regarding its nature and function. Hence, the history of criticism of comedy is generally treated to be a chronological recording of a series of triumph over whatever is inimical to human or social good, with certain amount of modification here and there. But by and large in nearly all the theories the critics have traced two significant functions of a comedy, first the subversive function in which the notion of laughter is of vital significance and the second the normative function where the notion of laughter is equally important but with a totally different intention. The first theory relates comedy to festive rejoicing, where laughter is convivial and fooling in order, hence the potentially anarchic and subversive spirit of carnival is licensed as a celebration of the life-force triumphing over its enemies. But in the second function laughter is both scornful and aggressive, causing a painfulness, which is usually mitigated in theory by an appeal to its instructive or corrective function. None of the critics however, have denied the concept of enjoyment in a comedy totally and hence comedy as literary genre has come to be universally accepted as a medium of ideal entertainment.

Promulgation of literary theories of comedy seems to have begun with the brief remarks of Plato (in *The Philebus* and *Epinomis*) and Aristotle (in *The Poetics*). Plato expressed his disapproval of the art form while Aristotle stated that like tragedy, comedy, too was an essential agent for the rectification of the ills of human society. Treating the genre contemptuously Plato claimed, that ignorance of human beings about themselves really leads to all comic situations and thus ignorance of self which is extremely odious and repulsive, injures in the long run both the comic characters themselves and also their neighbours.[1] Aristotle agrees with Plato about the concept of imitation in a comedy but feels that such an imitation would not necessarily corrupt the viewers. Comedy to him is:

> an imitation of men worse than the average; worse, however, not as regards any and every sort of fault, but only as regards one particular kind, the Ridiculous, which is a species of the Ugly. The Ridiculous may be defined as a mistake or deformity not productive of pain or harm to others; the mask, for instance, that excites laughter, is something ugly and distorted without causing pain.[2]

Thus what proved to be odious and repulsive to Plato was gracefully acknowledged to be merely human deformity by Aristotle, and such a deformity, according to Aristotle is as inconsequential as the wearing of a mask temporarily during the seasonal festivities. In other words, what to Plato is a repulsive and corrupting art, and ought to be shunned by man, proves to be the ideal medium of harmless enjoyment to Aristotle, a medium that should be cultivated to the point of perfection.

Following Aristotelian arguments about comedy two basic ideas emerge very clearly to serve as the guideline for all later playwrights. The first, is the idea of laughter and the second, is of social structure. In a genuine comedy the quality that provokes laughter comes through "certain ugliness a defect or deformity"[3] of the characters; and this ugliness is of two kinds, physical deformities and the frailties, infirmities and follies innate in human nature. Yet, the laughter that is provoked is not born out of any malice for any one particular person or race, rather it is a general feeling of pure enjoyment. Similarly, the society in a true comedy is a universal society, and hence unlike the "particular"[4] society of a satire it does not arouse any pain in the heart of the audience. Both Plato and Aristotle seem to be quite unanimous about objectifying this feeling of pain in any type of art form, and it is this point of resemblance between them that is of interest to us. True comedy, according to them should be a light narrative centered round ludicrous figures but containing no harsh or vindictive strains to spoil their entertainment value by arousing any bitter feelings. In contrast, however, satire, an allied art form primarily achieves its end, being of a moral assistance, by evoking within the viewers those very feelings, which both Aristotle and Plato specifically wanted the comic playwright to avoid. In other words, satire fulfils the normative functions of a comedy whereas Aristotelian comedy lays more stress on the subversive elements of the genre.

Elucidating Aristotle's theory Wylie Sypher points out that the great critic being fully aware of the potentiality of the genre as "a Saturnalia, an orgy, an assertion of the unruliness of the flesh and its vitality"[5] thought it to be the ideal medium for establishing man's faith in rebirth, restoration and salvation. And because comedy is the transformed art form of the primal rite[6] originating from carnival rites and seasonal rites, which brought together the incompatibles of death and life, it is like tragedy no "less mithradatic"[7] in its effect. Its comic catharsis enables man to purge himself of bad feelings like lust, greed, anger and jealousy, which are the actual frailties of human beings, and ennobles him internally. And it is this process, which helps the human society to create better and fitter individuals. That is, the success of a comedy depends on the universality of its comic catharsis. Again, regarding this comic catharsis Sypher expresses the view that it is basically "homeopathic" in its effect, "curing folly by folly."[8] Says he:

> The tragic law works a transformation: from sin and suffering come calm of mind and resistance to disaster, to fears that weaken us. The transformation in comedy is equally miraculous: from license and parody and unmasking or putting on another mask-come renewed sanity.[9]

It is therefore, the subversive element of comedy, which assists man to unmask himself and regain his lost sanity that Sypher stresses in his analysis of the mithradatic impact of a genuine comedy. To him comedy is really a species of authorized license working as a "safety valve or outlet for disorderly passions including erotic passions."[10] And when in a comedy these apparently harmful passions are treated in a dismissive manner they tend to become extremely undisruptive socially, leaving the playwright perfectly at peace with his creation.

Traversing the well laid out path of Aristotle, critics and grammarians started formulating their own theories about comedy, which to a large extent influenced the creative talents of playwrights of entire Europe down the ages. Critics like Cicero, Horace, Evanthius, Dante, Sidney, Jonson, Congreve, Fielding, Hazlitt, Meredith and Bergson, belonging to different centuries and nations contributed their share to the development of the art of literary criticism. All of them had their own theories about comedy, which at times resembled the theory of Aristotle and at times differed from it to a large extent.

Cicero, a Roman orator and statesman was one such critic who like Aristotle realized the essentiality of comedy in improving the society. He admitted that comedy is capable of producing unexpected, instantaneous and unrestrained laughter, which is not always guided by any logic or reason, but this capability he felt often helps man to obviate dullness and austerity in his life and also enables him to overcome all the adversities his life bristles with. And because comedy lies in the blemishes of human beings "who are neither objects of general esteem nor yet full of misery, and not apparently merely fit to be hurried off to execution for their crimes"[11] the viewer can easily identify himself with the comic situations and thereby laugh at the folly of the characters on the stage. Like Aristotle, Cicero too felt that comic mirth is mainly aroused from the depiction of human beings who are worse than the average and that this depiction should not be aimed at causing pain to the viewers. Neither must the playwright be over enthusiastic about his picturisation so as to make his work appear as mere buffoonery or mimicry. Cicero's idea of comedy therefore, lays greater stress on the subversive aspect of the art form though he does acknowledge the beneficiary impact of it upon human society.

Though more than two centuries of Hellenistic civilization lie between Aristotle and Horace the latter's *Ars Poetica* occupies the second position of importance after Aristotle's *Poetics*, in the field of literary criticism. Like the *Poetics* Horace's work influenced both the playwrights of his age and those writing during the Italian Renaissance and all of them seem to be quite reverential in their acknowledgment of indebtedness to the great master.

After Horace it was Evanthius, whose comic theory promulgated in the fourth century A.D., helped many playwrights to build up their comedies in a well-defined manner. An ideal comedy according to Evanthius ought to be "a story treating of various habits and customs of public and private affairs, from which one may learn what is of use in life"[12] and what should be shunned for all practical purposes. The normative function of a comedy is of primary importance to the critic though the style he suggested the playwright to adopt, is quite akin to that of Aristotle's light narrative, which when practiced properly acts as behavioral therapy to man. Evanthius, does not completely negate the entertaining aspect of comedy but its role as a social rectifier is more important to him than anything else.

After a gap of nearly ten centuries Dante wrote his *Divine Comedy* following which he made an insightful analysis of the actual function of a genuine comedy. Maybe Dante was echoing the tastes of his age when, contrary to the theory of Evanthius, he expressly gave more stress to the subversive spirit of a comedy. In the process of distinguishing tragedy from comedy Dante in his 'Epistle to Can Grande' stated that comedy by definition was derived from comos oda, a village song and hence 'as a genre' differed from all other poetic narratives in its subject matter. Citing the example of Seneca's tragedies he wrote:

> tragedy is tranquil and conducive to wonder at the beginning, but foul and conducive to horror at the end, ...comedy on the other hand, introduces a situation of adversity, but ends its matter in prosperity, as is evident in Terence's comedies. And for this reason some writers have the custom of saying in their salutations by way of greeting, 'a tragic beginning and a comic ending to you'... Tragedy uses an elevated and sublime style, while comedy uses an unstudied and low style.[13]

To Dante, therefore, a happy ending was the prime object in a comic situation, where the entertaining part of the genre overruled its instructive role. And, because the origin of comedy lay in a village song, the playwright while constructing a comic play was expected to avoid the elevated style of tragedy and adopt an "unstudied and low style." With Dante however, the survey of the other European critics, except the English end and the focus henceforth is turned towards the representative English critics down the centuries.

In England the trend of literary criticism started gaining momentum first in the middle of the 16th century with the publication of Nicholas Udall's *Ralph Roister Doister*. Dwelling on the role of comedy in his Prologue Udall states:

> What creature is in health, either young or old,
> But some mirth with modesty will be glad to use,
> As we in this interlude shall now unfold,
> Wherein all scurrility we utterly refuse,

Avoiding such mirth wherein abuse:
Knowing nothing more commendable for a man's recreation,
Than mirth which is used in an honest fashion:
For mirth prolongeth life, and causeth health,
Mirth recreates our spirits and voideth pensiveness
Mirth increaseth amity, not hindering our wealth,
Mirth is to be used both of more and less,
Being mixed with Virtue in decent comeliness.[14]

To the first English comic playwright the aim of the genre was mainly to please the audience and revive within them the flagging life-force. And an honest usage of this mirth was the most commendable gesture, on the part of the playwright as it prolonged the viewer's life, improved his health, increased amity and also drove away pensiveness from his life. The subversive spirit was the presiding deity of Udall's work possibly reflecting the preference of the age and the nation.

After Udall there is no clear evidence of any critic devoting himself or herself to the study of the genre, till the latter part of the Renaissance. But with the publication of Philip Sidney's *The Defence of Poesie* the ball was again set rolling in the field of literary criticism. Sidney's work, though extremely erudite and an interesting documentation of the literary activities of the age, is mainly devoted to an elaborate analysis of poetry in general.[15] Incidentally, the work is primarily aimed at refuting the charges of the Puritans against poetry but in the process the author discusses at length the actual functions of all kinds of literary activities. And logically therefore, comedy being the most popular genre of the age receives his justified attention. Writing about comedy Sidney expresses the view that comedy primarily aims at imitating "the common errors of our life" represented "in the most ridiculous and scornful sort that may be as it is impossible that any beholder can be such a one."[16] Furthermore the essentiality of such imitation he points out:

> ... as in geometry the oblique must be known as well as the right and in arithmetic the odd as well as the even, so in the action of our life who seeth not the filthiness

> of evil wanteth a great foil to perceive the beauty of virtue. This doth the comedy handle.[17]

Therefore to view a genuine comedy is actually a way of enriching one's power of self-criticism, because the nobility of virtue is unfolded only when it is contrasted against evil. Lashing out at the Puritan accusation that poetry (comedy being an extended form of poetry) is immoral, lying, and provocative of debauchery and debilitating Sidney points out that in a work of art the expectation to view only the virtues in man is a total fallacy. Added to it, the idea that man tends to learn evil things through comic performances is also a gross misreading of human nature. In the comic genre the playwright by pointing out the human problems through his character, is in reality embarking on a mission of arousing a new kind of self-awareness in his audience. And since the normative function is not the sole function of comedy Sidney readily approves of the medieval comic figures of Herod and Devil on the stages, who in their ugly masks and with their comic dances seek to entertain the audience.

In the Jacobean age Jonson however did not indulge the comic poets to cultivate the subversive elements in a comedy. On the other hand, he felt it obligatory on the part of a poet to create a brave new world for the masses through his work of art. The "office of comic poet" wrote Jonson in his dedication to *Volpone* is to "imitate justice and instruct life as well as purity of language or stir up gentle affections."[18] Jonson of course, was not very gentle in the execution of his aim, rather like a ruthless satirist, about whom Horace had spoken centuries ago, he instructed his viewers about justice and all other human virtues. Yet in spite of his strong satiric vein Jonson's works can never be really styled as the dry preaching of a "sermonizing pedant"[19] because the element of humor is very strong in his writings. Thus Jonson's comedy of humors stands out as outstanding example of both satiric preaching and inexhaustible wit. And his dependence on the ancients is limited to only that part where they "conferred authority on deeply congenial modes."[20]

Next to Jonson was Congreve during the Restoration, who, as a successful writer of comedy of manners, had a very clear idea about the predilections and requirements of his audience, regarding the themes of all comic writings. As a true representative of the age he endeavored to refine his art to cater to the tastes of his contemporaries. To him drama and specifically comedy was not the portrayal of anything that was not in nature. Any freak in nature should be deliberately avoided because it might shock the sensibility of man and degenerate him. In a letter to John Dennis he expressed the view:

> Things that either are not in nature or if they are monsters, and births, of mischance; and consequently as such should be stifled, and huddled out of the way...; that mankind may not be shocked with and appearing possibility of the degeneration of Godlike species.[21]

In reality too Congreve's comedies never portrayed monstrous characters who could shock the tastes of his audience or degenerate people. His deliberate effort was always to present on the stage everything that was refined and polished. And it was through refinement that Congreve satirised contemporary society and pointed out to his audience the maladies inherent in it.

A similar approach is observed a few years later even in the field of novel writing in the novels written by Henry Fielding. Writing in the mid-eighteenth century Fielding's novels show this trend of refined satire, because like Congreve he clearly disapproves of monstrousness in works of art. To him anything that deals with inferior manners is no serious comedy at all; rather it is good to designate it as pure burlesque because of its tendency to demean the "God like" species.[22] Recategorizing comedy in his own terms Fielding writes:

> ...comic romance is a comic epic in prose; differing from comedy, as the serious epic from tragedy; ...It differs from the serious romance in its fable and action in this; that as in the one these are grave and solemn, so

> in the other they are light and ridiculous; it differs in its characters, by introducing persons of inferior manners, whereas the grave romance sets the highs before us; lastly in its sentiments and diction by preserving the ludicrous instead of the sublime.[23]

Though Fielding's overemphasis on refinement is quite akin to Congreve's patterned elegance in the comedy of manners, the novelist in his basic approach feels more at home with the Jonsonian theory of comedy which aims at condemning vanity and hypocrisy of man, because these two elements of human nature are the true sources of ridiculousness in a comedy.

In spite of all their refinements the 18th century comedy makers failed to produce serious or edifying literature, because by the Victorian period comedy clearly became a medium of portraying man's commitments towards his society. Postulating this view George Meredith observes:

> There are plain reasons why the comic poet is not a frequent apparition and why the great comic poet remains without a fellow. A society of cultivated men and women is required, wherein ideas are current and the perception quick, that he may be supplied with matter and an audience. The semi-barbarism of merely giddy communities and feverish emotional periods repel him; and also a state of marked social inequality of the sexes; nor can he whose business is to address the mind be understood where there is not a moderate degree of intellectual activity.[24]

Meredith's analysis of comedy is not only highly specialized, meant for the intellectuals alone, but is miles apart from its origin of primal or seasonal rites. Yet, in respect of social purpose it resembles all other theories of the genre in basic formulations. In a similar manner Bergson's theory of comedy expresses his belief in the evolutionary purpose of comedy on the moral plane and mentions its corrective purpose that shames the butts into some sort of moral recuperation. In both Meredith and Bergson, therefore the common argument about comedy is its edifying effect upon man and his society.

In the twentieth century, critics like Bakhtin sought to trace the beginning of comedy to the ancient comic sources of carnivals and primitive festivities. Pointing out the prominent position of fools in the old comedies Bakhtin writes in *Rabelais and His World*:

> Moreover, nearly every Church feast had its comic folk aspect which was also traditionally recognized. Such for instance, were the parish feasts, usually marked by fairs, and varied open-air amusements, the participation of giants, dwarfs, monsters and trained animals... Civil and social ceremonies and rituals such as the tribute rendered to the victors at tournaments the transfer of feudal rights of the initiation of a knight.[25]

This carnival festivity, Bakhtin points out is of great importance in man's life as man loves to live in it. It is an all embracing idea which appeals to men at large irrespective of their social status. "It has a universal spirit; it is a special condition of the entire world, of the world's revival and renewal, in which all take part."[26] The festivity of the medieval society not only predominated in the comedies of the period, but also trickled down and acted as the true source of man's rejuvenation. To Ian Donaldson, however, "Comedy is a living and evolving form always changing a shade faster than the definitions which pursue it, the wish to circumscribe comedy with a system of theoretical ideas..."[27] Illustrating his point Donaldson proceeds to cite examples of comedies down the ages, which all the more convince the reader of the strength of his argument. From this perspective, therefore, the desire to compartmentalize the comedies of a playwright like Shakespeare as mere romantic fancy is some sort of narrowing down the master's potentiality as a perfect craftsman.

One thing that becomes quite clear through this brief survey is the fact that as genre, comedy mainly prefers average men to be its characters, because their oddities in behavior pattern can rouse a sense of pleasure among the members of the audience. And while the subversive spirit in a comedy entertains the viewer with the ulterior motive of purging him of his undesirable qualities, the normative spirit very often in the name of instructing the audience, rouses a sense of pain through its biting and caustic device called satire. But the role of comedy as a social rectifier has been recognized by all critics, from Aristotle to Ian Donaldson and simultaneously the entertaining power of the art form has never been undermined by anyone of them. In other words, without the moral orientations of society a comedy can never really be successful and without the sundry oddities of is members it can never really be entertaining, and the same theory holds good even for William Shakespeare, whose comedies have proved both successful and entertaining.

III

The history of the development of comedy, when traced from its source, reveals that comedy initially was evolved from the ancient Dionysian rites and celebrations of song and revel. During such celebrations the actors dressed as satyrs with masks and wearing huge leather phalli, paraded about, making impromptu jests and mocking at the spectators. Eventually poets began composing phallic verses for the jesters to recite and from these, according to Aristotle, the stage comedy of Athens was derived, the first being performed in the fifth century B.C. as part of the city's competitive festival.

The earliest of the Greek comedies known as Old Comedy followed the exuberant tradition of the Dionysian comedians in ridiculing prominent people and events. The most famous of the writers of Old Comedy was Aristophanes whose delight in the use of fantasy was equaled only by the pleasure he derived from launching the most obscene and savage attacks on well-known Athenians, including Socrates. His plays not only provide a safety valve for disorderly passions but also portray the irreligious attitude of the ancient Greeks towards their gods and goddesses. David Barrett observes:

> The comedies thus give us an idea of what was regarded as impious and what was not, and provides a valuable side-light on the attitude of the Greeks to religion at this period. Some of the gods – in their capacity as

> personified 'characters'- had, it seems lost much of their sanctity and could be freely ridiculed .... Thus ...Dionysus in the *Frogs* is presented as an utterly ludicrous figure.[28]

Middle Comedies differed from the Old Comedies in revealing free imagination and realism. Everyday language, customs and events of everyday life became more important to the playwrights than any far fetched philosophy. Thus the trend of realism noticed in New Comedies actually began with Middle Comedies. But New Comedy developed far better plot mechanics than either of its predecessors. Moreover, the great ideal of Hellenism dropped their local color and turned to appeal to the universal human sentiments. It also exhibited the general pattern of Aristotelian causation:

> ...which must be sought in the general atmosphere of reconciliation that makes the final marriage possible. As the hero gets closer to the heroine and opposition is overcome all the right thinking people come over to his side. Thus a new social unit is formed on the stage, and the moment that this social unit crystallizes is the moment of the comic resolution.[29]

It was Menander who wrote New Comedies which stressed plots of intrigue and romance. The themes of his comedies were domestic and private, unlike the public/social/political themes of the Old Comedies. The form of New Comedy was however not restricted to the Greek playwrights alone. The Roman playwrights Plautus and Terence, writing years later, adopted the style, attitude and subject matter of New Comedy and infused in them their boisterous Roman spirit. The traditional Roman comedy revelled in the broad humour of stock characters and situations but both Plautus and Terence sought instead to reproduce the unique art of characterization and stylistic polish and family relations that they found in their Greek models, Menander, Alexis, and Philemon.

In England, comedy proper as mentioned earlier came into existence in the middle of the sixteenth century with the appearance of Nicholas Udall's *Ralph Roister Doister*. The play was an adaptation of Plautus's *Miles Glorious* with a mixture of English elements in it. The evidence of classical influence is closer in the play's five-act structure, contrasting with the loose episodic sequences of the native dramatic tradition. But the tradition of medieval drama appears to have been retained while constructing the character of Merrygreek, Sir Ralph's servant. He is a wily parasite given to practical joking and has obvious family resemblances to the character of Vice of the medieval drama. The country setting of the play and the names Udall assigns to the characters are also very much English and not derived from *Miles Glorious*. Similarly, the eventual outcome of the play, with Gawyn Goodluck trampling over the soldier Roister Doister, was an obvious compliment to the rising merchant class of England. Thus, while classical principles provide the five-act structure scene divisions, a basis for the chief characters and unity of place and time, it is Udall's blending of these with native elements that is the real strength of the play. The concluding song in praise of Queen Mary is an appropriate reminder that the patronage of drama extended throughout society up to court itself.

By the middle of the sixteenth century, however, two distinct comic forms developed in England. They influenced all the playwrights of the age and the form remained popular till the middle of the eighteenth century. These were the commedia dell'arte and the commedia erudite. The commedia dell'arte was performed throughout Western Europe especially in Italy by a number of companies of professional actors and the commedia erudite was restricted to those who preferred the content of learning in comedy. While the commedia dell'arte was derived from the New Comedy, making use of its improvisations and the stock characters and plot, the commedia erudite preferred to abide by certain rules supposedly framed by the ancients, of which "the ancients never knew, and which was fatal to all but the most rarefied academic players."[30] Both Shakespeare and Moliere preferred commedia dell'arte over commedia erudita. And even Nicholas Udall's *Ralph Roister Doister* the earliest English comedy resembled

Shakespeare's *A Midsummer Night's Dream, As You Like It*, and *Twelfth Night* in its combination of love and laughter in the narration.

The plays of Jonson and Jacobean age were specified as the comedy of humors, but like New Comedy or any other comedy for that purpose the comedy of humors was realistic in approach to people and society. About Jonson's comedies Bradbrook writes:

> Jonson's critical strength lay in his formulated restriction upon the license of popular art.... He made unceasing wars upon common taste, from the attack upon romance and 'York and Lancaster's longjars' prefixed to *Every Man in His Humour*, a Globe play, to his very last comedy, where he is still complaining of stuffed legendary adventures.[31]

The Restoration comedy of manners which came immediately after the comedy of humors aimed at satirizing the factitious norms of the sophisticated upper class of England. It was in France first that the comedies of social criticism came to be written in the mid-seventeenth century, but in England the form was modified and developed and finally adapted by the Restoration playwrights like Etherege, Dryden, Wycherley, and Congreve. Talking about their comedies L.J. Potts says:

> The comic dramatists of the late seventeenth century treat sex as an opportunity for pleasure but a potential source of trouble and their norm of conduct is to get a fair share of the pleasure with least possible distress to all concerned. For the most part their men and women are of the same class, and treat each other as equals; and in one respect their morality compared favourably with the average Victorian morality,... The Restoration wit was however...upon the whole humane towards women and respected them as equals; there were among them notorious rakes, such as Rochester; but the general feeling was against the extremes of debaucher.[32]

Potts of course, does not condemn the Restoration comic playwrights, but he insists on the viewer's developing healthy desires. A "desire to understand the behavior of men and women towards one another in social life, and to judge them according to their own pretensions and standards"[33] should be inculcated by the playwright. But the Restoration comedy makers felt that in their desire to teach their viewers the playwrights should not stoop so low as to present on the stage a low or vulgar aspect of human life. And it was this refined outlook of the Restoration playwrights that gave their plays a refinement rare in English drama. But although Wylie Sypher describes the comedy of manners as an excursion of man's self-consciousness[34] all the efforts of the Restoration comic dramatists to rouse the self-consciousness had a very short life. With the upsurge of the middle class the apathy against the moral laxity of the aristocracy started manifesting itself in the sentimental comedies of the mid-eighteenth century.

Sentimental Comedy also referred to as "Weeping Sentimental Comedy"[35] dominated the English stage during the middle of eighteenth century. The aim of this comedy was to depict on the stage ordinary human beings beset by misfortunes caught up in distressful situation, but ultimately triumphing over seemingly insurmountable difficulties, thanks to their virtue. The ability of the spectator to respond both emotionally and even tearfully to such fictional situation was known as sensibility. "The Sentimental Comedy" writes T.G.S. Nelson "comes near to denying our animal altogether. This may explain why it is so widely regarded as a self-contradictory mode."[36] And probably this is one of the major reasons why the form in its purest state declined in popularity. Human animalism, we have seen seemed to be the most effective theme of popular comedy and if a playwright decides to do away with it completely, then the effectiveness of his work is lessened to a considerable extent. This is precisely what happened with the sentimental comedies.

Although the type continued well in its purest form into the nineteenth century the popularity of sentimental comedy began to decline in the last quarter of the eighteenth century, because of the revival of laughing comedy written by Oliver Goldsmith and Richard Brinsley Sheridan. However, the sentimental impulse has never been absent entirely from the drama, for sentiment lies at the heart of melodrama, and melodrama of one kind or another had been the dominant serious genre of the nineteenth and twentieth centuries. In fact, in the latter part of the nineteenth century sentimental comedy was reborn as the drama of social consciousness or drama of commitment. The names themselves suggest the aims of these plays. Not only are these plays socially committed like the sentimental plays, but they also aim at arousing social awareness in their viewers. Oscar Wilde, Noel Coward, Terrence Rattigan, James Barrie, all have traces of the sentimental in their works, while Shaw with his propagandist outlook on society wrote his comedies in a different style.

Shaw's comedy, the social comedy of Dumas and the semi-tragic comedy of Chekhov highlight the late nineteenth century's egalitarianism and the trend towards naturalism in the field of comedy. In rebellion, perhaps against the serious tone of such plays there also developed the broader low comedy of the music hall and Vaudeville, which depended less on the character and dialogue than on the presentation of incongruities and exaggerated buffooneries so popular with the audience of Aristophanes and Plautus.

In the twentieth century a rebellion also occurred in the literary scene with Synge, O'Casey and others seeking to replace drab realism with poetry and fantasy. Later, a new type of comedy appeared in the works of Beckett, Pirandello and Ionesco, who portrayed the absurd existence with bleak and black humor. By mid-century man's view of his world had so altered that the heroic seemed comic, the comic seemed heroic and pure comedy no longer seemed possible.

Notes

1. Tr. A.E. Taylor, ed. Raymond Klibansky, Dawsons and Pall Mall, London, 1956 rep. 1972, p. 169.
2. Ingram Bywaters, *Aristotle on the Art of Poetry*, Oxford University Press, Delhi, 1977 rep.1992, p. 33.
3. S.H. Butcher, Aristotle's Theory of Poetry and Fine Arts, Kalyani Publishers, Delhi,1951 rep. 1987, p. 375.

4. *Ibid.*, p. 380.
5. *Comedy Meaning and Form*, ed. R.W. Corrigan, Harper and Row, New York, 1981, p. 34.
6. *Ibid.*, p. 31.
7. *Ibid.*, p. 35.
8. *Ibid.*, p. 35.
9. *Ibid.*, p. 35.
10. L.J. Potts, Comedy, Hutchinson University Library, London, 1948 rep 1960, p. 52.
11. Tr. E.K. Sutton, *De Oratore* I &II, ed. H. Rackham, The Loeb Classical Library, William Heimnan Ltd., London, 1942, p. 375.
12. 'De Tragaedie et comedia' tr. Mildred Rogers, *European Theories of Drama*, ed. Barrett H. Clarke, Appleton, New York, 1918 rep. 1936, p. 43.
13. Tr. & ed. Robert S. Haller, in Literary Criticism of Dante Alighieri, Lincoln Nebraska, 1973, p. 100.
14. Early English Dramatis, *The Dramatic Writings of Nicholas Udall*, ed. Johns Farmer, Charles W. Traylen, England, 1966, p. 3.
15. It will not be wrong to point out here that Sidney's arguments followed quite closely the arguments of Aristotle in *The Poetics*, hence it cannot be called a deviant from the master's viewpoint.
16. *English Critical Texts,* eds. D.J. Enright and Ernest De Chickera, Oxford University Press, 1962, Delhi, p. 24.
17. *Ibid.*, p. 24.
18. Ed. David Cook, Metheun, 1962 rep. 1982 London, p. 58.
19. L.C. Knights, 'Ben Jonson the Dramatist', *New Pelican Guide to English Literature*, Penguin, London, 1955 rep. 1982, p. 405.
20. *Ibid.*, p. 406.
21. *William Congreve: Letters and Documents*, ed. John C. Hodges, Macmillan, London, 1964, p. 178.
22. *Joseph Andrews and Shamela*, ed. Douglas Brook-Davies, Oxford University Press, Delhi, 1966 rep. 1987, p. 4.
23. *Ibid.*, p. 4.
24. 'An Essay on Comedy and the Uses of Comic Spirit', *The Works of George Meredith*, VII, in *Comedy*, A case-book, ed. D.J. Palmer, Macmillan, London, 1984, pp. 57-58.
25. *Ibid.*, p. 95.
26. *Ibid.*, p. 97.

27. *The World Upside Down*, Clarendon Press, London, 1970, p. 1.
28. *The Wasps, The Poet and the Women, The Frog*, ed. David Barrett, Penguin, London, 1964, p. 27.
29. Frye Northrop, 'The Argument of Comedy', *English Institution Essays*, New York, 1948-1949, pp. 58-73 in *Comedy*, A case book ed. D.J. Palmer, Macmillan, London, 1987, p. 75.
30. M.C. Bradbrook: *The Growth and Structure of Elizabethan Comedy*, Cambridge University Press, Cambridge, 1953 rep. 1973, p. 77.
31. *Ibid.*, p. 103.
32. *Op. cit.*, p. 103.
33. *Ibid.*, p. 56.
34. *Op. cit.*, p. 29.
35. Oliver Goldsmith, *The Collected Works of Oliver Goldsmith* III ed. Arthuf Friedman, Clarendon Press, Oxford, 1966, p. 209.
36. *Comedy*, Oxford University Press, Oxford, 1990, p. 36.

2

SOCIAL REALISM IN SHAKESPEAREAN COMEDIES

Shakespeare, if an idealist, was also above all else a realist in art, and lurks almost impregnably behind his work ...Shakespeare possessed the most baffling of self-defence-humour. Just when we have laid hold of him he eludes us, and we hear only distant ironical laughter.*

Shakespeare's Romantic comedies, like those of Lyly, Peele and Greene, were characteristic of the Elizabethan age. This was because of the exclusivity of the age itself, when the audience clamoured for comedies which treated romance and all kinds of love interest with sympathy and understanding. Comedies which contained characteristics like romantic love as the central action, pastoral or idealized settings, multiple sets of lovers, with heroines frequently disguised as boys, lovers beset by great difficulties and reconciliatory or happy endings became extremely popular. But Shakespearean comedies do restrict themselves to these characteristics alone; apart from them, these comedies incorporated within their romantic framework — surprises, contrasts, intrigues, disguises and confusions which helped the playwright explore the general human nature. Even in his early comedies, *Love's Labour's Lost* and *The Comedy of Errors*, where Shakespeare had not fully mastered the art of characterization and was dealing with rather intransigent material, there are momentary flashes of his

* Edward Dowden, *Shakespeare A Critical Study of His mind and Art*, Routledge and Kegan Paul Ltd., London, 1875 rep. 1967, p. 6

creative genius which was later developed to the full. In *Love's Labour's Lost*, for example, the playwright's workmanship is perhaps not impeccable, but the tendency to explore the general human nature is very strong. Hence, at the end of the comedy one realizes that there is certainly an awakening of emotion in the characters who till then have tried to suppress it.

Critics in their efforts to analyse Shakespearean comedies from all plausible angles have developed over the years many new theories and parameters. Particularly, since the mid-20th century there has been a good deal of Shakespearean criticism, which for the sake of convenience may be divided into three distinct phases. In the first phase, before the 1950s, Shakespeare's comedies were generally regarded as 'happy comedies,' a term coined by John Dover Wilson.[1] The comedies then were seen as mere revelations of characters, a trend which tended to both moralize and psychologize the comic characters, treating them, as if they were real people and not dramatic representations. The critics of this school speculated on the motives and behavior patterns of the characters both on and off stage. The second phase, which dates from the 1950s is especially associated with the critical works of Northrop Frye, who studied Shakespearean comedies from the perspective of mythos, while the elements of carnival and ritual festivity predominated the critical writings of C.L. Barber. Both of them stressed the subversive elements of Shakespearean comedies and in the process related them to contemporary Elizabethan society. But in the third and latest phase of Shakespearean criticism, comedies along with both canonical texts and those outside the canon have been increasingly read within the retheorizing discipline of English studies that had occurred since the late 1970s. Feminism and psychoanalytic criticism have raised fundamental questions about comedies, concerning gender and family structures and also the functions of both of them in relation to both individual and collective fantasies. The rethinking of historical approaches to literature by Feminism, New Historicism, and more politically focused Cultural Materialism has revitalized the consideration of the comedies in their own time and in the history of their subsequent reception.

According to the older and conventional school of criticism, before the 1950s, Shakespearean comedies were considered to contain more of romanticism undoubtedly but, underlying the delightful entertainments and effusions of romantic celebration there managed to survive a deep tragic overtone, which actually reflected the prevailing moral code. And though the romantic themes were often expected to reflect aspects of the history of Shakespeare's time, they had in reality very little connection with the material practices from which the play grew. The critics of this school, therefore, felt that since "Elizabethan romantic comedy did emerge through a process of natural evolution; it was the product of an obligation imposed ruthlessly on the dramatists by their own age,"[2] it was not really necessary to investigate the material practices from which the comedies grew. Moreover, comedies being widely seen as revelations of characters, the method of character criticism adopted by these critics tended to both moralize and psychologize Shakespeare's characters. And elucidating their viewpoint H.B. Charlton opined that because:

> Shakespeare's play embodies a literary manner and moral code; its actions are conducted according to a conventional etiquette and are determined by a particular creed; and every feature of it, in matter and in sentiment, is traceable to the romantic attitude of man to woman.[3]

Love in Shakespearean comedies, unlike as in the traditional comedies of Europe, not only assumed the form of a "force making for proper happiness and actual reconciliation over a wide area of human experience"[4] but also acted as a joyous release in the plays to serve as a model to the audience of the basic rhythm of life. This mithradatic effect of love in Shakespearean comedies actually performed the vital social function of purging men of their detrimental instincts.

Explaining the other forces of Shakespearean comedies which make this social reconciliation possible V.Y. Kantak writes:

> It is also recognized that the social norm of the Shakespearean comic vision is not conservative like that of classical comedy. It does not assume an order that is regarded as sacrosanct, an unquestioned propriety in the established fitness of things, but rather speculated imaginatively on modes not of preserving a good already reached, but of enlarging and extending the possibilities.[5]

So there was an element of flexibility in Shakespearean comedies which did not presuppose any codified norm, rather speculated imaginatively a state that had far reaching possibilities. Added to it his explorative attitude in comedies actually provided him ample scope to improvise all his plots according to both public and artistic requirements. Thus, in *The Comedy of Errors* he took the classical plots and induced in them his ingenious comic vision and produced a play that was completely different from its sources.

But in most of the early romantic comedies of Shakespeare, neither the plots are strongly united, nor are the characters properly developed, yet the Elizabethan audience, we are told, highly appreciated them. J.R. Brown explains the reasons for this appreciation as thus:

> The audience of a Shakespearean comedy is not led towards an intimate knowledge of a single character but towards a wide view of the whole stage. It will sympathize with several of the characters in turn...but when all has been experienced in the due sequence of performance and is thus truly summed up, then the audience must sit back and be aware of the whole effect, must take it all in the relation of character to character the contrasts in attitudes, words and silence.[6]

Properly developed characters were, therefore, not deemed necessary factor for the Elizabethan audience to enjoy the comedies of Shakespeare. The final reconciliation, contrasts in attitude, word and silence were all what they desired and no amount of disproportion in plot or lack of development in character drawing deterred their sense of enjoyment and mode of participation. A festive atmosphere permeated the plays, infecting the whole surroundings. Dwelling on this special feature of Shakespearean comedies, R.W. Corrigan observes:

> The central intuition of comedy is an innate and deeply felt trust in life....The spirit of resurrection and joy that comes from the realization that despite all our individual defeats life does nonetheless continue on its merry way.[7]

The spirit of resurrection that vibrates in all the characters of Shakespearean comedies creates in them a kind of moral undertones. They celebrate the joy of living and provide assurance to lost souls and remind them of the silver linings behind all dark clouds. In other words, the plays act as saviours, redeeming faith in life.

The approach to evaluate Shakespearean comedies as celebration of life continued even in the second phase of Shakespearean criticism, with only a change in the perspective. The society and its rituals became the focus of study for critics like Northrop Frye and C.L. Barber, but not the actual social factors. The critical works of Northrop Frye and C.L. Barber initiated the second phase of Shakespearean criticism, when they attempted to survey the comedies as socially produced forms of literature. Comedy to both of them was nothing but the expression or enactment of a society's most profound myths and rituals. And Frye elaborating more on schematic insights focused his attention on a recurring pattern: a movement from disorder into a green world (represented by forest or countryside) and the ultimate establishment of a renewed society. His essay 'Mythos of Spring' provides a detailed appraisal of the comedies in general from this viewpoint. Here Frye observes:

> The plot structure of Greek New comedy, as transmitted by Plautus and Terence is in itself less a form than a formula, has become the basis for most comedy, especially in its most highly conventionalized dramatic form, down to our own day.... In the first place, the movement

> of comedy is usually a movement from one kind of society to another. At the beginning of the play the obstructing characters are in charge of the play's society, and the audience recognizes that they are usurpers. At the end of the play the device in the plot that brings hero and heroine together causes a new society to crystallize around the hero and the moment this crystallization occurs is the point of resolution in the action....[8]

The final society is the ultimate and ideal society for which both the characters and audience aspire throughout the comedy. But in Shakespearean comedies the connotation of society is wide, including natural and supernatural (*A Midsummer Night's Dream*, and *The Tempest*), to carry the action forward. Thus when Titania and Oberon (*A Midsummer Night's Dream*) appear on the stage with their retinue of fairies, they are as readily acceptable as the Duke and his subjects. Similarly, Ariel and his followers prove to be far more subservient to Prospero than the half-monster in that lonely island, where human beings, half-human beings and supernatural elements form a single homogeneous society. Even the rustics for that matter in *As You Like It*, peacefully coexist with Duke senior and the courtiers to form an integrated society in the forest of Arden. And to make the social amelioration more convincing Shakespeare finally marries off Audrey the rustic maid to Touchstone the court jester. But this social movement in comedies does not occur radically; it continues through the odds and disparities and finally succeeds in constructing an ideal society.

C. L. Barber's Shakespeare's Festive Comedy, relates comedy to pre-modern community festive rituals, in which existed a clear pattern of tension, its release, clarification and celebration. Reflecting on the subversive elements in Shakespearean comedies C.L. Barber observes:

> But the whole body of this happy comic art is distinguished by the use it makes of forms for experience which can be termed saturnalian. Once Shakespeare finds his own distinctive style, he is more Aristophanic

> than any other great English comic dramatist, despite the fact that the accepted models and theories when he started to write were Terentian and Plautine. The Old comedy cast of his work results from his participation in native saturnalian tradition of the popular theater and popular holidays.[9]

Shakespearean comedies undoubtedly demonstrate a saturnalian experience because the principal aim of all of them is mithradatic. Hence, their festive extravagances are expressed through many variations which involve inversion, statement and counter statement, finally leading to a release through clarification. Community rituals and festivities, for that matter, also aim at such a release and clarification of the society by providing a common platform to men from all walks of life, but there the purgation effected is temporary, whereas in Shakespearean comedies the purgation is of longer duration, if not permanent. In other words, Shakespearean comedies could reconstruct within themselves an ideal atmosphere of festivities which did not end with the "community observances of period sports and feast days."[10]

The essentiality of festive abandon in a community life can hardly be overemphasized, observes C.L. Barber in this context:

> A Saturnalian attitude, assumed by a clear-cut gesture towards liberty, brings mirth, an accession of Wanton vitality. In terms of Freud's analysis of wit, the energy normally occupied in maintaining inhibition is freed for celebrations.[11]

Shakespeare being aware of this feature of human psychology which seek wanton vitality, preferred to pattern his comedies on various festive motifs. The disguised heroine in *As You Like It*, for instance speaks more of carnival festivity while the bohemianism of Sir Toby in *Twelfth Night* is not merely his "personal idiosyncrasy, but...the pattern of the *Twelfth Night* occasion."[12] Yet, festivity is certainly not the last word in any Shakespearean comedies. Throughout his career Shakespeare appears to have conscientiously infused in all his plays serious social messages which cannot be missed by any reflective audience. The message of primogeniture, for example, rings out clearly in the cases of Orlando (in *As You Like It*) and Sir Toby (in *Twelfth Night*). Similarly, Petruchio's attempts to tame Kate (in *The Taming of the Shrew*) or Ford's distrust of his wife (in *The Merry Wives of Windsor*) speak explicitly of male repression in a patriarchal society. Likewise, issues like the economic crisis of English aristocracy, leading to their moral degeneration (Sir John Falstaff in *The Merry Wives of Windsor*) and English hostility against the aliens (Shylock in *The Merchant of Venice*) crop up time and again in the Romantic comedies of Shakespeare, eclipsing, at least for the time being, their carnival spirit.

The third phase of Shakespearean criticism which began since the 1970s tends to consider Shakespearean comedies in their own time and in the history of their subsequent reception. Among the disciplines of criticism, Feminism, (including Psychoanalysis), New Historicism and Cultural Materialism are given the greatest importance in this chapter, because these three disciplines reinterpret Shakespeare's comedies from the perspective of Elizabethan society. According to the conventional Feminists, Shakespearean comedies are actually a contention of gender issues, which deal with the problems of sexual identity, gender roles and family relations. And again, out of this contention of gender issues there emerge three distinct Feminist approaches of which the first and the most moderate one, views Shakespeare as a proto feminist, who loves portraying strong attractive heroines with distinct individualities. The critics adopting this approach refer to Portia and Helena to illustrate their point of view. Juliet Dusinberre's *Shakespeare and the Nature of Women* follows this line of argument as she contends that with the revival of humanism in England, Elizabethan women received a comparatively high social status and were encouraged to take part in the improved educational system (thus Bianca in *The Taming of the Shrew* is provided with a tutor by her otherwise conventional father Baptista Minola). Added to it the advocacy of the Puritans to marry for companionship allowed Elizabethan women to gain greater authority and freedom. Analyzing Shakespearean comedies from this angle Dusinberre states:

> Shakespeare knew that the tough intellect behind the raillery of the court ladies in *Love's Labour's Lost* of Beatrice and Rosalind or behind the self-awareness of Helena in *All's Well that Ends Well* had plenty of basis in real life.[13]

And this interest in women's roles and improved status, says Dusinberre, is not restricted to Shakespeare alone, "dramas written from 1590 to 1625 were all feminist in sympathy."[14] But Dusinberre's argument is definitely one-sided because it ignores the evils inherent in a patriarchal society, of which Shakespeare was fully aware. *The Taming of the Shrew* can be cited as a perfect example of the male repression that existed in Elizabethan society. Kate is an independent human being who is completely misunderstood by the society. (IV iii 77-80)[15] Even her father Baptista Minola has no sympathy for her as she is not ready to conform to the prevalent social codes and customs of bowing her head before every suitor who crosses her way. In contrast, Bianca her sister is more submissive at least before her marriage, and hence easily wins the men to her side. But Baptista's impatience with Kate, hints the playwright, is just characteristic of the patriarchal order, which is not ready to accept a well-developed personality in a girl.

The second approach of Feminist criticism as reflected in the works of Coppelia Kahn, C.T. Neely and Peter Erickson tends to view Shakespeare's comedies as ideal pictures of the patriarchal assumptions which sought to marginalize the Elizabethan women. In the process of interpreting Shakespeare's treatment of the problems of sexual identity and family relationships, Coppelia Kahn observes:

> In the action of his plays, he explores the unconscious attitude behind cultural definitions of manliness and womanliness and behind the mores and institutions shaped by them. Leontes' horns, Macbeth's "unmannerly breech'd dagger," Kate's hand beneath her husband's foot and Cariolanus's wounds are prismatic ambivalent images at the center of works that examine sexual

> identity as shaped by the patriarchal culture in which the playwright lived.[16]

Kahn's analysis is both psychoanalytic and feminist, because she lays greater stress on the behaviorial patterns of the characters in the comedies, which are born out of their unconscious conformation with the cultural values of a patriarchal society. And Kate's ready submission to place her hand beneath her husband's foot, when analyzed from that perspective, is a justified "emblem of wifely obedience"[17] to establish the manliness of Petruchio and make him the indisputable master. Marriage in *The Taming of the Shrew* is, therefore, an ideal means to achieve social harmony in the patriarchy.

C.T. Neely's *Broken Nuptials in Shakespeare's Plays* illuminates another facet of Elizabethan marriage in relation to the patriarchal society. To an Elizabethan, marriage was more important than the mere selection of a spouse who was good to look at. How far the girl would be able to assist her husband both physically (i.e., through healthy procreation) and socially was of primary importance. And elucidating this aspect Neely observes:

> The prescriptive literature, while urging men to marry and providing them with detailed instructions on the choice of their wives, rarely provides assistance for women beyond a vague admonition to choose a spouse wisely.[18]

The Elizabethan patriarch did not reckon it necessary to advise women about their marriage because choosing the spouse was not their prerogative; rather it was their parents who completely controlled all their premarital affairs. At times, parents would fix up the betrothals of their children "before they reached the age of consent"[19] and these betrothals would continue even after their death. Portia's protest in *The Merchant of Venice* is just an example to show the pointlessness of this arbitrary law of the patriarchy:

> .. O me the word "choose" I may neither Choose Who I would, nor refuse who I dislike, so is the Will of a

> Living daughter curb'd by the will of a dead father; is it not Hard Narrisa, that I cannot choose One, nor refuse none? (I ii 22-26)[20]

Marriage also failed to liberate the Elizabethan women since, sexually the Renaissance men thought that it was their sacred duty to subjugate their wives' wills. "Many Shakespearean husbands among them, Petruchio, Benedick, Othello, and Leontes manifest the desire to control their wife's will and appetite."[21] Furthermore, a strange kind of "conflict between male-female relations and male-male relations"[22] in the patriarchy achieved to complicate the gender issues of the plays. And, hence, until the characters in the comedies were able to overcome or mitigate the male bonds, which had behind them the force of patriarchal social norms, there could be no marriage or any other kind of resolution. The male-male relation in *The Two Gentlemen of Verona,* illustrated by the intimate friendship between Proteus and Valentine at one stage of the play, proves to be a dangerous proposition. Valentine's amorous alliances with Silvia, in fact, temporarily snaps their friendship, because, Proteus, overcome by sudden infatuation for Silvia, forgets all his past commitments and forswears both Valentine and Julia.(II iv 1-43)[23] But strangely enough, the price he pays for his betrayal is very little compared to his offence. The moment Proteus apologizes (V iv 73-77) all the male characters are overjoyed and they forgive him unconditionally, and even Julia readily accepts him. "Proteus, Bear witness, heaven/I have my wish forever./Julia. And I mine" (V iv 118-119). And this happens only because the key issue in such a society "is the tendency of male characters to have a primary attachment to men rather than to women."[24] No Shakespearean heroine committing a similar offence could ever imagine getting away so easily. In fact, Elizabethan men, at times even presuming the adultery of their wives, did not hesitate to torture them in public. Thus, in *The Merry Wives of Windsor,* Ford's unjustified suspicion and public humiliation of his wife is hardly censured by the society (III iii 145-147)[25]. Ford calls his insanity a "sport" (III iii 157) while his friends and observers derive lots of amusement from the situation (III iii 158).

The critics of the third approach of Feminist criticism relate the contradictions in Shakespearean comedies to both residual patriarchal assignments of gender and emergent feminist practices. They find in all the Elizabethan plays that these two factors are always held in contention, because the age itself was characterised by change in gender roles and authority within the family. *Twelfth Night* illustrates their views because the central focus of the play is on cross-dressing, which as in *As You Like It*, effectively blurs the sexual difference at the heart of the play. Both Viola and Rosalind are not merely women disguised as men, but also equally desired as partners by both men and women alike. In *Twelfth Night*, Olivia takes an instant liking for Cesario (disguised Viola) and she confesses it quite candidly (I v 296-302).[26] In the same way at the end of the play, when a final resolution is nearly reached, Viola discards her disguise much to the joy of Orsino, who instantly shifts his affection from Olivia to Viola (V I 319- 325). In *As You Like It*, correspondingly, Ganymede (disguised Rosalind) automatically evokes the emotion of love in Phebe which rather confuses her (III v 72-75) but at the end when she steps out of her disguise, she becomes Orlando's dearest Rosalind. "If there be truth in sight, you are my Rosalind" (V iv 118). In both the comedies the girls play roles that provide counter-roles for the men and finally draw them into the sphere of participation. Hence, by the end of both the plays, characters of both sexes are alternately actors and audience, cooperating in a relationship of mutuality. There fictions have helped to express truths like sexuality, physicality, diversion, dependence, flexibility and above all compromise. Both Viola and Rosalind repeatedly compromise with the alien world by disguising their true identities to protect themselves. In both the plays the heroines suppress their true identities in order to present themselves in circumstances where they will be either rebuffed or subjected to injury. And, being women of exceptional ability, they venture to cross the boundaries defined by the stipulations of a conventional patriarchal society.

Dwelling on the sexuality, physicality and diversion in Shakespearean comedies, Stephen Greenblatt observes:

> Shakespearean comedy constantly appeals to the body and in particular to sexuality as the heart of its theatrical magic; "great creating nature" – the principle by which the world is and must be peopled is the comic playwright's tutelary spirit. But there is no unmeditated access to the body, no direct appropriation of sexuality rather sexuality is itself a network of historically contingent figures that constitutes the culture's categorical understanding of erotic experience. These figures function as modes of translation between distinct social discourses, channels through which the shared commotion of sexual excitement circulates.[27]

Elizabethan men never acknowledged the erotic potentials of their women, because to them women were mere agents of procreation and it was not necessary that they should "experience any pleasure at all to conceive."[28] And possibly it was this belief on their part that assisted the patriarchy to marginalize women so easily. Citing the evidence of many Elizabethan medical texts to prove his point Greenblatt concludes:

> The medical texts that we have been examining suggest that the generative power of nature centers on fruitful, pleasurable chafing, and I want to propose that this notion...resonates in the fashioning of Shakespearean character, particularly in comedy. The theatrical representation of individuality is in effect modeled on what the culture thought occurred during sexual foreplay and inter-course: erotic chafing is the central means by which characters in plays like *The Taming of the Shrew*, *A Midsummer Night's Dream* and ... *Twelfth Night* realize their identities and form loving unions.[29]

But because women did not require any erotic pleasure, the pleasurable chafing was one-sided, enjoyed by men alone, and understandably, therefore, Olivia's views after the shocking revelation of Sebastian's true identity was not really asked for by the audience. To the patriarchy either Cesario or Sebastian would do for her, but because Cesario was a girl she had to be substituted by her male counterpart, her twin brother Sebastian. And whether Olivia finally accepts him remains unresolved at the end of the play, because she is absolutely mute on this problematic issue.

The critics of the New Historicism movement originated by Greenblatt, however link the texts of Shakespearean comedies to a network of cultural forces with historical material. Diaries, legal records, anecdotes and patterns of political or religious authority are cited by them as articulations of the society's dominant cultural forces. According to the New Historicists all individual texts and individual subjects are both imprisoned and legitimated by a rich and tightly-bound culture. No creative artist is therefore, capable of rising above it and more so a comic playwright, because the genre he cultivates is totally committed to human society and its culture. The general tendency of a New Historicist essay is to begin with an historical anecdote "what Jean Howard terms as illustrative example"[30] to the literary text under discussion to "demonstrate the connections and inter-weavings of the lines of power across disparate culture practices in the society."[31] Karen Newman's essay 'Renaissance Family Politics and Shakespeare's *The Taming of the Shrew*'[32] written in the style of New Historicism with a strong feminist undertone, begins with recounting of a tale from *Wetherden Suffolk*, Plough Monday, 1604. It is a story about a drunken tanner, who on being beaten by his wife for his drunkenness, is avenged by his neighbour Quarry in a woman's clothes. "The entire incident figures the social anxiety about gender power which characterizes Elizabethan culture."[33] Like the wife in the quoted story who lacks an identity of her own, Kate is also referred to in *The Taming of the Shrew* as an animal who cannot be carted (I i 55). This attitude was possibly prompted by a historical phenomenon which Karen Newman calls the "crisis of order" generated by the "fear that women were rebelling against their traditional subservient role in patriarchal culture."[34] This fear inevitably generated in the patriarchy a troubled gender relation, which in turn affected the whole matrix of family relations. And the only solution the patriarchy found to this problem was to subjugate women by both physically assaulting them and mentally torturing them to utter submission (*The Taming of the Shrew* IV i 175-198).

Leonard Tennenhouse's *Power on Display* provides another evidence of the New Historic criticism of Shakespearean drama. It reads the comedies in terms of an inescapable, hierarchical view of power. Tennenhouse begins his analysis with a detailed survey of the court politics of the Elizabethan age and then citing instances of monarchical arbitrariness, infers that most of the Elizabethan playwrights, including Shakespeare, fashioned their plays in accord with Queen Elizabeth's preferences. Commenting on the conventions of Elizabethan marriage Tennenhouse observes that because Elizabethan marriages were political alliance of wealth and connection it:

> was considered an overtly political activity, certainly not something to be left to the whim of the children – often barely in their teens – by means of whom alliances were made and the value of blood perpetuated.[35]

Thus, in *A Midsummer Night's Dream*, when Hermia requests Theseus to allow her to marry Lysander against the wish of her father, Theseus threatens her, "Either to die the death, or to abjure/ Forever the society of man" (I i 65-66).[36] No argument of Hermia can move Theseus because the law of Athens permits the father's will to overrule a girl's preference (I i 117-121). Marriage was also a means to "keep property within a family" and hence, rich heirs and heiresses "in their minority sometimes found themselves married off by their uncles within days of their parents' death."[37] Sir Toby's incessant strife to get Olivia married to Sir Andrew in *Twelfth Night* is possibly a hint at this practice. But Shakespeare's commitments to the court were not without a trace of sarcasm, and his romantic comedies were aimed at mocking the excesses and absurdities of the courtly tradition. Hence pertinently Tennenhouse observes:

> His (Shakespeare's) comedies invoke courtly tropes as a way to mock the communication situation of the court

> in which these tropes were used in all earnestness. One need only look at the excesses of the courtiers at Navarre's court to see the element of parody which enters into courtly discourse when Shakespeare reproduces it upon the public stage. But there is a host of characters who materialize the courtly lover just as absurdly: Lucentio from *The Taming of the Shrew*, the lovers in *A Midsummer Night's Dream*, Bassanio in *The Merchant of Venice* as well as figures as Orlando and Orsino.[38]

The trend however, discontinued by the time James came to the throne, and in place of the lighthearted treatment of aristocratic love came the tragicomedies and dramatic responses.

In a critical approach based on Cultural Materialism the central tendency is to lay greater stress on "potential growing points and contradictions, both referred to within the text or which, as it were, lurk on its margins."[39] Marxist theorists like Althusser, Macherey and Williams exerted the greatest influence on the Cultural Materialistic readings of Shakespearean dramas. Gary Waller tells us:

> Cultural Materialism investigates resistance to power rather than its apparent dominance, focusing on marginal groups like women, witches, the sexuality or economically disenfranchised, on conflict among class factions and racial minorities – in short on the marginal but insistent forces that challenge and may eventually break down a monolithic construction of power. The characteristic agenda of Cultural Materialism is the quaternary of gender, race, class and agency issues that arise from distinctly contemporary struggles, but which still acknowledge the historical differences between our society and that of Shakespeare. Consequently, where 'power' is a key word for a New Historicist, 'ideology' is the central focus for Cultural Materialism.[40]

Kate's ostracization by the patriarchy (*The Taming of the Shrew* I i 57-58) in Cultural Materialistic analysis is therefore, an attempt by the dominant power to disenfranchise her. Her rebellious temperament that seems to subjugate her in considerations of gender – just as it inveigles Shylock in *The Merchant of Venice,* into a ruinous situation on considerations of race and religion.

Elucidating the process of materialist criticism Jonathan Dollimore writes:

> Three aspects of historical and cultural process figure prominently in materialist criticism: consolidation, subversion and containment. The first – refers, typically to the idelogical means whereby a dominant order seeks to perpetuate itself; the second to the subversion of that order, the third to the containment of ostensibly subversive pressures.[41]

The incessant conflict inherent in Shakespearean comedies at times does corroborate Dollimore's analysis of consolidation, subversion and containment. The conflict between Oberon and Titania in *A Midsummer Night's Dream* over the Indian Prince is clearly an ideological conflict between the dominant order and the subversive pressures. Titania's dotage (II i 118-121) questions the authority of Oberon the monarch and hence he punishes her. Like Kate, Titania temporarily flashes a striking individuality which threatens Oberon and taking it for an open rebellion he instantly tries to crush it. Citing the example of *Measure for Measure* Dollimore further observes:

> The authoritarian demonizing of deviant behaviour was common in the period, and displacement and condensation— to and around low life— were crucial to this process ... But what made displacement and condensation possible was a prior construction of deviancy itself, so, for example, diatribes against promiscuity, female self-assertion, cross-dressing and homosexuality construed these behaviours as symptomatic of a impending dissolution of social hierarchy and so, in effect, of civilization.[42]

A strange decree of sexual abstinence (I i 119-130)[43] marks the beginning *of Love's Labour's Lost,* indicating an 'authoritarian demonizing of deviant behaviour.' The king and his friends readily conform to it, but the imposition of such a strict measure upon common people is clearly unjustified. When a low menial like Costard with no desire for any intellectual attainment momentarily transgresses the state machinery comes down heavily upon him: "Arm: Thou shalt be heavily punished" (I ii 141). Paradoxically, the very next instant Armado himself falls ready victim to the charms of Jaquenetta (I ii 157-160) establishing the fact that any amount of authoritarian subversion cannot dominate over human instincts.

Terry Eagleton's *William Shakespeare* is another materialistic criticism based on the ideological analysis of some of Shakespeare's plays. Dwelling on the theme of love from the perspective of sexual desire Eagleton observes:

> Desire in Shakespeare is often a kind of obsession, a well-nigh monomaniacal fixation on another which tends to paralyes the self to a rigid posture...There is something anarchic about sexual desire which is to be feared, and the fear is less moral than political: in exposing the provisional nature of any particular commitment, Eros offers a potent threat to social order.[44]

Understandably, therefore, Theseus in *A Midsummer Night's Dream* misunderstands Hermia's love for Lysander as an interplay of 'Eros'. Hermia's persuasion perhaps appears to him as a potential threat to social order, provoking him to threat her with dire consequences (I i 65-78). Likewise Malvolio's aspiration to marry Olivia in *Twelfth Night* is treated by contemporary world as a manifestation of 'a well-nigh monomaniacal fixation' forcing Sir Toby and his associates to imprison him both physically and morally. But in his treatment of both these cases Shakespeare appears to be a nonconformist. Hence, at the end Hermia is allowed to marry Lysander and Malvolio is made capable of disturbing his wrongdoers with threats of revenge.

In Terence Hawkes's analysis of *Twelfth Night* it is Malvolio the potentially tragic figure who poses a threat to contemporary aristocracy. His moral righteousness and overwhelming virtuosity, especially in regard to Sir Toby's behaviour (I iii) bespeak his Puritanical antecedent. In his heart of hearts he naturally detests the conspicuous lasciviousness of the members of the aristocracy who patronized the theater itself. Very significantly Hawkes observes:

> Shakespeare's comic plays can thus be seen not merely to assert the topsy-turvy values of Festival and Carnival in the face of a hegemonic 'everyday' but to do so in quite specific terms, asserting the interactive values of orality and community in the face of literate, book-committed Puritan to the theater. And they also assert the central importance of drama's oral mode as a model for, and emblem of, a 'good' participating, creating society, in the face of a 'bad', passive, inert society of consumer— spectators.[45]

The basic premise of all Shakespearean comedies, therefore, appears to be an effort at the recreation of a 'good' society free from all vices. Right from *The Comedy of Errors* to *Twelfth Night* the playwright has incessantly striven to present a set of standardized values which would enable the audience in the long run to form an ingenuous homogeneous society. Malvolio's attempt to check Sir Toby's noxious conduct has definitely been endorsed by the playwright himself. But, according to Hawkes, Malvolio's punishment is also ironically his excessive dotage on Puritan idealism. His single-minded Puritanical denial of cakes and ale is the denial of a considerable part of reality that can hardly be encouraged or supported.

The world of Shakespeare's Romantic comedies is the ultimate analysis of the world of Renaissance, where with the change of the feudal structure to rising bourgeoisie, the social values were also changing rapidly. Individual freedom, which apparently was a product of this change, was more relevant to the male characters of the plays because the existing patriarchy continued to marginalize women and treat them as an extension of male property. Heroines like Portia, Viola, Julia and Rosalind did try to create a ripple in the otherwise tranquil patriarchy, but ultimately all of them had to conform to the existing order of society. Parental control over their wards especially in marital affairs, manifestation of the arbitrary patriarchal law, governed nearly all the Shakespearean comedies with only a few exceptions. But romantic love ultimately triumphed in many of them, possibly because of the playwright's inclination for it. Money was another determining factor of marriage in the merchant plays of Shakespeare, a subject not really dealt at length, but merely hinted. The elements of romantic imagination and fantasy are relatively less frequently used in the early comedies than in the middle comedies, because the plots in the early comedies are slender as compared to those of the middle comedies. But with the development of his dramatic skill Shakespeare excelled in blending realism and romanticism in a well balanced manner. But the most striking aspect in all the comedies is the benevolent attitude of the creator towards his character, whether it is a Prince or a dark villain. Thus, the Windsorites are all eager to welcome the comic villain Falstaff at the wedding feast of Anne Page. In all these comedies, therefore, one finds that "Princes and dukes, lords and ladies, jostle with merchant weavers, joiners, country sluts, friendly rogues, school masters and village policeman" and no one is incapable of a "generous impulse."[46] Exceptions are there in *The Merchant of Venice* where Shakespeare appears to uphold "a mirror to man's inhumanity to man"[47] The law of the land cannot forgive an alien in spite of Portia's speech about "the quality of mercy" (IV i 180-210).

Chronologically speaking *The Comedy of Errors* is generally presumed to be the earliest of Shakespearean plays. And an in-depth analysis of it also reveals a wonderful fusion of realism with romanticism thereby establishing the fact that the playwright right from the beginning of his comic career conscientiously adhered to the basic premises of a comedy. The plot of the play however is not a totally ingenious one, having based itself largely to the materials of two Plautine comedies. But the final effect is certainly, not Plautine but completely Shakespearean with its central focus on the Renaissance mercantile class and its social values.

Notes

1. *Shakespeare's Happy Comedies*, Cambridge University Press, Cambridge, 1938.
2. H.B. Charlton, *Shakespearian Comedy*, Methuen, London, 1938 rep. 1979, p. 23.
3. *Ibid.*, p. 27.
4. G.K. Hunter, 'Shakespeare The Writer and His Works' in *Shakespeare Survey* 22, p. 7.
5. *Ibid.*, p. 8.
6. 'The Presentation of Comedy. The first Ten Plays' in *Stratford-Upon-Avon Studies* 14, eds. Malcolm Bradbury, David Palmer, and Edward Arnold, London, 1972, p. 9.
7. *Comedy Meaning and Form*, Harper and Row, New York, 1981, p. 8.
8. *Ibid.*, p. 48.
9. *Shakespeare's Festive Comedy*, Princeton University Press, New Jersey, 1954 rep. 1972, p. 3.
10. *Ibid.*, p. 5.
11. *Ibid.*, p. 7.
12. *Ibid.*, p. 6.
13. Macmillan, Hong Kong, 1975, p. 2.
14. *Ibid.*, p. 5.
15. All textual reference to *The Taming of the Shrew* are to the Arden Shakespeare *The Taming of the Shrew*, ed. Brian Morris, Methuen, London, 1981.
16 *Man's Estate, Masculine Identity in Shakespeare*, University of California Press, Berkeley, 1981, p. 1.
17. *Ibid.*, p. 117.
18. Yale University Press, New Haven, 1985, p. 11.
19. *Ibid.*, p. 10.
20. All textual references to *The Merchant of Venice* are to the Arden Shakespeare *The Merchant of Venice*, ed., J.R. Brown, B.I. Publications, Delhi, 1964 rep.1983.
21. *Op. cit.*, p. 15.
22. Peter Erickson, *Patriarchal Structures of Shakespeare's Drama*, 1985, University Press, Berkeley, p.1.

23. All textual references to *The Two Gentlemen of Verona* are to the Arden Shakespeare *The Two Gentlemen of Verona*, ed., Clifford Leech, Methuen, London, 1972 rep. 1986,
24. *Op. cit.*, p. 6.
25. All the textual references to *The Merry Wives of Windsor* are to the Arden Shakespeare *The Merry Wives of Windsor*, ed. H.J. Oliver, Methuen, London, 1973 rep.1985.
26. All the textual references to *Twelfth Night* and *As You Like It* are to the Arden Shakespeare. *Twelfth Night*, ed. J.M. Lothian and T.W. Craik, Routledge, 1975 rep. 1994, London. *As You Like It*, ed. Agnes Lotham, B.I. Publication, Delhi, 1975 rep. 1988.
27. *Shakespearean Negotiations The Circulation of Social Energy in Renaissance England*, Clarendon Press, Oxford, 1988 rep. 1990, p. 86-87.
28. *Ibid.*, p. 87.
29. *Ibid.*, p. 88.
30. In *Shakespeare's Comedy*, ed. Gary Waller, Longman, U.K., 1991, p. 9.
31. *Ibid.*, p. 26.
32. *Ibid.*, pp. 39-53.
33. *Ibid.*, pp. 41-42.
34. *Ibid.*, pp. 44-45.
35. Methuen, London, 1986, pp. 26-27.
36. All textual references to *A Midsummer Night's Dream* are to the Arden Shakespeare *A Midsummer Night's Dream*, ed. Harold F. Brooks, Methuen, London, 1979.
37. *Op. cit.*, p. 27.
38. *Ibid.*, p. 37.
39. *Shakespeare's Comedies*, ed. Gary Waller, Longman, London, 1991, p. 20.
40. *Ibid.*, p. 20.
41. *Political Shakespeare: New Essays in Cultural Materialism* eds. Jonathan Dollimore, and Alan Sinfield, Manchester University Press, Gt. Britain, 1985, p. 10.
42. *Ibid.*, p. 74.
43. All textual references to *Love's Labour's Lost* are to the Arden Shakespeare *Love's Labour's Lost*, ed. R.W. David, Methuen, London, 1968, rep. 1985.

44. Basil Blackwell Ltd., Oxford, 1986. p. 20.
45. In *Shakespeare's Comedies,* ed. Gary Waller, Longman, London, 1991, pp. 171-172.
46. Nevill Coghill, 'The Basis of Shakespearean Comedy' in *Shakespeare Criticism,* 1935-60, ed. Anne Ridler, 1963, p. 201.
47. Margaret Bennell, *Shakespeare's Flowering of the Spirit,* Lanthorn Press, London, 1971, p. 111.

3

THE COMEDY OF ERRORS

> Since money, as the existing and active concept of value, confounds and confuses all things, it is the general confounding and confusing of all things— the world upside down— the confusing and confounding of all natural and human qualities.*

The Comedy of Errors was first printed in the First Folio edition of Shakespeare's plays in 1693, consisting of about 1800 lines and was Shakespeare's shortest play. Though the exact date of its composition is unknown, its first recorded performance was at Gray's Inn on 28 December 1594. Quiller-Couch and Dover Wilson editors of the New Cambridge text, however, place it within the limits of the French civil war, which ended with Henry of Navarre becoming Henry VI of France in July 1593. In that case, of course the jest in Act III might have appeared very appropriate to the Elizabethan audience. The lines are,

> Antipholus of Syracuse: Where France?
> Dromio of Syracuse: In her forehead, armed and reverted, making, war against her heir (I ll 120-122).[1]

This assumption again.establishes a clear link between *The Comedy of Errors* and *Love's Labour's Lost. Love's Labour's Lost* set at the court of the King of Navarre is also thought to have been written when Henry of Navarre was engaged in the

* Karl Marx, *Works* III in J. P. Brockbank, *On Shakespeare,* Basil Blackwell, Oxford, 1989, p. 11.

civil war with the support of the English government and forces between 1591 and 1593. Two other plays that bear close affinities to *The Comedy of Errors* are *The Two Gentlemen of Verona* and *The Taming of the Shrew*.

Shakespeare's principal source for *The Comedy of Errors* was Plautus's *Menaechmi,* presumably in an English translation. The play, in fact, provided a natural starting point for the study of Shakespeare's use of inherited materials in that it was clearly structured upon a classical comedy and, therefore, lay closest to the type of creative adaptation implanted persistently in the Tudor schoolroom. And Plautus's *Menaechmi* (originally a Greek play of unknown origin), being extremely popular and frequently edited and acted in the Renaissance, proved to be Shakespeare's ideal material for a creative adaptation. But the brevity of the classical comedy would not satisfy the audience of the Elizabethan stage. Therefore, Shakespeare, seeing it as a play of errors, increased the number of misadventures and added other ingredients more English than Roman. And in this process of enlarging the play's scope Shakespeare adapted a few incidents and characters from another Plautine play, namely *Amphitruo*.

Menaechmi enacts the hilarious sequence of misunderstandings that spring from the arrival of one member of a pair of twins in a town, in which his brother unknown to him happens to be a leading citizen. The first Act of the play is devoted to an exposition of the estrangement between his brother (Menaechmus the citizen) and his shrewish wife whom he proposes to spite by giving one of her garments to a courtesan. The second Act introduces the second twin (also Menaechmus) who is instantly taken for the leading citizen both by the courtesan and her servant. Though he accepts their hospitality and pretends to be the man they take him for, he nevertheless remains sceptical about their sanity. In the third Act things become more complicated when the newly arrived twin is entrusted with a garment and a gold chain appropriated by his brother. In the fourth Act, the resident Menaechmus is challenged by his wife over both the garment and the chain. The confusion mounts high in the fifth Act and all the characters regard one another as mad before the source of the errors is revealed. With the unravelling of the situational complexities, all the problems are sorted out and the brothers joyfully united.

Plautus's *Amphitruo,* however, highlights the love-rivalry between two men identical in appearance. In the play, Jupiter takes the place of A*mphitruo* in his house, and sleeps with his wife, Alcmena, who unsuspectingly takes him to be her husband. Meanwhile Mercury, disguised as Amphitruo's slave, Sosia, at first confuses and then drives away the real Sosia. A good deal of fun comes from Alcmena's bewilderment when her real husband returns from the wars only a few moments after the false one has left her in the second scene of the second Act, and from Amphituro's suspicion that she has betrayed him. In the third Act, Jupiter returns as Amphituro, and the climax comes when Amphitruo tries to enter his house while Jupiter is within and is refused admission by Mercury disguised as Sosia. By transferring the identical slaves of Amphitruo to the plot of *Menaechmi,* Shakespeare more than doubled the possibility of error, much to the bewilderment of both the audience and the characters of his play.

In his fusion of the Latin plays Shakespeare follows a very interesting pattern. He certainly adapts incidents and characters from the two plays of Plautus, but very often changes the order of the events. For example, in the first Act *of The Comedy of Errors* he scrupulously follows *Menaechmi's* Prologue and introduces Egeon the Syracusan merchant who (in Menaechmi as well) is the father of twin sons and from whom he has been estranged for quite sometime. But Shakespeare introduces Antipholus of Syracuse in the very first Act, whereas Plautus introduces Menaechmus the citizen in the first Act. And the first confusion of identity occurs in the first Act of *The Comedy of Errors,* while in *Menaechmi* it occurs in the second Act with the arrival of Menaechmus the second twin. For the third Act of his play Shakespeare relies more upon *Amphitruo* than *Menaechmi.* In the third Act of *Amphitruo* the real Amphitruo is refused admission to his own house by Mercury disguised as Sosia. In a similar fashion

Antipholus of Ephesus is driven away from his own house by his wife and servants in the third Act of *The Comedy of Errors*. Many such similarities and dissimilarities are observed throughout the play, establishing clearly the fact that Shakespeare's adaptations of his sources were based upon the needs of his comedy.

Apart from Plautus, Shakespeare seems to have derived from another important source while composing *The Comedy of Errors,* St Paul's Epistle to the Ephesians in the *Holy Bible.* St Paul's exhortations to wives and husbands and to servants and masters "Wives, submit yourselves unto your husbands, as unto the Lord"[2] to maintain a proper harmony in their relationships seems to have influenced many passages in the play. A man is the master of his liberty; but in the given comedy it appears that time is actually their master, for instance when they see the appropriate time, "They'll go or come": (II i 9) which in turn essentially echoes St Paul's Epistle to the Ephesians (V). Similarly, the quarrel between Antipholus of Syracuse and Dromio of Syracuse:

> Antipholus of Syracuse; Yes, dost thou Jeer and flout me in the teeth?
> Think'st thou I jest hold take thou that and that (Beats Dromio)
> Dromio of Syracuse: Hold sir, for God's sake now your jest is earnest (II ii 22-24),

reminds the audience of another exhortation of St Paul: "Servants, be obedient unto them that are your master" (Ephesians vi).[3] And probably it was this source again which inspired Shakespeare to change the setting of his play from Epidamnum to Ephesus, because, according to the *Holy Bible,* Ephesus was a city where witchcraft and curious arts were extensively practised (Acts xix: "Many of them which also used curious arts brought their books together and burned them before all men").[4] And in the context of the magical tricks of Ephesus, Antipholus of Syracuse is made to think of the land as peopled with "nimble jugglers that deceive the eye,/ Dark-working Sorcerers that change the mind, /Soul-killing witches that deform the body"(I ii 98-100). The mistakes of identity which befall him seem like a nightmare of supernatural deception (II ii 199-201).

Shakespeare's interest in family relationships, however, compels him to make some deliberate alterations of his sources. And since Elizabethan family was very different from the ancient Roman family such alterations were not only inevitable but also essential. Analysing Shakespeare's alterations Geoffrey Bullough observes:

> He tells his Ephesian tale in terms of modern novella, which usually included some moral touches in an English version. In Plautus the Citizen's Wife is a figure of fun, a 'nagger' whose father blames her for being too ferocious, 'masterful and obstinate' and in the end she is dismissed with a laugh when her husband says he would sell her if he could find a bidder. Shakespeare builds on this considerably; his play deepens from farce, touching on the relations of husbands and wives, parents, children, in a moralizing way.[5]

Therefore, it is hardly surprising to find Adriana raising her voice of protest against male supremacy: "Why should their liberty than ours be more" (II i 10) or even against the infidelity of husbands: "His company must do his minions grace/Whilst I at home starve for a merry look"(II i 87-88). The introduction of Luciana is, of course, an important alteration which Shakespeare deliberately makes to satisfy the romantic yearnings of the Elizabethan audience. The Elizabethans loved to see a beautiful, gentle-hearted girl whose "lips speak in the sweet new style singers and sonneteers were consecrating to lovers and love-making."[6] Therefore, it was expected that they would welcome and appreciate the amorous approaches of Antipholus of Syracuse: "Are you a god? Would you create me new?/Transform me then, and to your power I'll yield" (III ii 39-40). The Renaissance saw the upsurge of a romantic spirit which Shakespeare mirrors in the love that develops between Luciana and Antipholus (of Syracuse). And since women could no longer be treated as commodities that could be sold off at their husband's will *(Menaechmi* V) both

Adriana and Luciana express a few definite opinions about the roles their life partners are expected to play (II ii 130-146 and III ii 17-24).

Shakespeare's characterization of the two Dromios is another instance of his alteration of the sources. Plautus's Messenio *(Menaechmi)* or Sosia *(Amphitruo)* differ from the two Dromios in their modes of function. Unlike their Roman counterparts the two Dromios can never engineer the story forward. Almost "invariably they are merely its clowns"[7] who only adorn the English stage and entertain the Elizabethan audience. Such a change of function, however, was inevitable since the sixteenth-century bourgeoisie had no place for Plautine man-servants who often shared the confidential and personal secrets of their masters. Rather, the English masters of the sixteenth-century kicked and beat them at frequent intervals. Therefore, through their ineffectiveness in the plot, Shakespeare probably wants to reflect upon their wretched conditions in real life.

Unlike Plautus's *Menaechmi* or *Amphitruo, The Comedy of Errors* is clearly a story of the English merchant-class. The English middle-class of the Renaissance who relied heavily on trade and commerce for sustenance had surely influenced Shakespeare's creative alteration. And to make his plot effective for this purpose he almost naturally transports the setting of the play from the busy Plautine Mediterranean seaport to the coast of England with which he was very familiar.[8] The result of such a transition has proved to be extremely happy. Shakespeare's Ephesus is a far more living city than Plautus's Epidamnum. Ephesus, in fact, turns into a contemporary living place "where men encountered the perennial problem of how to live together."[9] And the problems the characters of the comedy face in this setting are singularly similar to those faced by the Elizabethan middle-class. Therefore, it can be safely assumed that Shakespeare's alterations of sources were propelled by a permanent instinct of the playwright to portray the Elizabethan society in his comedies. And it was not the compulsion of his audience but rather his own instinct which insisted on connecting and demonstrating a unified whole of all human experiences. Thus even in the small and ordinary town of Ephesus we find that "everybody knows everyone else's business, where merchants predominate and where dinner is a serious matter."[10]

Shakespeare differs from the majority of his contemporaries in the way he extends the method of adaptation to his own plays. Not only does he follow the accepted method of structuring his plays on literary sources; he also looks back to his own plot material, utilising old devices in new ways, and re-using situations for different effects. The traditional comic structure assumed a far different and deeper meaning in his compositions. The apparently simple romantic plot of comedy is utilised to delineate the multiple facets of human relationship. The shrewish wife Adriana, for example, turns into an instrument of the playwright to portray the multiplicity of women's nature. And her jealousy and possessiveness are:

> treated by Shakespeare with an effort at psychological plausibility which on occasion surpasses the hard-boiled attitude which we might have expected him to take over from his originals.[11]

Therefore, what to some appears to be merely a romantic comedy of Shakespeare is in reality a play presenting an insightful study of human relationship, human psychology and human society. Structurally, the play is undoubtedly successful as it presents a harmonious blend of both the subversive and normative elements of a comedy. The normative elements may not be visible at first, but on closer analysis of the subversive elements the reader and the audience alike realize that, beneath the comic situations there is something more the playwright wants to say. For example, the play begins on a serious note (Egeon's impending death-sentence) giving a direct hint to the realities of the cruel world, but a comic intermission in the very next scene (the confusion of the identity of Antipholus of Syracuse) covers it up deftly. Dromio of Ephesus's mistake in thinking Antipholus of Syracuse to be his master instantly moves the audience to laughter. Though we are aware of his mistake, Dromio is certain that he is his master and so goes on insisting: "My charge was but to fetch you home from the mart home to your house, /The Phoenix, sir, to dinner my mistress and her sister stays for you." (I ii 74-76) Antipholus of Syracuse who commits the same mistake is vexed beyond limits "I shall break that merry scone of yours / That stands on tricks when I am undispos'd" (I ii 79-80). But before he can act Dromio plays it safe, and runs off stage, leaving the dumbfounded Antipholus to mumble to himself: "this town is full of cozenage" (I ii 79). The description of Nell the kitchen maid by Dromio of Syracuse to his master is a hilarious occasion which entertains the audience. The description (III ii 93-145) may not be very refined, but the groundlings definitely found it very entertaining. Antipholus of Syracuse's proposal to Luciana (III ii 29-52) and her subsequent refusal provide another comic situation for the audience. All these and many more incidents successfully wipe out for the time being the seriousness of the impending death-sentence of Egeon. But the aim of the playwright is not restricted to the evocation of laughter alone; he desires to rouse in the viewers the feelings of compassion, sympathy and understanding for unfortunate characters like Egeon, the victims of circumstances. And, therefore, at the end of the play (V i) Shakespeare brings in Egeon and also the unfortunate Adriana who for no fault of hers has been wronged by the Abbess who has shut her gate against her and will not allow her to look after her ailing husband (V i 155-160). R.A. Foakes observes in this context:

> The comedy proves, after all, to be more than a temporary and hilarious abrogation of normality; it is, at the same time a process in which the main characters are in some sense purged before harmony and the responsibility of normal relationships are restored at the end.[12]

Therefore, even the arrest of Antipholus of Ephesus brings about something other than mere fun. Like Malvolio in *Twelfth Night* he is punished temporarily, though for no fault of his. Malvolio's punishment was at least the result of the misdeeds of other characters of the play but poor Antipholus was punished because of a deep-rooted misunderstanding. And Shakespeare may have deliberately indulged in such a misunderstanding to drive home to his audience the crass idiocy of another misconception about the birth of twins. Twins, it was believed from ancient times, could only be born of an immoral mother. Elucidating the misconception Michael Grivelet observes:

> Twins it appears were always, for early humanity a subject of scandal and concern. In his study of the *Double* Otto Rank, the follower of Freud has collected evidence showing that primitive societies regarded the birth of twins as something supernatural, both evil and holy....As late as the Middle Ages, it was believed that twins could only be born of an adulterous mother....For reasons obvious enough in a context of Christian and highly domestic ideals, Shakespeare has toned down this aspect of the plot. But even then his Adriana, dutiful though she is narrowly escapes going to bed with the wrong Antipholus. And thus the case reveals itself as not one of mere dissipation but of potential incest...[13]

Plautus, however, is more desperate in this matter. His Alcmena goes to bed with the wrong Amphitruo (Jupiter disguised as Amphitruo) and conceives a child. Shakespeare being more cautious prevents Adriana from committing any such blunders, as the Elizabethans would not put up with heinous moral laxity on their stage. Therefore, despite following the Plautine play-structure the playwright very consciously avoids such occurrences. Antipholus of Syracuse, a true representative of the Elizabethans, is highly romantic, while his brother is very much a man of the world. Alexander Leggatt, however, has a different explanation for the differences that exist between the two brothers. To him Shakespeare's explicit desire was to emphasize the conflicting values of the commercial world and the world outside Ephesus through the differences of their outlooks on men and things. Thus, Antipholus of Syracuse is showered with all items of good immediately after his arrival at Ephesus, though he does not even ask for them, and his romantic spirit, though surprised, accepts them easily, while the extra-cautions Antipholus of Ephesus (who marries also according to the dictates of the Duke and not according to the dictates of his heart) is constantly being deprived of his own possessions. Their experiences vary according to their natures:

> ... throughout the play there are several small touches conveying the Ephesians' narrow concern with money. The merchant who talks with Antipholus of Syracuse in the second scene is kind enough to warn him against the law; but he refuses an invitation to keep his company and join him for dinner, on the grounds that he is already engaged 'to certain merchants/Of whom I hope to make much benefit' (I ii 24-25). The Officer who arrests Antipholus of Ephesus refuses to release him even when told he is mad and needs treatment 'He is my prisoner; if I let him go,/The debt he owes will be requir'd of me' (IV iv 14-15).[14]

It is in this world of money and benefits that Antipholus of Ephesus lives as a very respectable citizen. His marriage also is no romantic fancy but rather based on the approval and sanctions of the ruler of the place, the Duke. In such a money-oriented world disruption of normalcy in both domestic and social spheres is an unsettling and unpleasant experience for the victim but broad fun for the audience. In contrast the amorous approaches of Antipholus of Syracuse towards Luciana appear irrational and even crazy (III ii 52-53). Leggatt is again right when he says:

> What is enchantment and enrichment for one brother is simply confusion for the other, a confusion that must be put right. The only party to gain something is the audience; since commercial life has been depicted in such unflattering terms, we are bound to take a special, mischievous delight in seeing it disrupted.[15]

Yet, in spite of their differences the brothers are happy to be united, and a bright happy future of a united family is predicted by Shakespeare at the end. At last the search of the other half is complete and Antipholus of Syracuse instructs his servant, "Embrace the brother there, and rejoice with him" (V i 413), and in turn leaves the stage with his brother.

This search of Antipholus of Syracuse is interpreted by the psychoanalytical school of Shakespearean criticism as a search for one's own identity. W. Thomas MacCarey, an exponent of this school, draws our attention to certain uncommon features of *The Comedy of Errors*. Unlike the typical romantic comedies, this play does not end in a happy marriage. Rather the existing marriage of the couple Adriana and Antipholus of Ephesus remains unreconstructed. Therefore, it is quite likely that Shakespeare's main objective here is to focus the spectator's attention upon a family reunion and also a reunion of the twins. This major deviation occurs, argues MacCarey, because the playwright consciously desires to portray through the search an unconscious yet eternal pursuit of all human beings to unite oneself with one's ideal ego. And since all human beings are in search of such an ideal union the play appeals to all the audiences, irrespective of time and place. And once such an ideal self-identification occurs all the viewers are exhilarated, which purges them of all evil emotions.[16] Therefore, when Antipholus of Syracuse identifies himself with a drop of water: "That in the ocean seeks another drop/Who falling there to find his fellow forth,/ (Unseen inquisitive) confounds himself."(I ii 36-38). "He speaks to us in terms which are frighteningly real. The plight of the protagonist is felt almost physically, his yearning for his double accepted as natural and inevitable."[17] If the comedy is then approached from this angle this quest of an individual transcends all limits of time, place and society. It is an eternal phenomenon which affects men of all ages and is therefore a real issue which should be recognized and accepted in all the societies of the world.

The play, in fact, begins on a note of quest by Egeon. From the very onset the protagonists of *The Comedy of Errors* are aware of themselves as moving towards a condition of isolation. Egeon expresses his grief to Duke Solinus of Ephesus over the progressive disintegration of his family in the very first scene, Antipholus of Syracuse feels lost in the course of his search for his missing relatives (I ii 33-40), while Adriana his brother's wife, is found lamenting over her growing distance from her husband (II i 87-101). A serious conversation between Egeon and Solinus marks the beginning of *The Comedy of Errors.* Solinus, following the law of Ephesus which punished all the citizens of Syracuse, who stepped into Ephesus, is about to punish Egeon. The punishment is heavy; the citizen either pays a thousand marks or (in case of failure in procuring the money) be hanged. Solinus's sympathy cannot overrule the law. All he does is to relax it a bit after a patient hearing of Egeon's tale of woe:

> Therefore, merchant, I'll limit thee this day...,
> Try all the friends thou has in Ephesus,
> Beg thou, or borrow, to make up the sum
> And live; if no, then thou art doom'd to die
> (I i 150-154).

In the very next scene Antipholus of Syracuse arrives at Ephesus, of which his father is totally unaware. He talks to a merchant who informs him about the harsh law of Ephesus of which Solinus has just spoken in the previous scene. Dromio of Syracuse is found to accompany the new comer. Taking the advice of the merchant Antipholus instructs Dromio to take all his money to Centaur and wait there till he reaches it for his day's shelter. Dromio leaves and the two continue their talk when Dromio of Ephesus walks in to beckon the wrong master home to dinner. The first confusion occurs. Dromio of Ephesus, thinking Antipholus of Syracuse to be his master, says: "The clock hath struck twelve upon the bell;/My mistress made it one upon my cheek" (I ii 45-46). The common Elizabethan dinner-hour was between 11 and 12 noon and dinner was considered the biggest meal of the day. Antipholus is astonished; he thinks that his servant is teasing him. He asks for the money and Dromio of Ephesus replies, "0, six pence that I had O' Wednesday las" (I i 55). The use of pence here is a clear indication of Shakespeare's effort to make the classical plot speak out in contemporary accents. Antipholus of Syracuse is furious, their conversation, though weird to each other, vastly entertains the spectators. The confusion continues till the end of the scene.

Adriana and Luciana are introduced to the audience in the first scene of the second Act. Adriana the jealous, possessive wife of Antipholus of Ephesus is seen conversing with Luciana about the inordinate delay of Antipholus for his dinner. Adriana is impatient, while Luciana tries to convince her of man's need for greater liberty (II i 7-25). Though Luciana's words echo the exhortations of St Paul (pointed out earlier) the possibility of what she says as being converted into contemporary ideology cannot be ruled out. Dromio of Ephesus's entry at this juncture interrupts their conversation, which takes a different turn altogether when the servant reports that his master is "horn mad" (II i 57). He has refused to come home for dinner and is absolutely crazy about some mysterious gold. Adriana's jealousy is instantly roused: "His company must do his minions grace / Whilst I at home starve for a merry look" (II i 87-88).[18] All the soft soothing words of Luciana fail to pacify her wrath.

The Second scene of the same Act finds Antipholus of Syracuse grumbling at the irresponsibility of his servant, when Dromio of Syracuse walks in. The master bursts forth, "How, now sir, is your merry humour alter'd?" (II i 7). Dromio is taken aback. He denies all charges levied against him and pleads innocence. Antipholus is toned down a little, and they start conversing about time and its rule,

> Dromio of Syracuse: There's no time for a man to recover his hair that grows bald by nature.
>
> Antipholus of Syracuse: May he not do it by fine and recovery?
>
> Dromio of Syracuse: Yes to pay a fine for a periwig and recover the lost hair of another man (II ii 71-75).

Their talks about the lost hair of another man' or 'loss of his hair' probably referred to two contemporary things, one to the practice of buying and selling hair to make wigs, and the other to the consequence of syphilis which was a menacing evil quite rampant in Elizabethan society. While they continue talking, Adriana and Luciana walk in only to catch hold of the wrong master and his servant. Antipholus of Syracuse tries his best to convince Adriana that she has committed a terrible mistake but the lady concerned refuses to listen to him. Adriana's possessiveness propels her to fasten ... "on this sleeve of thine/Thou art an elm my husband, I a vine" (II ii 173-174). Elm was a creeper plant and this fixing of elm plant can be interpreted as an indication of her complete reliance on her husband for sustenance. Finally both Adriana and Luciana succeed in dragging the master and his servant to their house.

Shakespeare introduces Antipholus of Ephesus for the first time in Act III, scene I. He is seen talking to Angelo the goldsmith about a gold chain, of which Adriana had already spoken in the previous Act (II i 106). Antipholus of Ephesus appears to be trifle confused when Dromio of Ephesus alleges that he had beat him in the mart a few moments ago. He dismisses Dromio by calling him an ass and turns to Balthasar to invite him to dinner. The lengthy discussion that follows is an example of common place courtesy that was exchanged between men in the Elizabethan age. On reaching home, however, Antipholus of Ephesus finds the doors locked against him. Calling his wife a whore Antipholus then tries hard to convince the gatekeeper about his identity and open the gate for him. Finally utterly exasperated the master of the house decides to break in. What is interesting here is the abusive language used by Antipholus while referring to his wife. Nobody present there seems to take it amiss. In a bourgeois society where money was the prime mover it was quite likely that such faults could easily be overlooked. Balthasar however intervenes and stops Antipholus from being hasty, saying "... let us to the Tiger all to dinner" (III i 95). 'Tiger' perhaps was the name of either a London inn or a brothel of Shakespeare's England. Antipholus listens to the good advice and decides to visit a famous courtesan and present her the gold chain which was meant for his wife, Adriana. So this again was a significant gesture indicating his priorities and commitments. What was meant for his wife should never have been offered to a courtesan but he does it to spite his wife.

In the very next scene, Antipholus of Syracuse proposes to Luciana, who mistaking him to be her brother-in-law, reminds him of the obligations of a loyal husband. But Antipholus refuses to listen and the scandalized Luciana snubs him; "Gaze where you should, and that will clear your sight" (I ii ll 57). The sight regarded as the chief of the senses suggested a common poetic convention, inherited from the literature of courtly love. Luciana then leaves the disappointed Antipholus to fetch her sister, and Dromio of Syracuse enters to inform his master of the household gossips. By the end of the scene both the servant and the master decide to leave this strange place of magic and witchcraft.[19] And just when Dromio leaves his master to search for a ship that would take them back home Angelo the goldsmith enters and delivers the gold chain to the wrong Antipholus.

The confusion due to mistaken identity reaches its climax in the fourth Act of the play. The Act opens with Angelo talking to a merchant and an officer about Antipholus who has taken a gold chain from him but has not paid him yet, but he expects,

> ...at five O'clock
> I shall receive the money for the same
> Pleaseth your walk with me down to his house
> (IV i 10-12).

Shakespeare here takes care to point to this hour as indicative of the resolution of action. It was the usual supper hour. Angelo, however, does not have to wait that long; before he can even go off stage, Antipholus of Ephesus bursts in, full of rage. He is seen instructing Dromio to fetch a rope with which he plans to enter his house to teach his wife a harsh lesson. Angelo seizes this opportunity and asks Antipholus to pay him for the gold chain, and when Antipholus denies, he hands him over to the officer. Antipholus's astonishment is, however, not shared by the audience, who realize Angelo's mistake. Things worsen much to the amusement of the spectators when Dromio of Syracuse comes in to inform the wrong Antipholus about a ship that was to sail for Syracuse that very night.

In the second scene Luciana informs her sister about her brother in-law's amorous approaches, and while the sisters are thus busy analysing the strange behaviour of Antipholus, Dromio of Syracuse rushes in to inform his mistress about the misfortune of his master:

> He's in Tartar limbo, worse than hell
> A devil in an everlasting garment hath him,
> One whose hard heart is button'd up with steel;
> A fiend, a fury, pitiless and rough,
> A wolf, nay worse, a fellow all in buff;
> A back-friend, a shoulder-clapper, one that countenance...
> (IV ii 32-38).

Dromio is perhaps talking about Tartus the prison house and his everlasting garments' certainly refers to the dress of the sergeants of the sixteenth and seventeenth century England.

Antipholus of Syracuse is found talking to himself at the beginning of the third scene, when Dromio of Syracuse walks in with the money he got from Adriana to rescue her husband from the prison. Antipholus is at a loss, he can hardly understand Dromio, "Here are the angels that you sent for to deliver you" (IV iii 38-39). 'Angels' here refer to the gold coin worth between 6s, 8d and 10s according to the accepted rates of the period and having on one side inscription of the figure of St Michael conquering the dragon. Just then a Courtesan walks in and challenges Antipholus the wrong one in this case,

> Well met, well met, master Antipholus;
> I see, you have found the goldsmith now;
> Is that the chain you promis'd me to-day?
> (VI iii 43-45).

Both Antipholus and Dromio feel that she is nothing but an agent of the Devil himself and both run off stage, leaving the mumbling courtesan behind. The audience is of course convinced about the perseverance of the lady who decides to retrieve her forty ducats worth ring in lieu of the promised gold chain.

In the fourth scene Antipholus of Ephesus is on his way to the prison with the Officer. As ill luck would have it, Dromio of Ephesus enters to meet his master with a rope in his hand. And when Antipholus starts beating him mercilessly, Adriana and Luciana walk in with a school master named Doctor Pinch. Pinch, a Latin scholar, is a conjurer too who can deal with spirits and apparitions. Assisted by Adriana and Luciana Pinch succeeds in binding up Antipholus as he appears to be insane to them.

In the fifth Act both Egeon and Antipholus of Ephesus are totally estranged from the social group. Egeon, on facing Antipholus of Ephesus recognizes him as his son but the son fails to recognize him, and the Duke seizing the opportunity, dismisses his case, "I see the age and danger make thee dote" (V i 329). To the Duke, Egeon has been suffering from senility. Similarly, Antipholus of Ephesus is charged with certain offences which he has not committed and which he can never commit as he is a respectable citizen of Ephesus. Therefore, his contradictory actions too appear strange to the world who doubt his sanity and threaten to imprison him. The humorous aspects of mistaken identity are now overlooked for once and the audience becomes aware of the precariousness of the situation. According to Leah Scragg:

> Antipholus of Ephesus' frustration is strongly felt, while his father's plight reveals the vulnerability of human beings in a world in which a recognized place within the community is dependent not simply upon the individual's awareness of selfhood, but upon external endorsement of it. Deprived first of his wife and son, and then of a second son and his servant, Egeon is lost in an alien world in which his interpretation of actuality both isolates him and defines him as mad, in that it meets no answering response from his fellow men.[20]

But fortunately for both these lost souls, things do not remain that grim. Finally with the arrival of Antipholus of Syracuse and his proper servant all the knots are untied and once again the lost family is reunited.

The Comedy of Errors, therefore, can be called a play which shows how Shakespeare's romantic genius works on the unromantic material supplied to him by Plautus. He turns the classical plays into a play of the merchant class, where the chain, the ring, five hundred ducats and a thousand marks define the play's society. Ephesus may not have been defined precisely in terms of geography, but studded with English taverns like, Centaur, Phoenix and Tiger and topped by the Duke and served by the Dromios, its society is sharply outlined on the basis of its merchant class. Ephesus is an international trading centre whose tone is set up by the unnamed merchants. As in Venice *(The Merchant of Venice)*, there is political stability in the town, a free movement of capital and reliable and equitable laws which the local judiciary cannot change at their convenience. Thus, Solinus is seen to apologize to Egeon even though theoretically Egeon is his captive:

> Now trust me, were it not against our laws,
> Against my crown, my oath, my dignity,
> Which princes, would they may not disannul
> (I i 142-144).

Even the law-keeping policemen (the Officer) of Ephesus are extremely alert and take immediate action against complaints of improper trading practices. Thus, even a respectable citizen is arrested for a charge brought against him by a goldsmith. "I do arrest you, sir, you here the suit." (IV i 80). But the time-spirit of the place is underscored by the First Merchant, when he regretfully declines a dinner invitation on the ground that "I am invited, sir to certain merchants,/Of whom I hope to make much benefit" (I i ll 24-25). A business engagement is more important here than a social one. The business of *The Comedy of Errors* is, therefore, business only where it is only money that matters, and where the debt of a kin also cannot be exempted, "I would not spare my brother in the case" (IV i 78). Hence Egeon's punishment cannot be annulled if he fails to pay a thousand mark (I i 21-22) or Antipholus of Syracuse may have to face problems if his money is not safe. "I greatly fear my money is not safe'" (I ii 105).

In a commercial world such as this, where material wealth is the prime mover, a gold chain or even a gold ring cannot be treated as just a gift-object. It indicates something more serious. Antipholus of Ephesus initially purchases the gold chain to pacify his wife, but with the development of the play's action it comes to symbolize "the cohesion of society, as it asserts its orderly supremacy over prostitutes, wayward husbands, shrewish wives and lost brothers."[21] And it is probably this cohesive force of the chain that prevents Antipholus from giving it to the courtesan, despite his strong determination. The chain is delivered to his brother who is yet to be married, indicating probably his social commitments which are soon to take shape through his marriage to Luciana, "What I told you then/I hope I shall have leisure to make good" (V i 374-375). And after drawing Antipholus of Syracuse into the Ephesian society, the chain finally completes it function. Similarly, the ring, instead of merely adorning the finger of the courtesan, acts as an:

> appropriate symbol of the sexual and economic ambiguities in Antipholus's extramarital relationship. The exchange of chain for ring is a commercial transaction, as is sex for a courtesan. The distracted woman spends much of the play trying to recover her ring, expressing her dismay in unconscious innuendo, as when she complains that 'a ring he hath of mine worth forty ducats (IV iii 83) or tells Adriana that her "husband all in rage today/Come to my house, and took away my ring' (IV iv 135-136).[22]

Apart from these commercial transactions at all levels, there is another important engagement which all the characters like to enjoy and that is their dinner. Right from the second Act onwards the dinner time gets an unusual attention. Forgoing one's dinner or being late for dinner indicated a disruption of normal activities in this otherwise tranquil world of commerce. And disruption of any kind we know is fatal to all business deals. As Gamini Salgado observes:

> Dinner as the principal Elizabethan meal marks the chief event of the normal domestic day. Being usually taken around noon, it divided the day symmetrically in terms of clock time. Dinner and the dinner hour may therefore aptly stand for routine, unhurried normality,

> when public and private time kept a congruent rhythm. It is not surprising that they should figure prominently in a story which deals with the breakdown of that congruence. [23]

Thus, Antipholus of Ephesus's being, late for dinner, indicates a breakdown of the routine life of his family. A man who visits a courtesan or squanders his wealth in other wayward activities cannot be a successful businessman. Adriana unconsciously tries to inculcate in him this sense of discipline which will reinforce his commercial deal further. But, surprisingly enough, the other characters like Angelo or Balthazar take no exception to Antipholus's decision to visit a courtesan (III i 109-110). It might have been a normal practice for the Elizabethan business community to visit intelligent women for the sake of entertainment. Therefore, except Adriana who sees in such a visit a positive threat to her domestic sovereignty, none of the other friends of Antipholus seems to mind such a proposal. And Antipholus of Ephesus, in spite of such waywardness, is acknowledged by them as a respectable citizen. Says Angelo:

> Of very reverend reputation, sir
> Of credit infinite, highly belov'd,
> Second to none that lives here in the city;
> His word might bear my wealth at any time.

It is his wealth again that is of prior importance and makes him the leading citizen of Ephesus. Similarly, when he publicly calls his wife a harlot both the audience and the other characters do not protest. "Dissembling harlot, thou art false in all" (V i 205), and "While she with harlots feasted in my house" (V i 205), such sentences come naturally to him, while both his wife and the characters in the play never consider it extraordinary or shameful, and do not think that they should be shunned in a social gathering (V i 5-8).

A robust materialism is observed even in the marriages and the marital relationship of the characters in *The Comedy of Errors*. As has been pointed out earlier, though the marriage of the couple Adriana and Antipholus of Ephesus remains unreconstructed at the end; nobody seems to be much disturbed by it, because to the commercially oriented people in the play marriage is a matter of convenience and to wed for one's wealth has nothing unusual about it. The society they live in gracefully overlooks Antipholus of Ephesus's occasional amorous escapades here and there as long as they do not disrupt his daily routine. And only when they upset the family's daily routine the females protest:

> Be secret false; what need she be acquainted?
> What simple thief brags of his own attaint?
> (Tis double wrong to truant with your bed,
> And let her read it in thy looks at board;
> Shame hath a bastard fame, well managed;
> Ill deeds is doubled with an evil word (III ii 15-20).

Disloyalty towards spouses, therefore, is not a matter of any consequence as long as it does not destabilize the family structure. And only those evil deeds need sanction which break the harmony of a family routine. In other words, no untoward incident which upsets the social or family equilibrium will be tolerated by the Ephesian society.

The servant-master relationship is perhaps the most interesting aspect of *The Comedy of Errors*. It is simple cruelty that coincides with the farcical element of the play, when at regular intervals— the cries of the Dromios (when beaten by their masters) vitiate the atmosphere of the otherwise tranquil world of Ephesus. They seem used to this kind of treatment and the audience treats it as funny, for to them the Dromios are mere dramatic fictions and nothing but human cartoons. And only when they reveal their innermost thoughts their individuality is clearly manifested.

> Ephesus Dromio: I am an ass indeed; you may prove it by my long ears. I have served him from the hour of my nativity to this instant, and have nothing at his hands for my service but blows. When I am cold, he heats me with beating; when I am warm he cools me with beating; I am waked with it when I sleep, raised with it when I sit, driven out of doors with it when I go from

> home, welcomed home with it when I return nay, I bear it on my shoulders as a beggar wont her brat; and I think when he hath lamed me, I shall beg with it from door to door (IV iv 27-37).

"It is a disturbing reminder of the human being behind the cartoon. Being sane in a mad world bears hard upon servants, the shock absorbers of the social system."[24]

The Comedy of Errors is basically a play of the merchant class whose central focus is on money and other business transactions too are connected to money in various ways. From the very onset the playwright makes it clear that, if a man suffers from a paucity of funds in Ephesus he is destined to die an untimely death. In spite of all his generosity the Duke of the land cannot overrule the existing laws and hence Egeon must accept a death sentence if at the end of the day he fails to procure the needful guilders. Egeon's fault is his poor economic condition because economic status controls the social position of the bonafide citizens of Ephesus. Antipholus of Ephesus is considered to be a respectable citizen because he is wealthy apart from being honest in all economic deals. People respect him and are ready to lend him money because he never fails to pay it back. And when in due course of the play's action they realize that Antipholus's honesty is beginning to wean, they lose faith in him and get ready to hand him over to the law-keepers. They become merciless because the social values of Ephesus are completely money-based and money oriented. But with the final resolution not only are all the characters redeemed but also their economic position is made sure by the society. Both the Antipholus' are assured of decent mode of sustenance and hence admitted to the city of Ephesus.

Notes

1. All references to *The Comedy of Errors* are to the Arden Shakespeare, *The Comedy of Errors,* ed. R.A. Foakes, Routledge, London, 1962 rep. 1986.
2. *The Holy Bible,* National Bible Press, Philadelphia, 1978, p. 1218.
3. *Ibid.*, p. 1219.
4. *Ibid.*, p. 1144.

5. *Narrative and Dramatic Sources of Shakespeare* I, Routledge, London, 1957, p. 8.
6. H.B. Charlton, *Shakespearian Comedy,* Methuen, London, 1938, rep. 1966, p. 20.
7. *Ibid.*, pp. 64-65.
8. Theodore Weiss, *The Breathe of Clowns and Kings*, Chatto and Windus, London, 1971, pp. 10-11.
9. E.M.W. Tillyard, *Shakespeare's Early Comedies,* Athlone Press, London, 1983, rep. 1987, p. 89.
10. *Ibid.*, pp. 54-55.
11. Derek Traversi, *William Shakespeare The Early Comedies,* Longman Green and Co., 1960, p. 42.
12. In The Arden Shakespeare *The Comedy of Errors,* Routledge, London, 1962, pp. 1-11.
13. 'Shakespeare, Moliere and the Comedy of Ambiguity', in *Shakespeare Survey,* 22, 1971, p. 15.
14. *Shakespeare's Comedy of Love,* Methuen, London, 1974, pp. 7-8.
15. *Ibid.*, p. 8.
16. '*The Comedy of Errors* A different kind of Comedy' in *New Literary History* XI No. 3, 1978, pp. 525-28.
17. *Ibid.*, 528.
18. It was an expected practice for men to visit the courtesans. Here even though Adriana does not approve of her husband's visit she is compelled to accept it. Society would not support her for obstructing her husband from visiting a courtesan.
19. Witchcraft and sorcery was widely popular and much heeded by the Elizabethans.
20. Leah Scragg, *Shakespeare's Mouldy Tales,* Longman, London, 1992, p. 22.
21. Richard Henz, '*The Comedy of Errors,* A Freely Binding Chain' in *Shakespeare Quarterly,* 1971, p. 35.
22. Edward Berry, *Shakespeare's Comic Rites,* Cambridge University Press, Cambridge, 1984, p. 183.
23. 'Times Deformed Hand in *The Comedy of Errors*' in *Shakespeare Surrey* 22, p. 85.
24. Ralph Berry, *Shakespeare and Social Class,* Humanities Press International, INC Atlantic Highlands, New Jersey, 1988, p. 22.

4

THE TWO GENTLEMEN OF VERONA

> In these days he is a gentleman, who is commonly taken and reputed. And whosoever studieth in the Universities who professeth the liberal sciences and to be short who can live idly without labour and will bear the port, charge and countenance of a gentleman, he shall be called a master.*

The exact date of composition of *The Two Gentlemen of Verona*[1] is difficult to ascertain since there is no conclusive evidence either in the history of the theatre or in the text itself. But, it will not be wrong to assume that the play being a romantic comedy, certainly belongs to the group of six comedies, *The Comedy of Errors, Love's Labour's Lost, Love's Labour's Won, A Midsummer Night's Dream,* and *The Merchant of Venice,* which are generally regarded as the early comedies of Shakespeare. Striking affinities, however, exist with many later comedies like *Twelfth Night* (Julia's disguise and her employment of Proteus as a messenger to Silvia), *As You Like It* (the forest setting and Julia's disguise) and the tragedy *of Romeo and Juliet* (the elopement plan, the rope-ladder, and banishment of the lover), indicating the continuing process and development of Shakespeare's art.

---

* Sir Thomas Smith, *De Republica Anglorun* quoted in Lawrence Stone, *The Crisis of Aristocracy 1558-1641,* Clarendon Press, Oxford, 1965, p. 49.

Regarding the sources of the play it can be said that a "great mass of friendship literature that extends through the Middle Ages to the seventeenth century"[2] served to be Shakespeare's source of inspiration for *The Two Gentlemen of Verona*. But among the entire mass two specific prose stories, *The Governour* written by Sir Thomas Elyott and Montemayor's *Diana* are possibly the primary sources. *The Governour* which chiefly deals with the theme of friendly love between two men, triumphing over the love between man and woman, may have served as a model for Shakespeare while he was characterising the love between Proteus and Valentine. Gissipus, one of the two friends, renounces his claims to the bride whom he has formally married and also helps his friend who loves the girl, to win her through bed trick by which the marriage is consummated by the friend. In *The Two Gentlemen of Verona,* however, Valentine does not have to go that far; he merely renounces his claims to Silvia, "All that was mine in Silvia I give thee." (V iv 83) and his renunciation is finally overruled thanks to Julia's intelligent intervention. The other story, *Diana,* on which Shakespeare probably modelled his subplot, is another romantic tale of an Amazonian woman who, crossed in her love by a curse of Diana, pursues her lover in male attire only to find him with a new mistress. After a series of adventures and at last by means of a magic spell she wins back her lover. Shakespeare's Julia of course does not have recourse to a spell; rather her sharp common sense assists her to win back her wayward lover.

Shakespeare has only partially borrowed the materials from these tales and after having rejected quite a substantial portion of them has made a new story where the main theme is "the conflict between the duties of friendship and love."[3] There is also an element of mild satire in the play on the extravagance of romantic love in the shrewd comments of Launce and Speed who are intentionally introduced by the dramatist to unsentimentalize the prevailing tenor. Even the two friends in *The Two Gentlemen of Verona* are very different from their counterparts in the sources, they provide a dramatic contrast in the play. Proteus whom we see as the lover boy at the beginning of the play uttering lines like —

> O, how this spring of love resembleth The uncertain glory of an April day, Which now shows all the beauty of the sun, And by and by a cloud takes all away (I iii 84-87).

turns into a crafty villain by the end of the story, while the level headed Valentine with all his arguments against love,

> To be in love; where scorn is bought with groans;
> Coy looks, with heart-sore sighs; one fading moment's mirth,
> With twenty watchful, weary, tedious nights;
> If haply won, perhaps a hapless gain;
> If lost, why then a grievous labour won;
> How ever, but a folly bought with wit,
> Or else a wit by folly vanquished (I i 29-35).

turns into a highly romantic human being finally. On the whole, *The Two Gentlemen of Verona* is a conventional Elizabethan comedy describing the uneven course of love, and man's triumph over all adversities in love, to win his bride and achieve a state of marital bliss.

The entire structure of *The Two Gentlemen of Verona* can be said to be a true representation of the basic structure of Shakespearean comedy. Romantic love is at the very core of the plot; tyrannical fathers try to repress the generosity and passion of youth; one character revives his drooping spirits in a pastoral forest setting; another disguises herself as a boy and woos her lover's new mistress assuming the role of his page. Even the other characters are the earliest examples of types, the readers find Shakespeare using repeatedly in the later comedies. Silvia, for example is the artful, but reasonable woman of the world; and Julia is the ardent girl who proves to be a more positive character than her lover Proteus. Both Proteus and Valentine on the other are immature but accomplished young men who begin their discovery of the world by discovering their love for rich and pretty young girls. And like that of the medieval heroes love for them "has become a ritual and expresses itself in social behaviour with an elaborate etiquette of courtesy, word and deed."[4] The whole course of their activities centers round love; for love alone Proteus at first renounces his love for Julia and then forswears his friend Valentine and helps the Duke to banish him to the forest. The entire action of the play seems to be determined by the values that are attached to the love of a man for a woman. And since Proteus defies its most important value, loyalty, for merely satisfying his lust "I'll woo you like a soldier, at arm's end,/ And love you 'gainst the nature of love: force ye" (V iv 57-58), Shakespeare reprimands him through Silvia, "Had I been seized by a hungry lion, / I would have been a breakfast to the beast" (V iv 33-34). To force a lady to yield to a man's desire is, therefore, an act that is worse than being a prey to a ferocious animal. Actually it is the society that is condemning the act of Proteus as he is taking an unfair advantage of his allowed status. And like any other social malefactor his activities hamper all norms of social amelioration, towards which a comedy always aspires.

Just as loyalty is considered to be the noblest virtue in medieval chivalry, so also perjury is treated as the blackest crime. But cowardice seems to override even perjury in a world where conduct is guided by romantic ideas alone. Therefore, even Proteus's betrayal to his friend and falsity towards his lady love become somewhat insignificant when Shakespeare portrays Thurio's unwillingness to jeopardize himself for the woman he intends to marry. And it is this non-chivalrous attitude of his that shocks the Duke and he immediately decides to bestow his daughter on the gallant Valentine:

> The more degenerate and base art thou To make such means for her, as thou hast done, And leave her on such slight conditions (V iv 134-136).

Consequently, Valentine proves to be the gainer as the Duke open-heartedly declares, "Take thou thy Silvia, for thou hast deserv'd her" (V iv 145). And such an impasse is due to Thurio's "poltroonery" which "consists in his bringing practical considerations into a world where conduct is expected to be guided by romantic ideas alone."[5] But Shakespeare's objectivity is expounded through the speeches of minor characters like Launce, Speed and Lucetta who indicating the absurdities and excesses of this highly idealized world frequently express their disapproval of their masters and mistresses. For instance Speed's analysis of love as observed in Proteus:

> Marry sir by these special marks: first you have
> Learned (like Sir Proteus) to wreathe your arms like a
> Malcontent; to relish a love-song, like a robin-redbreast;
> To walk alone, like one that had the pestilence;
> to sigh like
> A schoolboy that had lost his ABC; to weep, like a young wench
> That had buried her grandma; to fast,
> like one that takes diet; to
> Watch like one that fears robbing;
> to speak pulling like a beggar At Hallowmas (II i 17-25).

It is clearly Shakespeare who presents such a vivid picture of the absurd behaviour of a lover. Love is here considered to be a pestilence that incorporates loss of vision, appetite and other such untoward habits, making the lover thereby both physically and psychologically an oddball for the real world. But these minor characters appear to be forever ready to bring their masters back to the real world, where one has to be nourished by victuals and not by air alone. Even Lucetta playing the role of a thoroughbred psychologist on the eve of Julia's departure seems to be a little skeptical about the fidelity of Proteus.

> Better forebear, till Proteus make return....
> I do not seek to quench your love's hot fire,
> But qualify the fire's extreme rage,
> Lest it should burn above the bounds of reason
> (II vi 14 21-23).

Lucetta here is clearly skeptical about Proteus's commitment the moment he leaves the place. Though she does not provide an explanation for her inference yet we may presume that perhaps some gesture of Proteus had led her to conjecture

Proteus's potential infidelity in the long run. Julia, of course is not ready to accept Lucetta's arguments and instead of waiting for Proteus's return she is ready to undertake the hazardous journey in the guise of a page boy.

These characters can therefore be said to actually voice the opinions of the dramatist, who is incessantly trying to strike a balance between the ideal and the real in his comedy.

Shakespeare's representation of romantic love is not a photocopy of the medieval ideals, rather his romantic love very decisively manifests a strong feminine element, and unlike as in the chivalrous ethics, the women here are given an essential role in determining human relations. Though the male characters like the chivalrous knights of the old willingly run a number of risks (Valentine's efforts at winning his lady, the rope ladder incident in Sc IV, Act II lines 176-181), it is the positive and active participation of the ladies that ultimately inspires them (both Silvia and Julia, unable to live without their lovers, undertake quite a perilous journey to meet them). Shakespearean women therefore can never be termed as sheer passive onlookers; they clearly express their views on men whom they prefer as life partners. Apart from this deviation there is another theme that Shakespeare has introduced in *The Two Gentlemen of Verona,* the theme of masculine friendship, which depended more on the Renaissance social ideals than on the medieval world of love and chivalry. "Shakespeare consciously introduces both themes (and ideals) on somewhat equal footing, romantic love and masculine friendship."[6] Shakespeare however is not the trend-setter in this aspect, because masculine friendship was a widely discussed subject in Renaissance literature. Starting from Lyly to Massinger all the dramatists of the age loved to present the clash that arose out of the two conflicting ideals of love and masculine friendship. And it was up to the dramatist to portray the victory of either both these ideals or, the triumph of any one of them. Consequently, when Proteus in *The Two Gentlemen of Verona* betrays his friend for his love for Silvia he is actually violating one of these ideals and as a result vitiating the world based on the fundamentals of trust and integrity in friendship. While, by renouncing his claims to Silvia Valentine tries to counter this evil and reinstate the noble values of friendship.

The minor characters of *The Two Gentlemen of Verona* as mentioned above are actually introduced to represent a different set of ideals. While their masters are engaged in defending the medieval ideals they address the audience through their comic actions and comic asides and not only manifest a "dramatic interplay between the wit of the audience and the wittiness of the clown"[7] but also establish a link with the real world of everyday life. Thus when Valentine and Silvia exchange high flown compliments Speed communes with the audience through the comic asides (II i 89-113) and both enjoy different perception of awareness, not restricted to the play world. Launce, however, directly addresses the audience in his famous leave-taking speech (II ii). Speed and Launce, therefore, serve two-fold purposes, first they establish a direct link with the audience, and second they incessantly strive to bring their masters down to the real world, where the old world medieval values of romantic love and chivalry cannot sustain the whole being of a man:

> Ay, but hearken, sir;
> Though the chameleon Love
> can feed on the Air,
> I am one that am nourished by
> my victuals (II ii 162-164).

Therefore, it can be assumed that Shakespeare's inclusion of these minor characters was also possibly to present two contradictory views of life. Proteus and Valentine represent the idealistic views of an age that had long passed off, while their own servants represent the contemporary real world, and only when a man can strike a balance between these two worlds can he and his fellow men live happily together in society, because an "unswerving and uncompromising sticking to a specialized line of conduct makes men difficult to fit in with their fellows."[8]

A conversation between Proteus and Valentine marks the beginning of *The Two Gentlemen of Verona.* They converse about Valentine's forthcoming departure to the Emperor's court and Proteus in spite of his strong affection for his friend refuses to accompany him because, affection for his lady-love chains him down to his homeland. Valentine being unused to the course of love mocks his friend. "Tis true; for you are boots in love, /And yet you never swum the Hellespont" (I i 24-25). Here Valentine probably, ironically, compares Proteus's love to a game of boots that was played in Warwickshire and in which the forfeit was to be slapped on the breech with a pair of boots or with the torture of the boot. After a few more exchanges of friendly affection Valentine leaves and Speed who is actually the servant of Valentine enters to inform Proteus that according to his instructions he has delivered a letter to Lady Julia.

> Speed: Ay, sir; I (a lost mutton) gave your letter to her (a laced mutton) and she (a laced mutton) gave me (a lost mutton) nothing for my labour (I i 95-97).

Speed's reference to Julia as a laced mutton is very interesting since the expression was frequently used to mean a courtesan who was either tightly laced or wore lace as a part of her garment. And strangely enough, Proteus knowing the implication of the term takes no exception to it. Probably, the pages in late sixteenth century England spoke in that manner, without meaning any mischief. Julia the mistress of Proteus is introduced to the audience in the second scene of the first Act. Lucetta, her maid, is advising Julia about the noble virtues of Proteus who is one of her many suitors. Lucetta then slyly produces the letter about which Speed spoke in the previous scene, and Julia, like a typical Elizabethan maid, coyly chides her and refuses to see the letter. Lucetta leaves the letter behind while going off stage in order to give her mistress a chance to read it in private. The scene, however, ends with Julia trying to gather up the torn pieces of the letter and expressing herself quite unambiguously:

> Nay, would I were so
> Anger'd with the same.
> O hateful hands, to tear such loving words;
> (ll 04-106).

While she is brooding thus Lucetta enters to beckon her to dinner where her father is awaiting her. In the third scene Proteus's parent Antonio decides to send him to the court of the Emperor so that like Valentine he too is able to add a few more things to his already attained intellectual stature. Proteus hearing this is at a loss, he tries to dissuade his father, "My lord, I cannot be so soon provided: / Please you deliberate a day or two" (I iii 72-73). Nevertheless his father turns a deaf ear to all his arguments and fixes the following day to be the day of his departure. Here is again a typical Elizabethan father who does not deem it necessary to take note of his ward's request rather enforce his ruling, however arbitrary it maybe, upon the child.

The first scene of the second Act begins with the love sighs of the straight thinking Valentine, and the audience knows that at last Cupid's arrow has hit another tough mark. Speed plays the role of the former Valentine who had mocked Proteus previously for being afflicted by the disease called love. Valentine is surprised; he can hardly believe that he has unconsciously betrayed his innermost thoughts so unequivocally: "Are all these things perceived in me." (II i 32). Speed declares that they do shine through him "like the water in an urinal" (II i 37). Since love here is considered to be a malady by Speed, it is but natural that following the practice of the day Valentine's disease will have to be identified by a physician by testing the color of his urine. Speed, however, avows his master that his feelings have been reciprocated by Silvia. Just after that the lady herself enters to talk to Valentine. Her pretext is to discuss about a letter which Valentine has written for her unknown lover. Silvia here very ingeniously hands back the letter to him, pretending to reward him for his pains. Valentine, blinded by love, fails to perceive the meaning of her action till Speed explains it to him (II i 154-159). Valentine is naturally overjoyed. The two small scenes that follow next inform the audience that Proteus after casting a longing, lingering look behind at his mistress, has set out on his voyage and Launce, his servant is accompanying him.

Thurio, a suitor of Silvia appears in the fourth scene of the second Act, and Valentine who cannot stand the very sight of his contender expresses his suppressed fury while talking to him. Silvia tries in vain to pacify both of them by pleading: "No more gentlemen, no more. Here comes my father" (II iv 43). The Duke comes in to announce Proteus's arrival and Valentine temporarily forgetting his antagonism is jubilant. As he starts praising his friend, his friend enters and Silvia as anticipated extends a warm welcome. And surprisingly Proteus too in rejoinder praises her rather fervently, "Not so, sweet lady, but too mean a servant/To have a look of such a worthy mistress." (II iv 102-103). The hint is clear – Proteus is already obsessed by Silvia. The lady concerned however does not remain long to enjoy the pleasantries since her father the Duke has sent for her. It is only after her departure Valentine gets the opportunity to talk to Proteus privately. After initial enquires about his dear ones at home Valentine honestly confesses to Proteus about his new found love in Silvia. But Proteus's response is unexpectedly inexplicable. Even though he pretends to mock Valentine's love as nonsense his interest in Silvia is clearly discernible: "No; but she is an earthly paragon" (II iv 141). Poor Valentine, little does he suspect this over enthusiastic Proteus! Instead of being cautious he proceeds to confide in him their plans to elope to the woods that very night. He gives him a detailed account about their modus operandi. Proteus listens to him in rapt attention and the moment he finishes Proteus looks for solitude. Valentine naturally leaves him behind allowing the audience to comprehend his iniquitous purpose. Proteus has already relinquished his love for Julia and is now contemplating a new relationship with Silvia employing all his resources. So the impending threat to unsettle the comic pattern of the play is imminent here.

The fifth scene is a comic one where one finds Speed and Launce conversing with one another. Contrary to the stance of his master, Launce here demonstrates a genuine pleasure on meeting Speed before they both rush off for a drink. The hint is clear the higher one is up in the social hierarchy the greater is the chance of backstabbing. Proteus's intentions become all the more clear — in the sixth scene when he plans to inform the Duke about Valentine's proposed elopement. And this is all because of his personal infatuation for Silvia. It is decided that hence forth his only endevour will be to win her favour by hook or by crook. Conscious of his sinful objectives Proteus appears to be indecisive at first. His love for Silvia means forswearing both Julia's love and Valentine's friendship, but finally lust getting the better of him he decides both to betray his friend and abandon Julia for good. Ironically, in the very next scene, that is in the seventh scene the audience finds Julia preparing herself to undertake a long journey in order to meet her beloved Proteus, little foreseeing how in the meantime he has renounced her for better pastures. Lucetta's word of caution before her departure sounds almost prophetic here. Although Julia remains impervious to what Lucetta has figured out about Proteus. Lucetta's apprehension may have been born out of a general distrust about men's fidelity, but Julia's devotion overrides such disbeliefs.

The act of betrayal occurs in the first scene of the third Act. After Thurio's departure Proteus gives the Duke a detailed account of the plans of his 'friend' Valentine, but cautions him not to disclose his name. "But, good my lord, do it so cunningly / That my discovery be not aimed at' (III i 44-45). Here a traitor is requesting not to be betrayed. But unlike Proteus the Duke is true to his words promising him in lieu, "Upon mine honour, he shall never know" (III i 48). Then observing the arrival of Valentine at a distance, Proteus hastily departs leaving behind the fuming Duke to expose Valentine and finally banish him to the forest far away from his court. Valentine is doomed; he cannot imagine a life without Silvia. Flying away from Silvia, means to "fly away from life" (III i 187). Yet the brunt must be borne and he escapes to the forest. Here one is reminded of Frye's 'green world'[9] and Valentine's banishment appears to be a deliverance from the world of reality to an artificial world of make-believe in anticipation that things will be better there. But in practice it is just the other way about because the moment Valentine reaches the forest he encounters many other young men who like him have been punished for very little offences. In other words it heralds the arbitrariness of the ruler. In Shakespearean comedies forest appears to be a shelter for social pariahs so it is expected it will be infested by all kinds of characters.

Proteus is next seen searching for Valentine, and pretending to be extremely disturbed by his misfortune. Trying to console him he promises, "Thy letters may be here, though thou art hence, /Which, being writ to me shall be deliver'd (III i 248-249). The intensity of the scene is relaxed a bit at the end when Launce informs Speed about his new found mistress. Launce's love, contrary to his master's is based on the maid's money and not upon her good looks. Another deliberate instance presented by the playwright of the down-to-earth attitude of the plebeians.

The beginning of the fourth Act finds Valentine reaching the forest and being acclaimed the leader of the outlaws, who welcome him with open arms. The other outlaws like Valentine are men of gentle birth and they too have been unjustly punished by the state for no fault of theirs. Expectedly therefore, none of them actually act as wayside plunderers. This again is a hint at the existing malaise of the Elizabethan society where men were often banished by the state if they dared to flout the existing social order (a fact well illustrated by the contemporary historians). In the second scene Julia arrives to meet her beloved only to find him courting another girl. But fortunately for her, Silvia, Proteus's new found love refuses to comply with his wishes. Julia as expected leaves the place with a heavy heart wondering about her fate. In the third scene Silvia plans with Sir Eglamour to flee from her father's house to the woods where Valentine has been banished and to reunite with her lover. This gesture of the lady is quite contrary to what we have seen in the courtship scene, when she feels embarrassed even to declare her feelings for Valentine openly. Silvia's gesture is also quite contrary to the social decorum of Elizabethan England. But many of Shakespearean comedies have similar heroines who to escape the highhandedness of their parents, especially their fathers often left the assured shelter of their homes.

In the fourth scene Julia disguised as Sebastian is employed by Proteus to act as envoy to lady Silvia, but inwardly she avers to do her duty only lackadaisically. "Yet I will woo for him, but yet so coldly, / As (heave knows) I would not have him speed" (IV iv 106-107).

The harshness of the play however is reduced in the final act of play and a happy resolution occurs when the Duke, realizing his lack of forethought decides to bestow Silvia to Valentine. But before the happy resolution many unpleasant incidents take place which tend to destroy momentarily the equilibrium of the play. At first Silvia's elopement is discovered and all three men, Proteus, Thurio and the Duke, proceed towards the woods. Silvia reaches the forest in the third scene and is attacked by the outlaws who decide to take her to their leader. In the fourth scene, significantly enough, Valentine is found lamenting for his lost love and yearning to meet his sweet Silvia, when all of a sudden he withdraws to observe unnoticed the arrival of a few newcomers. Silvia enters followed by Proteus and Julia, and Proteus is seen beseeching Silvia to bestow her favour to him forgoing her prior attachments to Valentine. Silvia is naturally refusing to submit thereby provoking the lecherous Proteus to decide, "I will for thee yield to my desire" (V iv 60). Valentine unable to remain a passive onlooker any longer instinctively springs forward and prevents the occurrence of any uncouth occurrence. Meanwhile, on the other side of the wood the Duke followed by Thurio is chased by the outlaws. And as can be expected of the coward Thurio, he departs because he feels that it is absolute stupidity to endanger one's life for a bride whose favours lie elsewhere. The Duke is shocked beyond limits; to him Thurio's attitude is utter blasphemy. Proteus, in the intervening time, being ashamed of his behaviour, repents for his dastardly act and Valentine comprehending this change of heart renounces all his claims to Silvia and easily bequeaths her to Proteus. Significantly enough Silvia at this juncture chooses to remain completely silent. All her preaching regarding freedom to choose ones life partner seems to have taken a nose dive and thereby vanishing for good. Following the diktats of the patriarchy Valentine, being the male superior, treats her as his commodity and hence feels completely free to bestow her to his friend just to appease the growing hostility between them. Conserving male friendship appears to be of primary importance here in contrast to his feelings for Silvia. Julia's timely intervention however saves Silvia from any further discomfiture. And Proteus in his bid to toe the trend of his friend also readily goes back to his prior commitments towards Julia the moment her identity is disclosed publicly. Proteus therefore, willingly accepts her as his wife while the Duke too, considering the magnanimity of Valentine declares "Take thou thy Silvia, for thou hast deserv'd her" (V iv 145). And what Silvia has to say here is of little importance. It's an all males world where the bartering of woman was socially and legally sanctioned much to the comfort of the patriarchy. The play consequently ends with a promise of, "One feast, one house, one mutual happiness" (V iv 171).

Analysed from a social stance *The Two Gentlemen of Verona* appears to be a Shakespearean experiment in the genre of the pastoral romance, which was considered to be a model of the high society in the late sixteenth century England. And Proteus was probably Shakespeare's initial attempt to adapt the Vice-figure to a contemporary social context, while Valentine's ready forgiveness of a perfidious but repentant friend can be interpreted as the representation of a masterless man of the sixteenth century, who was basically an outlaw and, was devoid of any power or privilege. But in contrast to the other characters, Shakespeare here explicitly discloses one basic fact – such an outlaw often proves to be morally far superior to his superiors in the social hierarchies and hence deserves the best of the world he inhabits (here it is his winning of Silvia). In spite of their negative aspects (as mentioned earlier in the discussion of the play) all the characters in the play speak and behave in ways that are, on the whole, totally consistent with their social positions, manifesting again, Shakespeare's general awareness of the tendency of the people to behave in a way appropriate to their social ranks and occupations and to reflect what others expect of them. Therefore, there is more in Proteus's pretended dislike to malign Valentine

"Tis an ill office for a gentleman" (III ii 40) than mere hypocrisy, which has been made explicit already (II vi). It is once again Shakespeare's awareness of the behaviour pattern of a gentleman that strikes the reader and audience alike. The word 'gentleman' however defies an exact definition, and of all social terms it casts the widest net covering the ideas of birth, education, wealth, behaviour and values. The word gentleman is not merely recognition of rank, it is rather an ideal of conduct, regularly noted in Shakespeare's plays (Hamlet, Ferdinand, Malvolio, Proteus, and Coriolanus are all gentlemen, irrespective of their social status). Therefore, it is through this concept of gentleman that Shakespeare brings into focus a wider problem of the social class of sixteenth century England.

For a young gentleman of the time, the transition from a grammar school to the university represented his first adventure into the world, "His initiation into the estate of manhood."[10] The different social rites are often indicators of this initiation process where by effecting transition, in the life of a person he has to undergo a spatial separation. This helps him to assume another social identity and thereby enable him attain a reasonable amount of maturity which makes him a better and a fitter man for the society. Hence both Valentine's and Proteus's departure to the royal court are not only aimed at removing their ignorance but constitute a process of their initiation into the estate of manhood. Spending a man's adolescence at home was considered to "be great impeachment" (I iii 15) to his age and "having known no travel" (I iii 16) in his youth would stunt his growth to manhood. Therefore, the senior members of both the families in the play follow the Elizabethan social custom and dislocate the two youths. The dislocation or the process of reaching one's manhood, however, proves to be a painful one, both to the youth and to his family. It not only involves an estrangement from the familiar world but also a snapping of all familial ties. Hence follow the lamentations of the entire household in Launce's family, (II iii 23-32), or the sighs and groans of both Proteus and his beloved (II ii). "Launce's mixture of rigidly conventional behaviour, great personal emotion and comic incongruity captures wonderfully the emotional complexity of such ceremonial occasions."[11] And how far they truly grow up to be perfect gentlemen, Shakespeare unfolds through the subsequent course of dramatic action. But the fact remains that after their process of initiation is complete the world expects them to change themselves from school boys to fully developed adults with wholly developed personalities, and if they fail to live up to the worldly standard of social etiquette, their reputation as gentlemen is likely to be endangered.

The concluding part of the play therefore is devoted to the completion of the process of initiation and the placement of the two youths as two fully developed gentlemen of Verona. But, strangely enough the end product seems to be radically different in the two cases. Valentine the cool-headed rationalist, is "metamorphosed with a mistress" (II i 130) and learns the values of tender emotions, ennobling himself thereby even to the extent of forgiving entirely the treachery of his friend, while the "lovely gentleman' (I ii 19) Proteus forgetting his previous commitments both to his friend and mistress becomes adept at the art of treachery and forswearing. The final reconciliation however is brought about by the noble gestures of the hero of the play, Valentine.

Unlike the male characters, the women of *The Two Gentlemen of Verona,* do not actually undergo any psychological transformation. From the commencement of the play, the playwright makes it obvious that for both Julia and Silvia marriage is vital and for marrying the men of their choice they are ready to undertake any amount of risk - Julia's disguise and repudiation of parental protection to follow Proteus and Silvia's fleeing to the woods incurring the wrath of her father. Prevailing social conditions probably, develop within them this marriage-oriented psychology, because in the Renaissance world only marriage was the parameter of determining a girl's social status. Explaining this feature Ian Maclean writes in *The Renaissance Notion of Women:*

> Marriage is the social content that centrally defines the female characters in Shakespeare's play; with few exceptions their conflicts, crises and character

> development occur in connection with wooing, wedding and marriage. Their roles and status are determined by their place in the paradigm of marriage— maiden/wife/widow— which likewise governed the lives of Renaissance women.[12]

Yet, what appears to be their free choice born out of romantic love is not really a complete freedom granted to them by the patriarchal society. They are not actually emancipated women; instead they are totally at the mercy of the male sovereigns. Hence, when Julia realizes Proteus's infidelity, she cannot come out of her disguise and take him to task. She is scared of exposition, because, she knows she will be "attacked by Elizabethan and Jacobean moralists for wearing men's clothes"[13] and for shamelessly following her lover to a distant land. As a result, Julia is silent throughout, unresistingly waiting for the opportune moment to win back her wayward lover and reclaim her lost status. And only when the right moment arrives she breaks her silence to rebuke Proteus for implicitly enforcing upon her this ordeal of transvestism. Julia:

> Be thou asham'd that I have took upon me
> Such an immodest raiment; if shame live
> In a disguise of love:
> It is the lesser belt modestly finds,
> Women to change their shapes, than their men their minds (V iv 103-108).

Similarly, when Valentine meets Silvia in the woods at the end of the comedy (V iv), there is absolutely no manifestation of their mutual affections, even verbally. Only Valentine mumbles a few words to himself. His mumbling is abruptly discontinued with the arrival of Proteus, who chases Silvia to persuade her to surrender herself. Valentine springs forward to save Silvia and then suddenly he barters her to regain Proteus's lost friendship. Silvia remains silent only to observe her lover, her seducer and her father discussing quite callously her future. Unlike Julia, she does not rebuke Valentine for using her as a pawn in the name of his masculine friendship. Then both Valentine and the Duke after a moment's reflection brush aside all possibilities of Silvia's opposition and decide upon her matrimonial possibilities.

Julia's disguise, as mentioned above, is another instance of male repression prevalent in Elizabethan society.

In The *Two Gentlemen of Verona,* Julia disguised as a page invents for her rival, Silvia, (now pursued by Julia's fiance Proteus) a story (VI iv 156-161), that describes her apparent male self playing "the woman's part" in the clothes of her real female self. The layers insulating this story from reality enable her to reveal herself through her disguise, express her deep grief at being abandoned, and to engender a sympathetic response from her onstage and offstage audience ..."Julia by playing male and female, actor and audience, herself and not herself, shares with Silvia grief of male betrayal and female abandonment."[14]

The plight of both the girls is exactly the same, with only Julia's disguise complicating her future temporarily and thereby making her situation worse in contrast to Silvia's, because, as Juliet Dusinberre explains:

> "A woman in man's clothes seemed to the Jacobians not simply eccentric in dress, but really in part a man, and thus monstrous and unnatural half-man and half-woman, a horrible counterpart to the homosexual courtier."[15]

This degradation possibly compels her to rebuke Proteus so severely, while Silvia, facing no such complexity hardly has anything to protest about when at the end of the play the whimsicality of their partners are set to rest. The questions raised in the play however remain unresolved finally even though the playwright hastily tries to bring about an amicable settlement. The first thing that strikes the reader in this regard is – will Julia be able to forget the lapses of Proteus? The second, is there any guarantee that Proteus will never again commit the same mistake? Third, how is it that Silvia chooses to remain absolutely silent when the male characters are negotiating amongst themselves about her proprietorship? So Shakespeare here, basically raises these uncomfortable questions and does not really take the pains to resolve it convincingly. Or is it because he deliberately wants to disconcert the easy going audience to ponder over these existing malaises of society? In all likelihood the second proposition seems to be more apposite.

Notes

1. All textual references are to *The Two Gentlemen of Verona* are to the Arden Shakespeare *The Two Gentlemen of Verona,* ed. Cifford Leech, Methuen, London, 1986.
2. *Ibid.*, p. xxxv.
3. Geoffrey Bullough, *Narrative and Dramatic sources of Shakespeare,* 2 Routledge, London, 1957, p. 203.
4. H.B. Charlton, *Shakespearian Comedy,* Methuen, London, 1966, p. 25.
5. S.C. Sen Gupta, *Shakespearian Comedy,* Oxford University Press, Delhi, 1950, rep. 1988, p. 86.
6. R.M. Sargent, 'Sir Thomas Elyott and the Integrity of *The Two Gentlemen of Verona'* in *P.M.LA.,* 1950, p. 1167.
7. Robert Weimann, 'Laughing with the Audience' : *The Two Gentlemen of Verona* and the Popular Tradition of Comedy', in *Shakespeare Survey,* 22, p. 37.
8. E.M.W. Tillyard, *Shakespeare's Early Comedies,* Athlone Press, London, 1983, rep. 1987, p. 127.
9. Northrope Frye, *Anatomy of Criticism, Four Essays,* Princeton University Press, New Jersey, 1957.
10. M.H. Curtis, 'Education and Apprenticeship', *Shakespeare Survey,* 17, p. 63.
11. Edward Berry, *Shakespeare's Comic Rites,* Cambridge University Press, London, 1984, p. 39.
12 In Carol Thomas Neely, *Broken Nuptials in Shakespeare's Plays,* Yale University Press, New Haven, 1985, p. 2.
13. Juliet Dusinberre, *Shakespeare and the Nature of Women,* Macmillan, Hong Kong, 1975, p. 231.
14. *The Woman's Part,* eds. C.R.S. Lenz, Gayle Greene, C.T. Neely, University Illinois Press, U.S.A., 1980, p. 13.
15. Dusinberre, p. 239.

5

THE MERRY WIVES OF WINDSOR

> They invent and devise all ways and means by which first they may keep without fear of loss all that they have amassed by evil practices, and secondly, they may purchase as cheaply as possible and abuse the toil and labour of all the poor.*

No one particular text can be cited as the source of *The Merry Wives of Windsor*. For nearly every incident or situation in the plot of the play, an analogue or a vaguely possible stories and translations are to be found. So instead of an illicit paramour which is the foundation of all the source stories, Shakespeare makes normal social relationships the focus of the play by ridiculing an amorous gallant, a jealous husband and two tyrannical parents who cannot themselves agree about the choice of a husband for their daughter. The play can be said to be one of Shakespeare's play that most obviously deals with lives of common men in Elizabethan England. And the theory that it was written to please the Queen who desired to see Falstaff the lover, after Falstaff the courtier in the two parts of *Henry IV* may be correct to a certain extent because certain episodes and remarks in the play are clearly designed with an eye to secure Royal Patronage.

---

* St. Thomas More, *Complete Works of St. Thomas More,* eds. Edward Surtz a J. H. Hunter, Yale University Press, New Haven, 1965, p. 241.

The horse-stealing episode is an example where (IV iii) Shakespeare quite discreetly approves of the Queen's reluctance to elect the Count of Mompelgard to the Order of the Garter, through his enquiry of the Host, "What Duke should that becomes so secretly? I hear / not of him in the court" (IV iii 45).[1] The Host voices the contempt of the entire court for such a nobleman. The speech not only supports the Queen's decision but also mocks at the burning desire of the Count to be elected to the Order of the Garter. At a time when the relations between England and Germany were deteriorating rapidly the Host's ironic remark, "Germans are honest men" (IV v 67) not only entertained the audience, but also pleased the Queen, by putting the blame squarely on the Germans for coming to such a pass. At the end of the play Shakespeare's desire to please the Queen is laid bare, and he cannot resist himself from referring to her in the most endearing terms (V v 56-75). To him both the Queen and her abode Windsor castle are divinely, and thus when Mistress Quickly instructs the children to search the sinful men, hidden in Windsor castle she refers to it most reverentially, "Worthy the owner, and the owner it" (V v 61). Misrule seems to be the motivating force of the play, and tried upon one another at all levels it forms to be the chief source of fun and hilarity. Falstaff initiates the movement by deciding to trick both the citizens, Page and Ford simultaneously, by pretending love to their wives and getting access to their purses. It not only reflects the unscrupulousness of the man but also hits directly at the moral laxity of the aristocratic class, to which he belongs. And to make his plot more credible Shakespeare depends heavily upon the medieval tales of gallants who seeking to seduce other men's wives were interrupted and hidden in strange places. But Shakespeare's gallant has something more in his mind than mere amorous adventures. Unlike his medieval counterparts Falstaff's seduction is totally directed towards mercenary gains. He feigns love, but, within his heart, desires to make both Mistress Ford and Mistress Page his exchequers: "I will be cheaters to them both, and they shall be exchequers to me:/ they shall be my East and West Indies, and I will trade to them both" (I iii 65-66). Therefore, love to Falstaff is a convenient garb to cover up both his mercenary motives and his dire poverty.

Plautus's *Casina* too seems to have influenced Shakespeare in creating the wooing scenes of Anne Page in *The Merry Wives of Windsor,* though unlike Casina (a slave girl in Plautus's play), Anne is the daughter of a respectable citizen of Windsor. But in both the plays the man and his wife desire two different suitors for the girls, while the girls themselves prefer some other young men. Shakespeare, however, has replaced the farcical intrigue of his source by the mercenary intrigue of the Pages, who negotiate the marriage of their daughter for money only. Anne, like Casina has three different kinds of suitors, two of whom having queer whims speak idiosyncratic English and resultantly give rise to many diverting complications. In both the plays a wedding is arranged and a man takes the bride's place to hoax two of her followers while the girl is able marry the young man she loves. Similar affinities are observed between Shakespeare's comedy and Thomas Dekker's *Shoemaker's Holiday*. Page's opposition to Fenton, "The gentleman is no having he kept company with the wild Prince and Poins./He is of too high a region"(III ii 65-6); echoes the very words of Dekker's *The Lord Mayor* when he opposes Lacy's marriage to Rose Oately: "Too mean is my poor girl for a high birth?" (I i).[2] Shakespeare's mode of observations has, however changed the source material into a plot that is more realistic and contemporary. From the beginning the marriage negotiations of Anne Page appear to the audience as a marriage of convenience. Fenton is not Page's choice as mentioned earlier, and if Anne dares to disobey the wishes of her father by marrying Fenton, and not Slender (her mather's choice), Page promises to be quite hardnosed:

> No he shall not knit a knot in his fortunes with the finger of my substance: if he takes her, let him take her simply: the wealth I have waits On my consent, and my consent goes not that way (III ii 68-7).

Mistress Page on the other hand does not approve of Slender either though for some other reasons. In spite of Fenton being well landed, to her he "is an idiot" (IV iv 85) and is, therefore, not fit to be her son-law. And since "The Doctor is well money'd, and his friends / Potent court; he none but he, shall have her" (IV iv 87-88). Both parents overrule the desires of their child, manifesting their rivalry in establishing two points (1) parental control over their child's marriage and (2) parental concept of marriage as a saleable product. Love to them is merely a commodity which can be easily procured if one wants to. And it is precisely this attitude that propels Page to order his daughter unthinkingly: "Now, Master Slender; love him, daughter Anne" (III iv 65). And it is hardly surprising to find Anne not registering an open protest against such an unreasonable command of her father because, that sort of a clout was quite normal for the Elizabethan fathers. Prisius the father of Livia in *Mother Bombie* manifests similar high-handed patriarchal control over his daughter. Prisius like Page is aware of his daughters' inclinations yet he insists that she will have to marry Memphio's son and

> It will not be long before She(e) will choose with her eye (eie), and like with her
> Heart, before she consent with her tongue (Uong;) (II 50-51).[3]

The horse-stealing episode, as has been hinted at earlier has its roots not in an ancient tale but rather in contemporary political history. It is a clear reference to Count Mompelgarde's notorious adventures forcing critics to describe him as "the indefatigable traveller, who made much use of port-horses and whose followers emulated his examples."[4] Like Falstaff here is another courtier who is apparently not very honest, and history further informs us that the Count was also quite crazy for a Royal title which the Queen for some reason or other hesitated to bestow upon him. And it is quite likely that Shakespeare was here trying to provide a probable explanation for the royalty's refusal to be pliable.

There is the same mixture of realism and romance in the fairy scene of the play, where we find local references to Dachet Mead or the Forest Park existing side by side with the fairies and Herne the hunter (disguised Falstaff). For this scene

Shakespeare may have relied on Ovid's *Metamorphosis* and Lyly's *Endimion.* Like the nymphs punishing Acteon by turning him into a stag, both the merry wives here pursue their knight with vengeance. At first he has to assume a disguise which in itself is a comic parallel to the metamorphosis of Acteon. Then little fairies burn and pinch the fat knight till he lies prostrate on the ground. The substitution of the fairies for Ovid's nymphs may have been reinvigorated by Lyly's *Endimion.* Lyly's fairies too pinch and dance round Corsites in order to interrupt his work and finally put him to an enchanted sleep (parallel to Falstaff's prostration). And it is highly significant that both these Elizabethans preferred fairies to nymphs for punishing their malefactors. "The tales enacted in Shakespearean drama are decided mouldy"[5] but they are by no means merely slavish reproductions of an existing work. They are rather a process of active imitation, through which the playwright's judgment and creativity are manifested. Shakespeare is engaged in a much more complex debate than were the authors of his sources, giving way to a succession of new meanings in the course of continuing a process of transpositions. Thus, in spite of his reliance on *Casina,* medieval tales or Ovid's *Metamorphosis* Shakespeare converts his *The Merry Wives of Windsor* into a typically Elizabethan merchant play.

The main group of characters of the play belongs to the typical families in a country town. Ford and Page, the two citizens of Windsor appear to be the true representatives of the Elizabethan country folks, who managed warehouses and cultivated their lands on the bank of the Avon. Shallow is a country Justice who takes keen delight in duels as well as in marriage negotiations of his kinsman (I i 23 and III i). Page, on the other hand, has rural tastes, likes a day's sport and has his hounds and hawks for that purpose (I i 81-87). But beneath this middle-class background it's a clear picturisation of the prevalent vices of society. *The Merry Wives of Windsor* is one of the few comedies in which Shakespeare somewhat criticises the society and its norms from the point of view of those characters, who through lack of intellect, or education or adaptability, cannot be designed as full members of society.

The play "represents the nearest Shakespeare came to writing a comedy after the fashion of Ben Jonson."[6] Unlike Jonsonian comedy, Shakespeare however, instead of censuring the characters like Falstaff introduces into it a certain amount of the romantic spirit of Elizabethan age. Anne Page and Fenton keep the love motive central and add a dimension to the mouldy tales of the play. Therefore, in brief, the play represents a well-balanced mixture of social criticism and romanticism. And nowhere in the play there is an overlapping of these two elements. When the playwright wants to censure Falstaff for his lechery he does so quite ruthlessly through the two wives (III iii and IV ii) and when he desires to emphasize the romantic spirit of the Elizabethan youth he makes Fenton say:

> No heaven so speed me in my time to come!
> Albeit I will confess thy father's wealth
> Was the first motive that I woo'd thee, Anne,
> Yet, wooing thee, I found thee of more value
> Than stamps in gold or sums in sealed bags;
> And 'tis the very riches of thyself
> That now I aim at (III iv 12-18).

Fenton's words really show both sides of the coin. As a suitor to Anne he was first allured by Page's wealth, but the romantic spirit in him prevailed over his mercenary calculations. In contrast, Slender's approach is simple and materialistic. It is simply her wealth that has encouraged his kinsman Shallow to negotiate the marriage between him and Anne Page (I i 55-58).

Yet, for all his romanticism in the sub-plot of his play Shakespeare gives the readers and spectators a vivid and realistic conspectus of the country he saw around him. For example, Sir Huge Evans a simple upright man deeply conscious of his vocation, is definitely a true representative of the Elizabethan clergy. His extreme awareness of his vocation inspires him to use all sorts of religious words or phrases in the most incongruous situations, thereby providing a source of tremendous fun to the audience. In fact, his use of colourful expletives and adjurations hardly befits his clothes. Expressions like "Got deliver to a joyful resurrection" (I i 49) and "Pless you from His mercy sake, all of you" (III i 40) hardly accord with his scholarly exterior. But that somehow does not prevent him from committing the same mistake repeatedly. Though by the 1590s, when Shakespeare was writing the play, these priests were no longer to be found, it will be wrong to underrate the memory of the Elizabethan audience by assuming that they had by then forgotten all about this class of whom Peter Milward opines:

> In any case the self-consciousness of their religiosity combined with their inability to command the respect of other characters suggests that they may well have given but one leap out of the shop into the church. In all of them too, there is a Puritanical flavour, even though they belonged to type of ignorant clergy criticized by the Puritan leaders.[7]

But Shakespeare's portrayal of the priest here cannot be in any way compared to the biting satire of Ben Jonson, because the festive element in the play is always centered around the theme of love as on initiation to marriage, and even when the play ends, it ends with the marriage bells ringing.

The entire action of the plot however, revolves round the unscrupulous fat rogue, Falstaff, who lies, cheats and behaves in a pusillanimous manner much to the amusement of the audience. Both in this comedy and the two parts *of Henry IV* Falstaff is seen to suffer from an incurable consumption of the purse. Therefore, it is hardly likely, that Shakespeare not withstanding the instructions of the Queen would portray this deceitful fellow with any genuine romantic preferences. And when we find Sir John Falstaff in *The Merry Wives of Windsor* deciding to dupe both the respectable citizens by pretending to love their wives, we are instantly reassured that this is the man who occupied such an important position in the two parts of *Henry IV*.

The play begins with a lengthy discussion of Slender, Justice Shallow and Sir Evans about the mischief of Sir John Falstaff. Slender's intention to "make a Star Chamber matter of it" (I i 1-2) speaks of the King's councils' sitting place where they acted as a judicial body. The unnecessary detailed discussions of "Custalorum" (I i 7) or "Ratolorum" (I i 8) and "Armigero" (I i 9) indicate that general craze for titles during the Elizabethan Age. The coat full of "louses" (I i 18) too indicate the same craze but there is another meaning inherent in it. It may either refer to the Fish Monger Company where stock fishmongers' coats displayed luces and those of the salt fishmongers which bore the symbols of dolphins, or it may simply refer to the lice which found shelter in men's old coats. In this context Evans's reference "It is a familiar beast to man and signifies love" (I i 19-20) probably satirically hints at the parasitic existence of men like Falstaff who thrived by mere sycophancy. That, however, was a normal practice of the day and the method of adding more louses to one's coat "by marrying" (I i 23) was the another usual trend of the Elizabethan youths, who in order to enhance their worldly assets were only too eager to marry girls who inherited their fathers' wealth or title. This becomes all the more clear when in the process of discussing the qualities of Anne Page Justice Shallow remarks: "She has good gift" (I i 56) clearly referring to Anne Page's worldly wealth and not to the wealth of her personality. This commercial approach of the Elizabethans towards marriage emphasises the patriarchal mode of treating women as mere commodities whose fate depended entirely upon their male counterparts.

Falstaff's entry encourages Justice Shallow to air his grievance against the aristocrats' misdemeanours. Not to be vanquished Falstaff replies "You'll complain of me to the king?" (I i 102). This may either be a teasing way of telling him that to report such a trifling matter to the King is ridiculous or may indirectly hint at his position of a courtier. The following dialogues, however, indicate the first assumption to be more relevant, "tware better for you if it were known in counsel: You'll be laughed at" (I i 110-111). Slender's faint efforts to malign the knight's reputation (I i 115-117) referring to his men as cony-catching rascals is met with a quick rebellion. Bardolph instantly responds, "You Banbury cheese"

(I i 118). Banbury was very famous in Elizabethan England for its thin cheese. But what is more important about the allegation is that, through it Shakespeare probably wanted to highlight Falstaff's degradation. The proverbial saying 'a man is known by the company he keeps' is highly applicable here in the context of Falstaff. All the three men, Nym, Pistol and Bardolph, protest against the titles conferred to them, but significantly enough Falstaff maintains a discreet silence here. Falstaff's muteness designates two things simultaneously one, for all practical purpose he was not really disapproving the charges leveled against his men. Two, this hard-heartedness towards his men reflects the general attitude of the aristocrats who utilized the service of their entourage without a trace of humaneness when it came to sheltering them from external aggressions.

At the end of the scene Slender is found longing for "songs and sonnets" (I i 180) for wooing Anne Page. This effort on his part to woo a girl is in itself very comic but apart from that through the expression of longing Shakespeare most probably wanted to make explicit the artificiality of the man-woman relationship of his time. Slender's approach to wooing is, however, not a singular happening, but was a common practice of the Elizabethans. Like Petruchio in *The Taming of the Shrew* Slender here is a professional suitor and not a romantic lover. Therefore when he says: "I keep but three men and a boy yet, till my/ mother be dead: but what though, yet I live like a/poor gentleman born" (I i 251-53) we assume that he is talking about his poor economic conditions which he wants to recover by marrying Anne Page. Yet in spite of their poverty these so-called aristocrats never for once forsake their portentousness, and thus Anne is forced to address her suitor as "your worship" (I i 254). Like all young men Slender, of course, tries to impress his would be wife, "I have seen Sackerson loose twenty times, and have taken him/by the chain; (I i 270-272). Sackerson was indeed one of the most famous of the bear used for bear baiting in Shakespeare's day. Therefore Slender's seeing Sackerson loose indicated his prowess, an essential ingredient to establish ones masculinity prevalent from the middle ages. But all his efforts fail to impress Anne and the final effect is his ineffective wooing which infuriates Shallow later. In the second scene of the first Act Mistress Quickly is referred to by Evans as: "one Mistress/ Quickly, which is in the manner of his nurse; or his/dry nurse; or his cook; or his laundry; his washer, /and his wringer" (I ii 2-5).

As an ordinary citizen, Doctor Caius, though more wealthy than either Falstaff or Slender, has employed one person to do all his household jobs, whereas the two aristocrats try to maintain their external show by engaging three men to look after them. But what is normally expected of Falstaff proves to be a source of criticism for Doctor Caius. Consequently instead of employing three different persons for performing three different tasks he has opted for Mistress Quickly who is three in one combined.

Further evidence of Falstaff's bankruptcy is found in the third scene of the first Act. He is no longer able to maintain his entourage and, therefore, informs the Host, "Truly, mine host, I must turn away some of my / follower" (I ii 4-5). And when the Host agrees to employ Bardolph Falstaff readily condescends. The reference to "froth and lime" (I iii 14), in this context can be explained in two ways. It may mean 'to go and earn ones living' or it may refer to the malpractice of cheating the customers serving more of froth than the drink. Apart from his economic crisis Falstaff also displays his unscrupulousness and lechery. In a way of self-justification he assures that the two innocent wives of Ford and Page of having "greedy intention" (I iii 62) towards him. Hence, to use them as his exchequers should not be condemned totally. Falstaff's derogatory remarks about two wives may also reflect the contemporary general misconception, about a woman's frankness and free disposition. And only such a guess can justify Ford's unfair suspicions about his wife's fidelity. Added to it one can say that Falstaff's approach is a reflection of the contemporary aristocrats' disposition towards the fairer sex of the commoners. He takes it for granted that they would be allured by his connections with the royalty and hence readily surrender to his charms. According to contemporary history of

England there were many such declassed aristocrats who by merely inheriting the title found it difficult to make a proper living like a common citizen. So the only recourse they had was to swindle the masses and make a living out of it.

The first scene of the second Act opens with Mistress Page reading a billet doux of Falstaff. She is flattered a little but is not totally carried away by the encomium (II i 1-3). Finally on seeing the signature Sir John Falstaff she loses her self-control and calls him "Flemish drunkard" (II i 23). Flemish here refers to the inhabitants of the low-countries and of course to the Danes who were alleged to be often drunk. At the end Pistol and Nym are seen to inform both Page and Ford about the evil designs of Falstaff. The reactions of the two men are extremely significant here. Ford instantly starts distrusting his wife while Page does not bother to think twice about such tittle-tattle. Page's rationality is however looked down upon by Ford. To him it is cuckoldry perhaps to place implicit trust in his wife. Wife beating being rampant at that point of history Ford's contempt for Page possibly rang a familiar note to the ear of Shakespearean audience.

The two men here apparently represent two different brands of Elizabethan men, one, treating women as commodities and the other with his inherent rationality treating his better half as his equal and believing his wife to have a distinct opinion of her own. This clearly is a reflection of Shakespearean effort to portray the growing Renaissance consciousness which preached spiritual equality of women and insisted that they should be given equal hearing by the society. In contrast, Ford's irrationality appears to be a reflection of the existing patriarchal order handed to him down the ages, and which tended to repress women from functioning. Therefore, later when he dares to flog his wife in public the general consensus seems to be for him. Even Page for that matter hardly protests for he knows such acts were considered permissible in the patriarchal structure.

The second scene opens with a quarrel between Falstaff and Pistol. They quarrel for money and one thing that becomes obvious from their quarrel is Falstaff's share in the booty of Mistress Bridgett's "handle of her fan" (II ii 11). Generally fashionable ladies of Elizabethan England used fans which had ivory or metallic handles and were, therefore, the most desired objects for thieves. Enraged, Falstaff accuses Pistol of having stolen such an item and not sharing the booty with him and hence he thunders to his men in such unflattering words: "cat-a-mountain looks, your red-lattice/ phrases, and your bold beating oaths, under the/ shelter of your honour" (II ii 25-27). Red lattice here refers to taverns or alehouses which normally had red painted lattice instead of glass windows. Falstaff immediately gets rid of Pistol: "Go thy ways; I'll make/ more of thy body than I have done. Will they/ yet look after thee?" (II ii 133-35). Since his men were employed only to help him swindle other men for his benefit Pistol's individual effort to rob the lady concerned and pocket the pillage all by himself proves to be insufferable for Falstaff. Hence, manifesting both his nastiness along with his natural, high-handedness towards his subordinates and plebeians alike he dismisses Pistol at a moment's notice. There is display neither of any compunction nor sorrow when parting from his long associate Pistol. Previously too when his men were accused of fraudulence Falstaff had manifested similar indifference and this incident only substantiates his general attitude towards them all the more.

The third scene of the third Act begins with the two Wives talking to one another and planning to punish the Knight. Their incensed behaviour is understandable. On one hand Falstaff is questioning their fidelity as wives, added to it they realise the innate contempt of the man towards their class. So both combined they do not hesitate to punish the pretentiousness of the man by pushing him into the buck-basket. And Falstaff little suspecting their ire readily steps into their trap by creeping inside the buck-basket. Buck-basket was meant to store the dirty linen of the house. And Falstaff indeed was the dirty linen of the society who required a thorough cleansing in the Thames. His creeping therefore not only amuses the audience but also establishes both his cowardice and symbolic insubordination of his immorality in presence of the two innocent women's chastity. As was planned before, John and Robert carry the basket to Datchet Mead or a meadow between Windsor Little Park and the Thames and empty its content into the Thames.

The second punishment of Falstaff is meted out in the second scene of the fourth Act. Both Mistress Ford and Mistress Page advise the knight to dress up as "the fat woman of Brainford" (IV ii 67), to avoid detection by Ford. But Mistress Ford knows the consequences of their jest well in advance because her suspicious husband will not spare a single chance of maligning her in public and thereby declaring her perfidious nature: "I would my husband would meet him in this/ shape. He cannot abide the old woman of Brainford;/ he swears she's a witch, forbade her my house, and hath threatened to beat her" (IV ii 76-8). Added to it his distrust for any person with occult power is likely to provoke him to take extreme measures. And that is precisely what happens when Ford meets the disguised Knight. This incident can, however, be interpreted in two ways. First Ford's belief that the woman of Brainford was a witch actually reflects a common belief of the day having its roots to the middle ages. And second it indirectly hints at the accepted Elizabethan practice of wife beating "Mistress Ford, good heart,/ is beaten black and blue, that you cannot see a/white spot about her" (IV v 106-08). The concept that a man should not for any reason torture the weaker sex physically or mentally was not accepted by the Elizabethan patriarchy even though Renaissance philosophy preached spiritual equality of women. Thus, when Ford pounds the innocent woman for no cause, the other male characters do not object to it. To them it is just a natural manifestation of male wrath and hence nobody troubles to stop him. "Domestic violence, far from being contained in the family, spills out into the neighbourhood, and the response of the community is an 'old country ceremony used in merriment upon such accidents,.'"[8]

The play ends on an ambivalent note, the Windsorites unite to defeat Falstaff in a fine demonstration of local solidarity and yet another courtier manages to carry off their own daughter defeating all their efforts (the marrying of Anne Page to Fenton). First of all being convinced of his wife's honesty, Ford insists on getting back all the money he previously paid to Falstaff. Secondly, while they are busy punishing Falstaff much to the chagrin of both Page and his wife Anne marries Fenton. But finally there is no ill-will against any one at the end and the audience is happy to find all proceeding to "laugh this sport off by a country fire,/Sir John all" (V v 229-230).

Not in the manner of his other comedies, Shakespeare in *The Merry Wives of Windsor* portrays the town's people and not the aristocrats. Windsor was, in fact, the sprawling little town which he knew well therefore, used it with unusual thoroughness as the play's background "The town sets the atmosphere of the play, since at every point it is court characters that are duped and the town characters that are successful."[9] The duping occurs at more than one level. Falstaff's decision to pretend love to the wives of Page and Ford is the first and the important deception of the play, resulting into all kinds of hilarious situations. The aristocrats' bankruptcy and immorality is quite explicit when Falstaff says, "I will be cheaters to them both, and they shall exchequers/ to me" (I iii 65-66). The two apparently, simple country wives, however, are clever enough to distrust Falstaff's amorous approaches and remaining quite loyal to their familial ties, take adequate steps to both deceive and punish him in turn for his offensive suggestions.

Falstaff's own men dupe him and try to extract money from him and failing to achieve their end go and inform both Page and Ford of their master's evil designs (I iii 91-98). Their unscrupulousness is at par with Falstaff's. Ford's deception of Falstaff in the guise of Brook is important for two different reasons. First, it clearly establishes the jealous nature of Ford which goes to the extent of flouting all social decorum, and second it gives the two wives ample opportunity to punish the gullibility of Ford and expose his weakness in public. In the sub-plot it is the Host of Garter Inn, who deceives both

Doctor Caius and Evans when they decide to fight a duel for winning the hand of Anne Page,

> Doctor Caius. By gar I vill
> Kill de Jack-priest; and I have appointed mine host of de Jarteer to measure our weapon (I iv 111-113).

This measuring of weapon was an old social custom in duels and it is quite possible that Shakespeare himself was not in favour of such unnecessary bloodshed on the stage and hence through the intervention of the Host made the two suitors two laughing stocks (III i 92-103). Yet, in spite of all his good gestures it is the Host who finally is deceived by some unknown Germans in the third scene of the fourth act (ll 8-10). And as mentioned earlier this deception indicated something far more significant and ominous other than merely cheating the noble natured Host, which presumably was appreciated by the Elizabethan audience.

Anne Page's and Fenton's duping however supersedes the rest and brings about the final reconciliation in the comic plot. Fenton is the true representative of the new romantic spirit of the age and Anne is his ideal partner who without openly opposing the parental authoritarianism ultimately rejects their choice and manifests to the world her new found identity. The marriage of Anne and Fenton is, therefore, not a marriage of convenience but a union of two romantic souls. At the end of the play the impression is one of open and cheerful spirit which makes the effects of comic devices all the more hilarious, but the Windsor's social consciousness in forming the comedy becomes an interesting comment on Shakespeare's critical approach to the society of his age.

Notes

1. All references to *The Merry Wives of Windsor* are to The Arden Shakespeare, *The Merry Wives of Windsor,* ed. H.J. Oliver, Methuen, London, 1971.
2. All references to *Shoemaker's Holiday* are to *The Dramatic Work of Thomas Dekker,* Cambridge University Press, Cambridge, 1953.
3. All textual reference to *Mother Bombie* are to *The Complete Works of John Lyly* III, ed. R. Warwick Bond, Clarendon Press, London, 1902, rep. 1973.

4 Geoffrey Bullough, *Narrative and Dramatic Sources of Shakespeare*, 2, Routledge, London, 1957, p. 15.

5. Leah Scragg, *Shakespeare's Mouldy Tales*, Longman, London, 1992, p. 1.

6. John Dover Wilson, *Shakespeare's Happy Comedies*, Faber, London, 1962, p. 1.

7. *Religious Background*, Sidwick and Jackson, London, 1973, p. 145.

8. Karen Newman, 'Renaissance Family Politics and Shakespeare's *The Taming of the Shrew*', in *Shakespeare's Comedies*, ed. Gary Waller, Longman, London, 1991, p. 41.

9. Marchette Chute, *Shakespeare of London*, Sovenir Press, London, 1977, p. 222.

6

LOVE'S LABOUR'S LOST

> Remember dear ladies, how these men call you frail, unserious, easily influenced but yet try hard, using all kinds of strange and deceptive tricks to catch you just as one lays traps for wild animals.*

No particular text can be cited as the source of *Love's Labour's Lost,* and, it will not be wrong to presume that the play like *The Merry Wives of Windsor* relies heavily upon contemporary history to serve as its source material. In fact, the characters of the play are clearly the living personages of English history, and the incidents and situations of the plot often echo certain definite incidents and situations of sixteenth-century England. For instance, Ferdinand and the Princess of France, the two central characters of the play round whom the entire action of the play revolves, were two well known figures of English history very familiar to the Shakespearean audience. Their names were of course, not the names assigned by the playwright (the real King of Navarre was Henri and not Ferdinand), but were often very close to the originals (Due de Biron changed to Berowne and Due de Longueville to Longaville). Moreover, the real King of Navarre did receive an embassy from France headed by a Princes Marguerite de Valois, in 1578 to discuss an important topic about the dowry of the Princess, which included the question of possession of

---

* Christine de Pisan, *The Book of the City of Ladies,* trans. Early Jeffer Richards, Pan, London, 1983, pp. , 256-257.

Aquitaine (II ii 28).[1] And on this occasion the royal envoy bent on reinforcing the norms of diplomacy sought to please the visiting royal dignitaries through coquetry (V ii). But their method to please them (to appear before the ladies in Russian disguise) was clearly the impact of the diplomatic exchange of ambassadors between Russia and England during the eighties and nineties of the sixteenth century, and also of the arrival of the special envoy of Czar Ivan the Terrible to seek the hand of Lady Mary Hastings in marriage in 1583. Thus, Shakespeare masterfully mixed facts with fiction to create dramatically convincing figures.

Even in the subplot of his play Shakespeare skillfully introduces such much discussed topics as the anti-alien riots in 1593 and the London plague of 1591-1594 because he knew his audience would appreciate them as known facts. As a true English citizen, Shakespeare possibly felt it to be his duty to highlight these social problems faced by his compatriots and thereby enlighten his viewers about the existing malaise of the society. Thus, Moth's question to his master Armado "Master, will you win your love with a French braw'l" (III i 6-7) assumes a different dimension in the given context. The playwright is actually referring here to the contemporary London riots which was deliberately launched to oust foreign refugees, for their presence meant a tough competition for the city's accommodation, food and employment for the residing citizens. Likewise, through Berowne pleading with Rosaline, "Lord have mercy on us" (V ii 419), Shakespeare sought to highlight the disaster that struck London during the epidemic of plague in the year 1591-1594.

Regarding the plot of *Love's Labour's Lost,* therefore, no single authority can be cited as its chief source. Rather the materials of the story seem to be scattered here and there in many books, contemporary events and historical data. The central story of the academic vow for example, may have been derived from *Academic Francaise* by Pierre d la Primandaya or may have been a reflection of the School of Night of the Copernicans. And the austerities observed by the French Academy like keeping away from women or other worldly affairs by the young scholars while pursuing their studies may have tickled the fancy of the playwright. But the flight of fancy does not stop at merely restricting the king and his courtiers from taking part in all other normal human activities; the promulgation of similar decree for the entire country is a deliberation on the part of the playwright to underscore the whimsicality of the monarch. It is only for registering fame upon 'his' brazen tomb Navarre inflicts a diktat upon his subjects thereby, undermining their actual preferences. It is true that his courtiers gladly accept to follow the austere measures of not sleeping more than "three hours in the night" (I i 42), or taking only one meal a day or not to communicate to any lady within a span of three years but the entire country does not show any such proclivity. The lesser mortals like Costard and Jaquenetta who have no desire "to study so, / to know the thing" (I i 60-61) are being forcefully deprived of the normal ways of life (I i 236-263). This certainly does not speak in favour of a fair and just ruler like King Ferdinand.

Apart from portraying the ruler's whimsicality Shakespeare also tries to expose the fallaciousness underlying the idealism that learning is tantamount to asceticism and barren verbiage. He clearly points out that love should not be mistaken for frivolity but should be treated as the experience of real life that helps man to act in the manner of a true man. Berowne, acting as the mouthpiece of the playwright, reminds the court of the hollowness of the ideal which does not recognize the basic facts of human life and points out its obvious unreality by saying that one of the articles will have to be broken immediately as the French Princess will visit the court on an embassy (I i 127-139).

The diplomatic exchange between the King and Princess that follows (II i 129-168) does echo a contemporary event of the dramatist's time:

> In 1578 Marguerite de Valois, who had been unwillingly married to Henry of Navarre and separated from him, went with her mother ... to meet the King at Ne'rac, where they discussed her dowry which included Aquitaine.[2]

This historical event in fact helped Shakespeare to highlight the common social system of accepting dowry in marriage, both in the royal household and in the merchant community of the Elizabethan England (The *Taming of the Shrew* I i 64-75). The difference is, of course, made quite explicit. Amongst the royalty it is the proposed bride who discusses her dowry while the discussion of dowry in the merchant class is restricted to the parents of the girl (The *Taming of the Shrew* II i 115-130).

The interest in Russia as mentioned earlier was intermittent in the eighties and nineties of sixteenth century England along with it reminiscences of Gray's Inn entertainment. So both these event combined might have acted as an incentive for the playwright to construct the scene of the Muscovite Mask (V ii) and provoked Berowne to declare, "Knowing a forehand of our merriment/To dash it like a Christmas comedy" (V ii 461-462). Even the comic conduct of the lover seems to have been directly borrowed from the reminiscence of the Gray's Inn and the current joke at the expense of the Russian ambassador whose ridiculous courtship of Lady Mary Hastings led to the lady being nicknamed the Empress of Muscovia. But, the mask, however, does not remain a mere mask, a mere source of entertainment, it rather assumes, a far deeper meaning which hits at the lightness of the amorous approaches of the king and his courtiers. Instead of wooing the French ladies in the downright way of simple courtship, they mask themselves and repeat their conned speeches and are rightly mocked for their pains. There has not been a test of their sincerity, nor have they confronted hazards of life and fortune as in *The Two Gentlemen of Verona* or *The Merchant of Venice.*

For the subplots of Armado and his fellows Shakespeare might have depended more upon the Italian commedia dell'arte than any other source, but their "relationship is generic rather than particular."[3] He, however, utilizes them to provide a variation on the theme of the play and reduce it to absurdity. Both Armado and Holofernes take barren verbiage for real learning, and similarly their betters in the court make the mistake of exalting learning over the realities of life. Later on,

Armado too, who giving himself the airs of a courtly sophisticated knight finally forgets his fanciful nobility and recognizes a plain man's desire for a plain maid, and like the courtiers who are placed on trial, undertakes a self-imposed penance of driving the plough for her for three years.

But to consider the comedy of *Love's Labour's Lost* as a topical satire on the Schools of Atheism of which Raleigh was the chief patron and Marlowe, Chapman and Harriot were members, is to remain impervious to the sympathy of the playwright in portraying his characters and also to give undue importance to the casual references to the School of Atheism. Unlike his contemporary, Ben Jonson, Shakespeare hardly censures the social or sectarian prejudices; rather his explicit desire seems to be to provide pure entertainment for his courtly audience and in the process to laugh mildly at their follies. Therefore, even though Shakespeare might have derived some hints from the controversy between the Essex-Southampton and the Raleigh-Northumberland groups, it was, at the most, an intellectual stimulus, and the satiric impulse was largely transcended by the broad human implications of the comedy. In a sense:

> Evolutions in *Love's Labour's Lost* express the Elizabethan feeling for the harmony of a group acting in ceremonious consort, a sense of decorum expressed in areas as diverse as official pageantry, madrigal and motet singing, or cosmological speculations about the order of the universe.[4]

And when the harmony or even the cosmological order is somehow disrupted, all unpleasant things tend to take place. For instance, the apparently unwise decisions of the king and his courtiers to abstain from all normal activities in order to know the things one is "forbid to know" (I i 60) will ultimately lead to all sorts of comic situations as found in the third scene of the fourth Act. The target of the playwright appears to be is always to make the characters move towards the achievable and the normal. And hence, the existing comic incongruity in the play in fact creates a gap between the affected and unrealistic on the one hand, and the sensible, on the other. The king and his men represent the former type, while the Princess and her retinue represent the sensible group.

Strangely enough, there is a curious absence of court servants and attendants in *Love's Labour's Lost,* except those found in the Princess's retinue. Instead, the villagers like the constable, the parson, the school masters and the country wench people the play in profusion. And the setting, as mentioned above, in the opening two scenes, the playwright envisages a manor house, a curious-knotted garden and a park which reminds the reader not of a royal court but rather of a large-estate where the lord of the manor consorts to a certain extent, with the people of the village. A royal court of Shakespeare's day would not normally be credited with such close involvement in the life of the village as portrayed in the play. And this probably happens because Shakespeare quite deliberately decided to make his play a "social comedy"[5] where four young men turning a blind eye to reality, attempt an act which rationality declares totally unfeasible. Though one among them tries to point out the impossibility of the feat, "O, these are barn tasks, too hard to keep" (I i 47) all the rest persist in their childish view of reality. But, fortunately enough, four clear sighted women representing the society give them a series of lessons and puts, them on the way to see things as they are. A similar distorted view of reality is found to individualise two other characters of the play, Holofernes and Armado.

They are fully grown up and set in their habits and yet unlike the young men,

> who are still malleable, they will continue to be comparatively harmless misfits in the society to which they belong; or to put their case more accurately in terms of the play, they will remain forever islanded in the park of Navarre which is made to stand so exquisitely for a state of affairs at odds with what prevails beyond its bounds.[6]

The return of the young men is, however, not very smooth or easy. A year of penitence awaits them to attain their cherished state of bliss, "Grant us your loves" (V ii 779). And only after a year of penitence, having completely renounced the boyish pursuits of dry book learning can the four young men become husbands, thus assuming the role of a full adult, in society. But the first requisite of a successful marriage is knowing one's own self, which can be "achieved only in society, in "the converse of breath" (V ii 727) which exposes the self to relationship and to the actualities of material existence.[7] The older citizens of the play are however finally denied this self-knowledge because the playwright is aware that they are beyond all learning.

This denial may presumably spring from the class consciousness that is often felt in the play for the commoners like Nathenial, Holofernes, Moth Armado, Dull and Costard being often treated quite contemptuously and even critically by the nobility. They are always the easy game for the noblemen, for their failings are made obvious by Shakespeare. Their affectations blind them to their own faults (IV ii 71-72), yet they all seem only to be too ready to criticise the faults of others. And it is this fault in them that makes them all the more vulnerable to the criticism of the lords who themselves commit the same error as the common village folks, "Costard the swain and he, shall be our sport," (I i 178). But the playwright does not take long to establish that these very young men who wanted to take Costard for a ride because he betrayed his affections for Jaquentta had been suffering from the same malady called love, "Saint Cupid, then; and soldiers, to the friend" (IV iii 362). The noble men are, however, oblivious of the fact that "the commoner's imperfections are, in essence, cruder versions of their own characteristics."[8] The commoner's misuse of language is in reality the wit of the noblemen and the over ambitiousness of the commoner is reflected in the pretensions of the noblemen. The difference between the two distinct class is simple— the commoners lack the sophistication of the noblemen and hence are not able to cover up their hypocrisy, and, it is this lack of sophistry on their part that are exploited by people like Berowne "Greater than great, great, great, great,/Pompey Pompey the Huge"

(V ii 677-678). One also recalls his sarcastic remark even after his exposure of his weakness for Rosaline, "Will these turtles be gone" (IV iii 208).

King Ferdinand's instructions to his courtiers about the strict implementations of their vows mark the beginning of *Love's Labour's Lost.* All agree, except Berowne who tries to point out the fallacy underlying the rules,

> This article, my liege, yourself must break;
> For well you know here comes in embassy
> The French king's daughter with yourself to speak—
> A maid of grace and complete majesty—
> About surrender up of Aquitaine
> To her decrepit, sick, and bed-rid father:
> Therefore this article is made in vain
> Or vainly comes th' admired princess hither
> (I i 132-133).

The King is at a loss, he has hardly foreseen such a situation in his hasty declaration of the diktat. Berowne's argument not only bowls out the entire court but also echoes the acknowledged fact (both by the Catholics and the Protestants) that man lacks the might to fulfill the law by himself. Berowne then proceeds to enquire. "But is there no quick recreation granted?" (I i 160) King Ferdinand assures him that there will certainly be some interesting interludes in the form of Armado who will entertain the court with his quaint tales of the world narrated in his unique style. Armado, the reader knows, is a Spanish traveler and by mocking his well-studied English the court manifests the highbrowed attitude of the Englishmen towards foreigners. The scene ends with the discussion of Armado's letter about the misbehaviour of Costard and a country wench called Jaquenetta. The letter proves to be a real treat for the courtiers and Berowne confesses that this is much better than he expected.

The second scene of the first Act begins with Armado conversing with Moth about sadness and melancholy. Armado confides in Moth about his intention to study with the King and his courtiers for three years and in the process live a life of abstinence. But Moth is not at all impressed he makes fun of him instead:

> Sir, is this a piece of study? Now here is three studies ere ye'll thrice wink; and how easy it is to put years to the word three and study three years in two words, the dancing horse will tell you (I ii 47-50).

The dancing horse to which Moth refers was probably a description of the trick-performing horse, famous in Elizabethan literature and popular down to the middle of the seventeenth century. Armado, however, is not at all disheartened by Moth's jeering, on the contrary, he proceeds to confide in him his love for the country girl whom he "took in the park with the rational hind Costard" (I ii 110-111). Though as a true soldier Armado feels that it is beneath his dignity to love a "base wench" (I ii 54) as an ordinary human being he cannot get rid off his baser feelings. Armado's attitude establishes two things quite clearly—first the existing class consciousness among the Elizabethans and second, the romantic love which had recently swept off the old ideals of love in Elizabethan England. Armado desirous of proposing to Jaquenatte despite his social position does not have to wait long. Jaquenetta's entry at the end of the scene gives him the right opportunity to fulfill his yearning.

The Princess of France and her attendants arrive at Navarre in the first scene of the second Act. A long controversy regarding the ownership of Aquitaine has brought her to Navarre, therefore, Boyet is sent to Ferdinand to inform him about their arrival. King Ferdinand along with his courtiers follows Boyet and is quite apologetic about his inability to welcome the Princess to his court: "Here me, dear Lady; I have sworn an oath" (II i 96). But the Princess seizing the opportune moment mocks him, saying: "Were my lord so, his ignorance were wide, / Where now his knowledge must prove ignorance" (II i 101-102). The sensible approach of the newcomer impresses the reader, and once again unlike the king he is reminded of the fallacy of the oath the young men have taken.

The king, however, returns to business after a few moments of diversion, "Madam, your father here doth intimate/The payment of a hundred thousand crowns" (II i 128-129). This reference to the payment of hundred thousand crowns seems to have a definite historical basis. History says that in 1420 Charles IV did have to pay an amount of 200,000 crowns to Charles of Aragon, King of Navarre, according to prior negotiations. Shakespeare being aware of this event sought to present it in his play to both authenticate his play and also to convince his audience. The Princess then states as a way of clarification:

> You do the king my father too much wrong,
> And wrong the reputation of your name,
> In so unseeming to confess receipt
> Of that which hath so faithfully been paid
> (II 153-136).

Boyet who has come in to rescue the Princess now promises to produce all the relevant documents regarding the debt the next day when the packet arrives. The satisfied King once again extends his welcome to his honoured guests and then departs, leaving his courtiers to flirt with the retinue of the Princess. At the end of the scene comes the characteristic forecast of Boyet : "Deceive me not now, Navarre is infected" (II i 22) Contrary to his vow of total abstinence the King has not only met a woman but has also fallen victim to the same disease of Armado, the malady of romantic love.

Armado is found confiding in Moth his love for Jaquenatte in the first scene of the third Act. Taking advantage of the situation Moth teases his master, first, by referring to the French brawl mentioned earlier, and then by explaining it to him as a "Jig off tune at the / tongue's end, canary to it with your feet" (III i 9-l0) Canary was a type of dance a great deal popular in Elizabethan England, and it had its roots in Spain. And, since Armado belongs to that country, Moth's explanation seems all the more appropriate to the audience. Moth then proceeds to instruct his master further about matters of love, and Armado is quite surprised at the immensity of his experience: "How have thou purchased this experience" (III i 24). Wise Moth's keen observation further helps Armado to realize the extent of his affection for the maid:

> Moth: A man, if I live; and this, by in, and without, upon the instant: by heart you love her, because your heart cannot come by her; in heart you love her, because your heart is in love with her; and out of heart you love her being out of heart that you cannot enjoy her Armado: I am all these three (III i 38-44).

The gallant knight hardly realizes that Moth is clearly teasing him and exposing him more and more, much to the delight of the viewers. Armado then asks Moth to fetch Costard for carrying his love letter to Jaquenetta and Costard completely conquering his previous fondness for Jaquenetta and hatred against Armado (I i 202-222) agrees to act as a go-between just for three farthings. And just when he decides to go off stage Berowne enters with a similar request, but this time the remuneration is a guerdon of a shilling and the lady is Rosaline, a gentle lady in the train of the Princess. Costard is overjoyed, "Gardon, O sweet gardon: better than remuneration;/a' leven—pence farthing better" (III i 164-165).

The fourth Act begins with the Princess talking to a forester about their king, and about deer hunting. The lady seems quite proficient in the art of hunting both men and animals. She is absolutely free and easy while talking to this ordinary person, and hence even teases him out of his wits. "Here, good my glass, take this for telling true;/Fair payment for foul words is more than due" (IV I 18-19). This again can be called a deliberation of the playwright to present a contrast between the King and his courtiers and the Princess. The arrogance of Berowne and his compatriots regarding Armado, Costard etc. clearly indicates their highbrowed attitude, but the Princess does not feel it demeaning conversing easily with a menial like a poor hunter. While she is busy conversing in this manner, Costard enters, and as expected of a comedy, delivers Armado's letter to Jaquenetta: "I have a letter from Monsieur Berowne to one Lady/Rosaline" (IV i 53-54). As instructed by his employer, Boyet opens the letter and starts reading it only to realize after a moment that the letter has been wrongly delivered. The letter, however, makes delicious reading and clearly indicates the fact that Armado, in spite of his over whelming affection for the country wench, has not really overcome his class consciousness, and that is why he compares his love for the ordinary girl with the love of Cophetua and Zenelophon (IV i 61-87). But whether Costard has deliberately delivered the wrong letter or it was a mere mistake on his part is not very clear, as at the end of the scene we find Costard not at all ashamed of his wrong doings. Rather we find him enjoying the stupidity of Armado's flamboyant expressions, so thoroughly discussed by Boyet and Rosaline and also to a certain extent by the Princess herself.

Dull, Nathaniel, and Holofernes are found discussing things about the sport of deer killing. Holofernes tries to prove in the next scene both to Dull and Nathaniel his superiority in Latin. Not to be bested Nathaniel, too, displays his vast knowledge of the language, and when poor Dull seeks to fathom the meanings of their words both Holofernes and Nathaniel condemn him : "O: thou monster Ignorance, how deform'd does thou look, /Nathaniel : Sir he hath never fed of the dainties that are bred in a book" (IV ii 22-23). Both Holofernes (the schoolmaster) and Nathaniel (the curate) are true representatives of their class, and are often sneered at by Shakespeare (Sir Hugh Evans in *The Merry Wives of Windsor).* Perhaps both the curates and the schoolmasters of Shakespeare's time often misquoted Latin in order to impress their audience and since their audience comprised men like Dull and Costard their wrong usage was never detected or exposed, and hence they were allowed to go off the hook.

The third scene opens with Berowne's attempts to compose another antic poem for his lady-love and while he struggles with the rhymes, King Ferdinand enters mumbling his love poem, addressed to Princess of France. Berowne hides behind a bush and listens to the poem and, just when the King has finished reading the entire poem, Longaville enters, and like both Berowne and the King, is found reading a love poem.

Lastly, Dumain enters in a similar manner and exposes his deepest secret to one and all. All these four young men at last have forsaken their life of recluse and are fully prepared to come back to the real world where natural human instincts are both recognized and appreciated.

At the beginning of the first scene of the fifth Act Holofernes is seen talking to Nathaniel about a dinner where they both had been, and as observed on the previous occasion, they once again compete against one another in their knowledge of Latin. It was the general tendency of the pedants of the day to exhibit their scholasticism by uttering Latin off and on and confounding the commoners. While they are conversing thus their discussion turns towards the general behaviour of Don Adriano de Armado, and Nathaniel is seen to draw out his table-book. The table book was generally used by the Elizabethans to note down anything worth noting and was mainly used by men who pretended to be considerably learned. Therefore, Nathaniel's drawing out his table book was intended both to amuse the audience and establish his pretensions of learning. Armado, along with Costard and Moth, is seen to enter the stage, and as expected he is found using bombastic expressions to impress his audience. The last eventful scene of the play consists of the Muscovite Mask and the desperate declaration of love for the French ladies by King Ferdinand and his courtiers and also the enacting of the Nine Worthies. The scene begins with a casual conversation between the Princess and her retinue:

> Princess: Sweet hearts, we shall be rich ere we depart, If fairings come thus plentifully in; A lady wall'd about with diamonds: Look you what I have from the loving king (V ii 1-4).

Fairings in Elizabethan England stood for almost anything that was purchased at fairs, and the lady wall'd about with diamonds' was a favourite design of Elizabethan jewellers. While the ladies are busy teasing thus, Boyet crosses the threshold to inform them about the approaching young men: "They do, they do; and are apparell'd thus, /Like Muscovites, or Russians, as I guess" (V ii 120-121). The Muscovy was much in news throughout the eighties and nineties of the sixteenth century England and consequently, it can be presumed that the audience too was quite thrilled to view the entertainment that was to be presented on the stage.

After some time the maskers arrive and in their ignorance woo the wrong ladies, as they too are masked. The following merry love-making scene, where the Princess and her retinue chaff their young suitors illustrates their superiority in contrast to the blind infatuation of King Ferdinand and his men in spite of their professed celibacy. Finally when they invite the ladies to dance, as decided earlier, the ladies refuse and the disappointed lords and their king depart, leaving the ladies behind to make fun of them in absentia. "Rosaline: Well, better wits have worn plain statute-caps" (V ii 281). The statute cap that Rosaline talks about was a part of the academic habit of Shakespeare's time. So the academic achievements of Ferdinand and his courtiers have now been restricted only to their statute-caps and nothing else. All whatever they have said and done so far did not manifest their intellectual superiority hence the ladies are absolutely right in mocking them in this manner. Their discussion however is brief, as Boyet warns them that the King and his men would return soon in their original attires to get a feedback from the ladies. The ladies, therefore, hurry off the stage to unmask and prepare themselves to counter the attack of the approaching royal dignitaries.

The King and his men arrive and Boyet receives them till the ladies return. Then follows a nother merry love-making scene, where the Princess and her ladies establish that all their oaths are bogus and that they have all wooed the wrong ladies. The men are consequently bewildered, much to the amusement of the audience and the mystery of the unknown Russians is readily acknowledged by them. A lengthy show of Nine Worthies follows immediately after that. But behind this carnivalesque atmosphere the audience is consistently made aware of the dark façade of these young royalties who have come to woo the ladies. And again it is the Princess who designates both the shallowness and the vindictiveness of the nobility while dealing with the commoners when they are busy presenting the show of the Nine Worthies. In contrast to the brusque manner of Berowne as noted earlier, the occasional encouraging remarks of the Princess: "Speak, brave Hector; we are much delighted" (V ii 657) to the commoners not only establishes her refinement but also makes her appear more civilized than their own ruler. The royalty of the land does not deem it necessary to maintain even a semblance of politeness when dealing with common folks. The women, therefore by exposing this hollowness of theirs implicitly also try to correct them. They themselves are not presented as perfect human beings, but they embody the norms of human conduct against which the aberration of the noble men are to be measured. Thus the play finally does not end on a note of reunion but rather with a promise of reunion in future only if they give up their impractical ideologies of life. Added to it, maybe rectify themselves when dealing with their subjects.

In conclusion, it can be said that the setting *of Love's Labour's Lost* is firmly rooted in a rural English community centering on the great house, of which the reader sees nothing. As mentioned earlier, Navarre and his followers appear to inhabit a house instead of a royal court, which in reality belongs to the owner of a large estate, and almost naturally consort with simple village people like Dull, Costard, Moth and the rest.

> The convention of place involved is 'about Navarre's Court', outdoors, it seems to be nothing more definite. The recluse King may walk there; the Princess may be met there ... a pricket may be driven near for shooting, a pageant be shown there, a measure trod on the grass.[9]

It resembles a deer park of an English country, and makes its owner certainly not a king but rather a minor Elizabethan noble man living on his estate. Therefore, studied from a social perspective, the play certainly appears to be dealing with the domestic realties of Elizabethan England, where royalty actually reflects the aristocracy. And if Navarre is a noble man attended by three young men, the Princess with her retinue is the female representative of the French nobility. The other characters fortunately do not have any such problems regarding their true identity, as Shakespeare makes them the fittest representatives of their class. The rustics however, being too literal, appear to be quite critical about the Spanish accents of Don Armado, a foreigner and often try to censure him for mispronouncing the words of their mother tongue.

> The schoolmaster's strictures on Don Armado suggest that upper class Englishmen in Shakespeare's time made a point of their mispronunciations, as they do in ours. The Don says "cauf for "calf," "hauf" for "half, and "nebour" for "neighbour." No doubt he also said "wescot" for "waistcoat" and "orffer" for "offer.[10]

Shakespeare's censure is, however, not at all malicious, nor is it destructive or contemptuous, Shakespeare's ridicule of the sentimental lords and their wild fancies manifests an indulgence which implies affection and not reprobation. "His play is more in the nature of a family diversion where private jests are exchanged for the fun of the thing."[11] And since the jests are private and at times totally topical the modern reader tends to loose clue of many of the play's witticisms and is even likely to overlook them. But that is not the fault of the playwright, rather it the fault of the genre which is totally dependent upon the society in which it is composed. And with the passing away of that social structure the problems treated in the comedy too tend to become dated. But in *Love's Labour's Lost* in spite of many topical references, the central theme is universal one, the theme of "the infirmity of human purpose."[12]

The story that turns on vows sworn and then forsworn under the pressure of circumstance is the universal story of man. Even in one's real life this infirmity generates many events of unpleasantness. Therefore, to condemn the King and his courtiers is to condemn one's own self, and to manifest a very unsympathetic attitude towards the realities of life. And this is exactly what Shakespeare feels when he tries to direct the action of the play towards righting the balance of nature, which the proud nobility with their one-sidedness, try to upset. The self-deceived nobility are forced to seek self-knowledge, because society in the form of sensible French ladies will never accept them with their artificial and distorted perceptions of life.

In spite of its countryside setting one cannot deny that *Love's Labour's Lost* is basically:

> a Londoner's play written for people, who knew all the latest jokes with words. It was written by a man who had been watching and listening even more intently than he had been reading.[13]

Hence, it is not at all surprising to find the playwright alluding several times to the controversy that existed between the Catholics and the Protestants regarding various religious interpretations. The vow of celibacy, the garden confession, the pageant of the Nine Worthies, and administration of penance and the deferred promise of festive joy are the few actions of the play that refer to the issues of that controversy. The King of Navarre who vows for celibacy was in reality a Protestant king, and his forswearing of the vow for trying to marry the Princess can easily be equated with the conversion of the real King to Catholicism for the purpose of becoming the King of France in 1593. And Shakespearean audience being fully aware of whole event, probably was greatly delighted to see the defeat of their Protestant hero. Similarly, in the unmasking scene the entire group of the King's courtier who had sworn celibacy with their leader, experience an edifying humiliation and thereby realize the fallacy of their vow.

> And the ladies on their part charitably lead their lords through games, comic rituals and direct humiliation into a humility which frees them to understand and forgive error in others, to rejoice in their common imperfection, and try to amend their lives.[14]

The approach of the ladies can be interpreted as the approach of true Catholic spirit, which acts as the eye opener to the socially estranged nobility. Shakespeare here of course displays a bias for the Catholics who according to him are always full of hope and charity. The pageant of the Nine Worthies is another instance, where the cruelty of the noblemen comes to surface and is instantly censured by the ladies. Berowne's remark about the performance "To have one show worse than the king's and his company" (V ii 512), is a clear hint of the presupposition of the aristocrats that anything the commoners present are bound to be inferior to their performance and hence not worth attending. Therefore, when Armado presents the pageant to please his esteemed audience the lords either ridicule the actors or remain indifferent. "Their behaviour finally provokes from Holofernes the deserved and surprisingly dignified rebuke, 'This is not generous not gentle, not humble' (V ii 629)."[15] Even though Holofernes's rebuke sounds a little affected and pedantic, he cannot be blamed for it, as imitations are totally based upon the action of those men whom they try to please. Moreover, his rebuke, echoing the gentle censuring of the Princess, "Nay, my good lord, let me o'er-rule you now. /That sport pleases that doth least know how" (V ii 512-513) can be interpreted as the voice of a Catholic spirit preaching the virtues of both tolerance and charity. Ultimately, however, the Princess mediates and a final resolution is reached and the two distinct classes of people learn to accept each other. As Ralph Berry observes:

> *Love's Labour's Lost* frames an idyll, an Eden within a park. And its social relations are, if not Edenic, a reasonably earthly approximation. The classes rub along well enough, with an endearing mixture of definition, mingling, containable friction, and acceptances of each other.[16]

The most interesting aspect of the comedy is perhaps its dependence on the contemporary social and political history of England. All the important characters are clearly living personages of sixteenth century England, whose life-style, sense of values, political strategies and lack of foresight seem to have inspired Shakespeare to write a comedy bordering on sarcasm. The male characters here are deliberately subjected to ridicule by the playwright. When in Act IV, scene III King Ferdinand and his court cautiously confess the reality of their amorous inclination towards the ladies, and in the process expose their vulnerability in spite of an austere exterior, the playwright's timely intervention by presenting all the characters together on stage convert all of them to undisputed butts. The hint is clear; to go against the law of society and nature actually is a sign of immaturity, a stage which cannot really last long. And it is the ladies and that too of a foreign origin who point out to them the mendacity of their vow of celibacy. Their very presence itself acts as an antidote to the men, who realize the pointlessness of their vow. As a king, Ferdinand is supposed to look after the welfare of his subjects and not subject them arbitrarily to any regulations that can contravene their individual rights. And unfortunately for Ferdinand without the intervention of the Princess, he could not have fathomed out the resulting social imbalance of his country due to his capricious verdict. Hence, to restore the balance of the play Shakespeare finally forces Ferdinand to realize his mistake and accept the Princess as his bride. But the Princess here plays her role most pragmatically as she lays the condition of a year's penitence for him before he can marry. And whether her promise will actually be fulfilled is left uncertain at the end.

Notes

1. All textual references are to The Arden Shakespeare *Love's Labour's Lost* ed. R.W. David, Methuen, London, 1985. *The Taming of the Shrew,* ed. Brian Morris, Methuen, London, 1981.
2. G. Bullough, *Narrative and Dramatic Sources of Shakespeare* I, Routledge, London, 1957, p. 29.
3. *Ibid.*, p. 27.
4. C.L. Barber, *Shakespeare's Festive Comedies,* Princeton University Press, Princeton, New Jersey, 1972, p. 89.
5. E.M.W. Tillyard, *Shakespeare's Early Comedies,* Athlone Press, London, 1966; rep. 1987, p. 73.
6. *Ibid.*, p. 74.
7. Malcolm Evans, 'Mercury Versus Apollo : A Reading of *Love's Labour's Lost* in *Shakespeare Quarterly,* 1975, p. 123.
8. J. J. Anderson, 'The Morality of *Love's Labour's Lost*', in *Shakespeare Quarterly,* 1973, p. 59.
9. H. Granvill-Barker, *Prefaces to Shakespeare* II. Princeton University Press, Princeton, 1946-1947, p. 305.

10. Robert Speaight, *Shakespeare : The Man and His Achievement,* J. M. De London, 1977, pp. 122-123.
11. D. John Palmer, *Comic Characters of Shakespeare,* Macmillan, London, 1949 p. 22.
12. Cyrus Hey, '*Love's Labour's Lost* and the Nature of Comedy,' in *Shakespeare Quartely* 1962, p. 31.
13. Marchett Chute, *Shakespeare of London,* Sovenier Press, London, 1977, p. 108.
14. Chris Hassel, *Faith and Folly* in *Shakespeare's Romantic Comedies,* The University of Georgia Press, Athens, 1980, p. 39.
15. Edward Berry, *Shakespeare's Comic Rites,* Cambridge University Press, London, 1984, p. 195.
16. *Shakespeare and Social Class,* Humanities Press, New Jersey, 1989, p. 30.

7

THE MIDDLE COMEDIES OF SHAKESPEARE

> Shakespeare's magnificent comic heroines thrive in facilitating marriages ... ones that restore the natural sex roles.*

It is unfortunate that the romantic strain in Shakespearean comedies right from their inception seems to have always beguiled critics and failed to create the necessary impact the playwright had possibly desired. Beginning with the neo-classicists critics of mid twentieth centuries found these romantic strains as mere Shakespearean efforts to present an idyllic world order. Without perceiving the host of sub-texts beneath each romantic effusion they felt the bard was deliberately evading reality. But, critics of the late fifties in the process of re-evaluating the works of the poet suddenly grew aware of their subterranean depths. And in the process of scanning each play categorically they singled out instances where the playwright's personal views overrode his romantic perception. Elucidating this deviation Edward Berry writes:

> These plays are romantic not so much because they exploit the conventions and themes of romance, although many do, but because they share a central romantic action: they chart the tortuous course of pairs of lovers through courtship to marriage.[1]

---

* T.H. Anderson, 'Thinking about women and their prosperous art: a reply to Juliet Dusinberre's *Shakespeare and the Nature of Women*, *Shakespeare Studies* II, 1978, p. 276.

So contrary to the traditional approach of treating Shakespearean romanticism as mere happy endings and idyllic world order critics now tended to re-evaluate this romanticism in Shakespearean comedies as the root cause of various social contentions and discords. Undeniably, conforming to the rules of Commedia dell' Arte[2] superficially Shakespeare did seek to highlight the paradigms of marriage in his middle comedies but his attempt did not end there in itself. In fact, he used all the parameters of marriage and courtship to explore the possibility of passing his well marked disapproval in this regard.

Marriage and courtship to which Berry refers has always been imperative for social amelioration hence, comic playwrights down the ages have thought it to be an ideal medium to express their views. And Shakespeare being no exception to this generalized rule thought it indispensable to utilize them in his plots to validate his judgment. Consequently, the social structure he wanted to represent in each of his comedies became for Shakespeare a means of transmitting human identity. Nearly all his characters therefore, not only represent the exclusivities of the groups or social classes to which they belong, even their speeches and behaviour for that matter simultaneously corroborate their social positions. Thus characters like the shrew,[3] the hen-pecked husband,[4] the prodigal,[5] the witty child,[6] etc, galore in nearly all Shakespearean comedies enabling the playwright to establish the "tortuous course" the Elizabethans lovers had to traverse before marriage.

The primary device Shakespeare used for socially authenticating his characters was their speeches uttered on different occasions. For instance, the sudden dive in Launce's soliloquy to his dog, a turn for pure vaudeville by Petruchio, the crudeness of the mechanicals and the manipulation of the fairies[7] all bespeak the playwright's deliberate effort to validate them in the given context. Significantly, cocooned by their own idiosyncrasies, Shakespeare never allowed these characters to continue independently. On the contrary, he perforce implanted them within the given framework of his plot by grouping them together and coercing them to interact with the other characters of the play. This process had one constructive effect, it helped them to develop themselves and thereby attain a state of desired maturity[8] . Thus, the society which Shakespeare finally developed in each of his comedies was an idyllic organic whole; where everybody took pains to ameliorate one another thereby making their world a better place to inhabit. Shakespeare's conscientiousness also helped him to portray them in such a manner that the contemporary audience was able to place them effortlessly into their desired statuesque with no trace of either discomfiture or apprehension.

Therefore, it is hardly surprising that even minor characters in many of his comedies are bestowed unusual importance in developing the plots. Because it is often through these minor marginalized characters the playwright feels comfortable to air his views about the world. For instance Antonio the sea captain in *Twelfth Night* is attributed not only a heightened stature as a human being–magnanimously sheltering an unknown youth Sebastian, but has also been assigned the power even to alter the balance of the play. Hence even his brief appearance in the entire play proves to be quite vital – to vindicate the claims of Viola and establish her in the patriarchy. While improvising his clowns however Shakespeare used the traditional parts of the countrymen in russet (for old Gobbo and Costard) and the comic constables (for Dogberry, Dull) because he was aware of the contemptuous attitude of his viewers in regard to the professionalism of the constables. Traditionally constables were considered foolish, while all shoemakers witty.

In his early comedies however, Shakespeare offers an uncomplicated account of these social classes by fixing up the ranks with interesting precision. But in the middle comedies he makes his plots more complex and dynamic by supplying far more detailed information about the key personages. Just as we find in Falstaff, combining within himself the braggart soldier, the parasite, the vice and the court jester. The characters of the middle comedies are, therefore, more complete portrayals of real individuals and their social interactions too are more down-to-earth, mirroring the intricacies of the society of sixteenth century England. There is, in fact, a greater cohesion of plot in the middle comedies of Shakespeare and they possess a largeness of significance not found in his earlier plays. In other words, the social realism of the early comedies of Shakespeare reaches a point of culmination in his middle comedies. Consequently, his dramatis personae include men and women of all sorts residing side by side. Kings and dukes, tinkers and bellow menders, pure London bred rogues, courtesans and bawds, a superman, spirits reside alongside forming a homogeneous whole in that settled institution of man which ensures his welfare and happiness – the society.

As observed earlier, Shakespearean comedy is basically a representation of action by normal individuals placed in situations altogether abnormal, but not recognized by them as such. This representation becomes more specific and acute in the middle comedies with the predictable result of a more detailed and explicit characterisation. Though Shakespeare shows great ingenuity in respect of plot handling, the plots of the early comedies do not contain any great characters. Characters like Berowne, Don Armado, Julia and Luciana appear to be shadowy sketches rather than full-length portraits. But the characters of the middle comedies have distinct emotional and intellectual life-patterns, revealed through amazing incidents. Thus the 'dramatis personae' in these plays include men and women of all sorts and conditions— kings and dukes as well as tinkers and bellow-menders, despicable rouges and gracious ladies, superhuman spirits and half-human monsters. Surprises, contrasts, incongruities, disguises and confusions are the varied dramatic techniques which Shakespeare employs to explore these, but at the same time ensuring that the techniques never supersede the characters themselves. Though Rosalind[9], Viola[10] and Portia[11] put on male attire which deceives even their nearest kinsmen, it is not the deception which is important for the comedy. Initially all these girls are found to be divorced from their familiar surroundings. Then transvestism helps them to assume a new identity and finally assisting them to be reintegrated into society with the materialization of marriage prospects. Marriage therefore often becomes the central concern in the middle comedies. And what is marriage after all – the movement of an individual from adolescent to maturity. The movement however is three-fold as hinted earlier – the individual is at first divorced from his familiar environment (Viola's undertaking the sea voyage with her brother which sinks near Illyria), then follows a transitional stage in which his old identity is destroyed and a new one created (her disguise to enter the service of Orsino) third and the final stage is of incorporation in which he is reintegrated into the society in his new role (Orsino's acceptance of Viola as his mistress in marriage). So the final effect always has to be reintegration whether be it a man or a woman. In *The Taming of the Shrew* for instance, the reintegration of Kate, the acclaimed shrew of Padua is the central motivating force and everybody seems to be working towards it right from the beginning of the play. And finally with the arrival of Petruchio when this reintegration seems possible the anxiety of her father Baptista is set to rest.

Going by the aforementioned category of incorporation we can therefore easily consider Kate's amalgamation into the society in the following manner. The first phase as mentioned above is the phase of separation where the individual is estranged from his/her familiar surrounding. Resultantly he/she suffers from a sense of loss of identity. The process being usually abrupt and at times even violent it often causes pain to the individual. Petruchio's attempt to tame Kate from day one of his marriage marks this violence. But Kate once married cannot do other wise except to relent. It has been observed that in initiating this process of separation the individual at times has to endure even physical violence like whipping, intoxication followed by literal journeys away from home. The event is sometimes characterized by a symbolic death as well. In Kate's case though Petruchio does not inflict any physical violence but forces his wife to undertake a journey far from her familiar world and the intervening journey that ensues certainly kills her shrewish disposition to a certain extent. And all this is deliberated to ameliorate her to the society which has so long ostracized her.

Unfortunately for Kate, even though society normally permits a period of betrothal where one gets time to test both the bride and the groom and educate one another in the process, she is given no chance to do so. Her partner neither visits her with gifts nor is she allowed to serve her in-laws[12] to demonstrate her worth and in the process learn the behaviour appropriate to a married adult. In western societies, since the commencement of romantic love during the Renaissance this was the common practice and Kate being stigmatized as a shrew is denied all these privileges because such initiation could prevent her from getting married finally. So the conventional courtship period is significantly absent in the play preventing the poor girl from enjoying the expected pampering and adulation. Even after her marriage she is not given the required time to attend the following sumptuous wedding meal, which is again a communal affair, and receive the wedding gifts or partake in the ritual dancing. Even though the community is ready Petruchio does not allow her to take part in the customary ritual. Assuming his new role of mastery it is now easy for him to deny his wife the expected privileges.

The Taming of the Shrew

As hinted above in *The Taming of the Shrew* Shakespeare magnificently covers the full blooded story of wife-taming by presenting the entire ritual of an Elizabethan wedding through consequent sequence of separation, transition and incorporation. The couple move from the prospective bride's house to the church (an attempt to snap the old family ties), in the church they are joined as man and wife and assume a new identity; then they move from the church to the bride's house where they feast and proceed to the bridal chamber to consummate their marriage and accept their new roles in society. But Petruchio temporarily hinders the final consummation. Kate, in spite of being married to him, is not allowed to assume her new role. Elizabethan patriarchy will not acknowledge her marital status unless she totally subjugates herself to the will of her lord, master and husband, the apparently insane Petruchio. Unlike Adriana, in *The Comedy of Errors,* Kate is a fully developed character. Her conversion is also concrete and complete, while Adriana's marriage even at the end of the play remains unresolved, allowing the union of the brothers to predominate.

Kate is introduced to the viewers at the very initiation as a shrew who has alienated herself both from her family and her potential suitors. But Petruchio by refusing to acknowledge her shrewishness and out maneuvering her not only unnerves her but also coaxes her to marry. But having decided to rejoin the society through marriage Kate realizes that her wedding in reality forces her father outside it. Petruchio by cutting off Kate from her social milieu also ostracizes Baptista to a certain extent. But everything is tolerated because Baptista has finally managed to shrug off his responsibility to his son-in-law.

Petruchio's decision to marry Kate however manifests another interesting aspect of Elizabethan marriage. Baptista's handsome dowry is the only incentive for Petruchio:

> As wealth is burden of my wooing dance—
> Be she as foul as was Florentine's love,
> As old as Sibyl, and as curst and shrewd. (I ii 67-69)[13]

Like any other Elizabethan youth Petruchio treats marriage as a commercial contract which should be a subject of bargain. "What dowry I shall have with her to wife" (II i 120). and only after he is satisfied, he decides to woo Kate and finally marry her. But Shakespeare never portrays Petruchio as a mean fortune hunter, not even when he is setting the financial terms and conditions with Baptista. On the contrary, he appears to be the most prudent wooer who promises to Baptista all his "land and leases whatsoever" (II i 125) in case of Kate's widowhood. He refers to the deed, the simple documents which generally closed the contracts of Elizabethan marriages. Elucidating this legal aspect M. L. Ronald observes:

> "*The Taming of the Shrew* is full of references to matrimonial law and ceremonial practice, treated with

> that easy familiarity that comes from common knowledge shared among writers and audience."[14]

Petruchio is therefore merely far-sighted wooer who comes to the point directly by asking his would be father-in-law: "Then tell me, if I get your daughter's love, /What dowry shall I have with her to wife?"(II i 119-20). The financial arrangements are rapidly concluded, because Baptista is not ready to take a chance for his shrewish daughter by haggling over terms.[15]

Both Petruchio and Baptista's insistence on convincing Kate here to marry Petruchio is another singular instance in the comedy, which apparently contradicts the patriarchal tradition of the age (II i 129). Elizabethan fathers were famed for bullying their daughters to marry the groom they preferred not the one their daughters wanted. But, knowing Kate as we do, Baptista's argument to win Kate's love first and then marry her appears very pragmatic. His fear of Petruchio ultimately backing out of the deal is born of his clear perception of his daughter's shrewish disposition, but as an Elizabethan he knows that once Petruchio strikes the deal with him neither of them can back out and legally break the contract. Marriage in contemporary setting thus turns out to be a social contract based on commercial terms. But, in the case of Bianca Baptista has no such dilemma. Since she had more than one wooer he decides like a cautious father to weigh the economic status of all and then to sell her off to the highest bidder:

> "Tis deeds must win the prize, and he of both/ That can assure my daughter greatest dower/ Shall have my Bianca's love." (II i 335-7)

To him the question of compatibility is immaterial because of the two suitors one is old Gremio as well. So regarding the marriage of both his daughters Baptista doesn't seem to manifest any fatherly concern for their well beings after marriage. Instead, he operates as an all powerful father who completely neglects a necessary pre-requisite for valid matrimony-the free and unforced consent of the girl.

The most important feature of the play perhaps is the singular status of Kate, which baffles her from the very beginning. She is a conceptual shrew whom the entire patriarchy abhors. But the playwright is not really convinced of her shrewish disposition. Like any other girl she too is inclined to marry but with a difference. She is a well developed personality contrary to the expectations of the patriarchy. Hence, unlike her apparently submissive sister she is categorical about her preferences. But this means a social segregation which undoubtedly scares her: "I must dance bare-foot on her wedding-day" (II i 33). This concept of dancing bare-foot was a common Elizabethan practice. In case the younger sister was married before her elder sister, the elder was expected to dance bare foot to establish her spinsterhood. In a world therefore, where a girl's social status is primarily determined by her marital status the thought of remaining a spinster frightens Kate and hence the resulting anguish: "I must dance bare-foot on her wedding day." Entire Padua has refused to accept her so an alien like Petruchio has to arrive to redeem her. Significantly Padua at that point of time was considered to be the sacred place of learning and in many plays of Shakespeare we find adolescent heroes being sent there to heighten their academic achievements and attain full maturity. So it will not be wrong to presume that even Petruchio had initially ventured there for the aforementioned reason. But on reaching Padua he thought it wise to marry. And what a marriage it was! Nonetheless marriage here can be accepted as a means to reach the aspired maturity of a responsible husband by carting a shrew.

The subjugation process again is a hard one as noticed during the marriage ceremony. First of all the image of unpredictability that Petruchio took care to promote reaches its summit then. He is late for the ceremony – keeping everyone on tenterhooks 'will he or won't he?' Added to it when he does arrive he is dressed so bizarrely that everybody present is simply astounded. After reaching the church when expected to avow as the legal husband of Kate he shouts: "Ay, by gogs-wouns" instead of the marriage vows. Then he cuffs the priest and throws the sops of the wedding toast "all in the sexton's face;" and kisses the bride "with such a clamorous smack/That at the parting all the church did echo" (III iii 157-182) stunning the entire congregation. Even a mere onlooker like Gremio slinks away from the shameful sight. The application of force symbolically representing ravishing the chastity of Kate shames an outsider but not her father Baptista. His silence at this juncture may be inferred to have been born out of his sense of relief at Petruchio's ready acceptance of his burden. Washing his hands off after his daughter is married seems to be another prerogative of an Elizabethan father. Even the entire patriarchy likewise seems oblivious of the potential threat to Kate's future with an apparently insane groom Petruchio.

The wedding feast then proceeds as mentioned above without either the bride or the groom for Petruchio draws his sword against any guest who is bold enough to detain them and abducts her. Kate's wedding then continues with a hazardous journey where she is dunked in mud and finally concluded with dinner thrown away and a lecture on continence by Petruchio in the bridal chamber. The overall effect maybe hilarious for the viewers, but for the girl it's a torturous path to traverse in the realms of marriage. These violent gestures however are deliberated by Petruchio to shatter Kate's dependence on social conventions and this can also be termed as her initiation to a new life which culminates in a kiss in broad daylight in the city streets.

Eventually Kate is subjugated by her husband and at the end her surrender seems complete. But, within is she really conquered? Though at the end of the play Petruchio challenging the other males to establish his supremacy beckons Kate and she does comply readily contrary to both Bianca and the widow who refuse point blank the question remains is Kate in fact conquered? Going by her antecedents it's a difficult proposition to digest. Can Kate in actual fact be conquered? Should we then presume that it is only her growing love for her husband that induces her to respond thus? Clearly, Kate is not scared of Petruchio then what compels her to submit? Or is it her diminution as an individual as the patriarchy loves to believe that coerces this subjugation?[16] Shakespeare however does not provide us with any such clue to infer for certain why Kate relents.

Understandably, the play with all its complexities has inspired directors and producers alike to represent Kate's subjugation as they perceived. For instance in a production where Peter O'Toole was playing the role of Petruchio, the weird man seemed to have appeared as:

> a man intelligent enough not to sit down the fate and human enough to be mightily relieved when his sabre rattling works. His strength makes Katherina surrender; his sensitivity makes her want to... When she resists him, a twitch of amusement hovers about her mouth. Her suffering before the submission is therefore nominal and fit to joke about; the submission itself is easily swallowed dramatically, and the whole effect is happier and kinder.[17]

So, according to this performance Kate willingly accepts the rulings of her husband because the director loves to believe that. Hence there is a smile hovering about her mouth when she tries to resist him. But whether the torture inflicted upon her is really fit for a joke is for the audience to decide. Surprisingly, Dame Peggy Ashcroft playing the role of Kate in the same production believed that:

> "Kate is a raging hoyden who with every shrug, every pout, every word, suggests that behind the habitual mask of the shrew, there breathes a woman simply dying to be tamed."[18]

Yet, going by the other previous circumstances it is hard to digest Petruchio's sensitivity or Kate's ready submission with a twitch of smile about her mouth. Dame Ashcroft however preferred believing Kate's amorous inclinations for Petruchio the moment she met him, and yet she managed to camouflage her feelings and fought him on her own level just for the sake of comic effects. While another noted actress Janet Suzman felt that they actually combated till they found an ally. But never did Petruchio allow any harm to come upon Kate and whenever he tortured her he stopped before any dangerous thing happened.[19] Both actually have a tendency to ignore one fundamental fact – the torture Petruchio inflicted upon Kate was a psychological pressure and not sheer physical violence. Other wise it is very difficult to explain the last speech of Kate where she instructs women about their attitude towards their husbands:

> Thy husband is thy lord, thy life, thy keeper,
> Thy head, thy sovereign, one that cares for thee,
> And for thy maintenance commits his body
> To painful labour both by sea and land,
> To watch the night in storms, the day in cold
> While thou liest warm at home, secure and safe,
> And craves no other tribute at thy hands
> But love, fair looks and true obedience,
> Too little payment for so great a debt.
> Such duty as the subject owes the prince,
> Even such a woman oweth to her husband
> And when she is forward, peevish, sullen, sour
> And not obedient to his honest will,
> What is she but a foul contending rebel,
> And graceless traitor to her loving lord? (V ii 151-67).

The speech clearly establishes Kate diminution. Since the husband is the bread winner it is his privilege to act authoritarian. And what is a wife after all, a toy for him. So the sense of equality between a husband and wife is entirely gibberish and she has no right to manifest her disapproval "peevish, sullen," and "sour" however much she may be agonized. With Renaissance humanism preaching spiritual equality for woman doesn't such vanquish sound a trifle strange? It is really hard for the reader to believe that Kate calls a woman traitor just because she has failed to comply with the wishes of her husband. Indicating the absurdity of this long uncomplaining speech rightly does Michael Mangan observe:

> "this crucial speech, this lynch pin of the play's structure, expresses a world-view and a vision of gender relations which is repulsive to the growing consensus."[20]

Induction of the play is another interesting feature of *The Taming of the Shrew*. Shakespeare's inclusion of the induction at the beginning of the play is a deviation in itself for nowhere else has he used this comic device. The central character of the Induction is Christopher Sly the tinker. He is an integral part of the play because the whole play has been enacted at his behest. "Christopher Sly must have been a part of Shakespeare's personal experience" opines Brian Morris "and his Warwickshire background-so richly evoked must be Shakespeare's own recollection of his native country."[21] No wonder therefore, Sly appears to the viewers as an earthy alcoholic whose sole past time is chasing lasses. He is a part of the widest social network comprising of a beggar, an innkeeper, a huntsman, an actor etc, which strikingly contrasts against the narrower bourgeois mercantile society of Padua where like Ephesus money is the prime mover and marriage is its executor. The induction is therefore, full of topical allusions like – "Burton heath," a village about sixteen miles south of Stratford where Shakespeare's aunt lived, "Marian Hacket the fat ale-wife of Wincot" (Ind ii 21-2), probably being the daughter of Robert Hacket of the hamlet of Wincot, in order to authenticate the artificiality of the main play. But even in the main play the playwright does not radically discard the use of topical allusions thereby dissociating it from his viewers. For instance, the play is set in Padua, a place actually renowned in the sixteenth and seventeenth century for its university which imparted excellent education on Aristotle's philosophy to youngsters. Petruchio's arrival there is therefore quite understandable. But once there he is more inclined to "cart" Kate (I i 55) rather than pursue Aristotle's philosophy. The word cart here is significant for it refers to a whipping at the cart's tail as a punishment for bawds and whores. Lucentio and Hortensio are the two other young men who unlike Petruchio do not dare to cart Kate. Instead they prefer to woo Bianca her younger sister for she is of milder disposition. Lucentio enters Baptista's house as tutor to Bianca. And since, (strangely enough though) Elizabethan fathers thought it wise to impart proper education to their female wards Lucentio is permitted in. The ensuing wooing of course culminates only after Kate is married off as desired by Baptista.

Finally, two other interesting aspects of *The Taming of the Shrew* points to the play's close affinity to Shakespeare's early comedy *The Comedy of Errors*. First, in both the plays absence of nobility is conspicuous. In *The Comedy of Errors,* the Duke of Ephesus appears only at the beginning and at the end of the play to initiate and conclude the action but not to take part in it. Similarly, in *The Taming of the Shrew* a lord is found only in the induction of the play, not in its course of action. In both cases the function of the nobles is vague and undefined. This deliberate omission on the part of the playwright may be attributed to his intention to portray a purely mercantile society, whose values differed radically from those of the prevalent feudal set up. Hence, throughout the comedies, no conflict of values is observed; all accept the social norms gracefully and try to conform to them without any questioning. Second, in both the plays it is the ladies who refuse to comply at first, Adriana and Kate, but sensing a potential threat from them the entire patriarchy rises against them and finally overpowers them. Both Kate and Adriana suffer from a feeling of insecurity which contributes to their shrewish natures. Kate's hatred against Bianca may have been backed by her sense of economic insecurity (II i 31-34). For an Elizabethan woman father and husband symbolized the two steady sources of economic security, but Kate fails to procure even one and hence all her anger is directed against Bianca, the favoured girl in the patriarchy. And Kate's threat, observes Karen Newman, "is truer than we have heretofore recognized, for it is that silence which has insured Bianca's place in the male economy of desire and exchange"[22] towards which Kate is constantly aspiring. Adriana's angry exclamations can also be attributed to her sense of insecurity because Antipholus of Ephesus, we know, had the unhealthy habit of visiting courtesans. But the central focus of *The Taming of the Shrew* observes Ralph Berry, is on "the marriage arrangements characteristic of the Padua/Verona gentry, which were strikingly similar to those of Elizabethan England."[23]

A Midsummer Night's Dream

Like *The Taming of the Shrew, A Midsummer Night's Dream* is another middle comedy, where Shakespeare's art of characterisation and his capacity to build up a romantic atmosphere reach a point of perfection. Unlike his previous comedies the playwright here welds together the stories of four different social classes of citizens, the citizens of the court, the lovers, the fairies[24] and the Athenian mechanicals. And though its society superficially appears to be ordered and stable but with the gradual unfolding of the plot the deeper layers of longing and antipathy, appeasement and hostility become quite apparent.

A contention between Lysander and Demetrius for Hermia marks the beginning of the play, (I i)[25] indicating a symmetrical dispute within a class. Both the youths are virtually identical in their social standing yet Egeus prefers one to the other for no conclusive reason. And instead of neutrally assessing this subjective preference, Theseus sides with Egeus and orders Hermia, "Be advis'd fair maid./To you your father should be as a god:" (I i 46-47). Theseus's reaction is again a reflection of the existing social order which licensed a father to bestow his daughter to anyone he preferred and not necessarily to the one approved by his daughter. And as a ruler of the land Theseus cannot flout this norm. Therefore, going by Elizabethan standard the behaviour of both Theseus and Egeus seems very normal. Even though Renaissance humanism preached spiritual equality of women but in practice the patriarchy refused to comply.

Likewise the argument between Lysander and Egeus (I i 29-31) appears to the reader more like a fight for masculine supremacy regarding the girl's possessionship than a squabble between would be father-in-law and a son-in-law. Who would come out to be the winner in being the rightful owner of Hermia is for the Duke to decide. Hermia's claim is therefore completely overruled both by the father and the state because a girl had no right to air her own opinion regarding marriage. As a woman she was only to legalize the offspring of a man and prevent his fornication. And hence it was not necessary to seek her approval. As in the early comedies, even here the patriarchy intervenes and prevents Hermia from choosing her own husband.

Egeus is the economic protector of his daughter and has the complete sanction of the state to inflict upon her his arbitrary rulings. Therefore, bringing her before the court he claims "As she is mine, I may dispose of her"(I i 42). Here he is stating only the common place Elizabethan parlance because in the sixteenth century England the patriarchal family was the foundation of a hierarchical concept of society which linked monarch and subject. The male head of a family was equivalent to the head of a state. Explaining this unique feature of England in spite of having a female monarch, Sir Robert Filmer observes: "As the father over one family, so the King as father over many families extends his care to preserve, feed, clothe, instruct and defend the whole commonwealth."[26] Therefore when the father refuses to give in to Hermia's wishes to marry Lysander and not Demetrius his argument sounds almost like Ralph Berry's analysis of the Elizabethan marriage which was nothing but a "square dance of changing partners, there is no room for individual movement outside the choreography."[27] And the state too toeing the lines tries to repress her.

Upsetting the family set up is analogous to upsetting the state and social hierarchy and this cannot be allowed to continue. The court here proves to be a direct version of the patriarchal authority and so to avoid this male environment, both Lysander and Hermia decide to escape to a female place of safety, to Lysander's aunt.

> Lysander: I have a widow aunt, a dowager
> Of great revenue, and she hath no child,
> And she respects me as her only son.
> From Athens is her house remote seven leagues.
> There gentle Hermia, may I marry thee,
> And to that place the sharp Athenian law
> Cannot pursue us (I i 157-63).

The aunt for sure would provide asylum to these wayward lovers because the place where she lived was outside the jurisdiction of Athens that is, an end to the patriarchal diktats. So the prevailing matriarchal rulings would allow the pair to marry in safety. Egeus's refusal on the other hand, meant a kind of highhandedness of the patriarchy, which considered the normal sensitivity of their young wards as something superfluous and hence not worth paying any attention. It is therefore in direct contrast to the promised assistance of Lysander's aunt.

Helena and Hermia are the two mortal female characters in the play employed by Shakespeare to unravel two divergent aspects of the aforementioned patriarchal structure. Both initially appear to be two guinea pigs of the same patriarchy and are made to undergo various tortures. Hermia has to face either death or perpetual abstinence for refusing to comply with her father's wishes (as mentioned above), while Helena is exposed to potential polyandry by being wooed by two men alternately. Even though Shakespeare assigns it to the foul play of Puck,[28] the mischief making fairy but the threat looms large till Oberon intervenes and solves the problem.

Prior to this ceremonial wooing by two most eligible bachelors, Lysander and Demetrius, Helena's status was exactly like Kate in *The Taming of the Shrew*. Would she finally find a husband to establish her statuesque in the society – because Demetrius who had loved her once is now inclined to marry Hermia at the instigations of Egeus? The anxiety understandably distraughts her and finding no other recluse she decides to follow her love even to the Forest of Arden risking her maidenhood. Demetrius threatens of ravishing her chastity yet she is unwavering. Being renounced by her lover what has she to loose other than her chastity?

In contrast, Hermia's dream in the Forest indicates another form of maidenly anxiety – of loosing her chastity. Since her position as a married woman in the patriarchy is almost assured chastity now becomes her prime concern. Chastity she realizes is now indispensable for her to remain in the folds of patriarchy because she has virtually renounced everything and even the protection of her father. Her stakes are higher compared to Helena. And maybe if she flouts the ruling even Lysander's aunt will not allow her to marry in dignity. Therefore in the dream, a serpent eating her heart away while Lysander 'sits at a distance' smiling, symbolically stand for her, two facets of Lysander's character, the sexual (before going to sleep Lysander had desired to lie near her) and the affectionate (normal love, courtesy and affection discernible before elopement). But both these images are hostile – one trying to ravage her maidenhood and the other distancing himself from her. Hence the anxiety following her waking-up in the forest and not finding Lysander by her side.

The other interesting aspect of this comedy is its inclusion of the working class. Prior to *A Midsummer Night's Dream*, Shakespearean comedies never contained characters like Quince the carpenter or Bottom the weaver who decisively influenced the play's story line.

But in *A Midsummer Night's Dream* the characters, belonging to a low stratum of society both control the action of the play and determine its social interest. Shakespeare defines only their social status without highlighting their working practices or their economic conditions. Their relation with the court is dubious; they are both loyal and apprehensive. Thus when they seek to entertain the court during Theseus's marriage their eagerness is marked by a strange kind of anxiety,

> And you should do it too terribly, you would fright
> The Duchess and the ladies that they would shriek:
> and that were enough to hang us all (I ii 70-72).

Their theatrical production, however, appears to the audience as a replay of the Nine Worthies pageant of *Love's Labour's Lost* with one essential difference : the courtly audience here shows them due courtesy, while the young men of Ferdinand's court had to be reprimanded by the Princess for their unseemly behaviour. There is no deliberate effort on the part of the Duke and his associates to undermine the affections of the Athenian mechanicals and hence no untoward comments thwart their spontaneity. In fact, cheerful audience reactions (V i 254-261) bespeak a deep harmonious accord that existed between the court and the rough mechanicals.

The social style of the court is governed by Duke Theseus. He can perhaps be called the model of princely accomplishments when he discharges his functions of an administrator. There is no sign of immaturity in Theseus when he passes his judgments over his subjects or patronises the works of art of the Athenian mechanicals. His relation with Hippolyta is also very normal and balanced apparently,

> Hippolyta, I woo'd thee with my sword,
> And won love doing thee injuries;
> But I will wed thee in another key (I i 16-18).

There is neither exuberance nor frigidity in their relationship. Yet, what the playwright here stops from elucidating is the question whether Theseus had really won the affection of Hippolyta. The question of wooing a woman with ones sword maybe symbolic representation of ravishing her chastity and a very probable assumption, going by Theseus's track record:

Oberon: Knowing I know thy love to Theseus?
Didst not thou lead him through the glimmering night
From Perigouna, whom he ravished;
And make him with fair Aegles break his faith,
With Ariadne and Antiopa? (II i 76-80).

But the questions that actually baffle the reader are two-fold: did Theseus following the ancient Athenian practice of marrying the queen having killed the king of a domain force Hippolyta to surrender? Hipployta after all was the queen of Amazon but no where is the reader informed about Hippolyta's previous marriage. Or following his sexual inclinations had Theseus in reality raped her in the name of wooing? And now the proposal of marrying in another vein is just an indication of his attempt to legalize his unlawful violence previously. Hippolyta's questionable silence here however prevents the reader to conjecture anything conclusively.

But as a ruler of the land the salient trait of Theseus is his unfailing diplomacy and tact as evidenced in his dealings with his subjects. When Egeus and Demetrius approach him for justice he cajoles the senior and tactfully imparts good sense to the youth so that both of them return satisfied. (I i 112-127). And when he chides Hermia, "For you, fair Hermia, look you arm yourself/To fit your fancies to your father's will" (I i 117-118). He is perfectly man-of-the-world who warns the young girl of the dire consequences she might have to face if she dares to disobey her father's will. Theseus possibly portrays the playwright's concept of an ideal ruler. Explicating the dire consequence Theseus says that Hermia's disobedience will bring upon her either death or complete banishment of male society by being sent to a nunnery. Surprisingly Hermia opts for the second. For her, life without Lysander is barren in itself so why not opt for nunnery? The threat to banish her to a nunnery is socially significant, indicates Valerie Traub. Even though it was mandatory in the "patriarchal ideology" observes Traub, to transfer "the governance of a father to the protection of a husband, almost twenty percent of adult women in northwestern Europe never married."[29] And these nunneries "offered women refuge from marriage" and provided "opportunities for political, emotional and erotic[30] independence."[31] Hence Theseus's threat of abjuration and enduring "a withered, barren virginity ... correlative to death," is daringly defied by Hermia: "So will I grow, so live, so die, my lord" (I i 79), asserting "the possibility of growth and life within a religious sisterhood."[32]

The supernatural regime of Titania and Oberon represent the fourth social group of the comedy. Unlike their human counterparts, the fairy king and queen suffer from a sense of marital maladjustment. Titania's affection for the Indian prince is misinterpreted by her husband as inexplicable dotage (perhaps bordering on sexual perversion), while the queen, instead of relenting to the wishes of her husband, tries to assert her matriarchal supremacy. But their extraterrestrial quarrel does not succeed in effecting a cataclysmic change on the surface of the earth, as did the quarrels of the Greek and Roman gods and goddesses. Their quarrels strongly reflect struggles for supremacy, and are interpreted as "a contention for mastery. Oberon asserting his male supremacy (Am I not thy Lord?) and Titania insisting in her turn on matriarchal rule."[33] Titania's response is very interesting, because it provides a direct contrast to the responses of all her human counterparts. None of the Shakespearean ladies, except the shrews, ever question the norms of male supremacy in the comic societies. But Titania's open rebellion is not overruled by the playwright and hence to punish her adequately he transfers her dotage to the ass-headed Bottom temporarily. And only after she realizes her mistake and is completely purged of all the undesirable instincts (according to the patriarchal ruling of course) Shakespeare returns her to her proper social status of a queen. Oberon's character, in contrast to his wife's is definitely more conventional. He appears to underscore the principles of Renaissance humanism rather than the whimsicalities of the supernatural beings. His wrath is justified by the playwright and, therefore, when Titania pleads guilty, he forgives her readily and converts Bottom to a normal human being. The fairies of *A Midsummer Night's Dream* may not be regarded as supernatural creatures rather the playwright's representation of a set of idealized human beings on earth. And, hence, summing up the behaviour of all the four social classes of *A Midsummer Night's Dream* one can opine like Ralph Berry,

> The play offers a model of the class extremes meeting with civility, good will, and harmony. It is not a model that can be adjusted to all circumstances, and it may look primitive when set against Shakespeare's later work. Within its own terms, the play's statement relations between rulers and ruled is wholly satisfying. And that ideal, of course, is presented within a *Dream*.[34]

Finally the forest in the play is presumed to be an idyll escape from the harsh realities – an aspect dealt in details by Northrop Frye.[35] Linking the early comedies with the middle comedies Frye terms Shakespearean forest as a green world where comic heroes and heroines tend to escape when confronting potential enemies of the real world. For instance,

Valentine in *The Two Gentlemen of Verona* escapes to the forest after having incurred the wrath of the Duke, so do Lysander and Hermia here. Incidentally in both the plays the playwright introduces a pair of lovers or potential lovers at the court of a Duke. The court then proves to be a place of threat for both, and its ruler their potential enemy. The result – the lovers run off to the green world, the forest, which offers them shelter. But in both the cases the forest is already inhabited and hence the lovers find themselves enmeshed in unforeseen stratagems. Likewise in *As You Like It* Orlando and Rosalind (potential lovers) are forced by the state to escape to Arden where they are confronted by the court-in-exile. In all three plays one common feature appears to be the antagonism between the court and the green world, which forces the characters to seek refuge in the latter world till reconciliation is reached between the two through marriage. It is a dramatic technique observes Frye which Shakespeare deliberately adopted from traditional sources:

> Shakespeare's type of comedy follows a tradition established by Peele and developed by Greene Lyly, which has affinities with the medieval tradition of the seasonal ritual-play. We may call it the drama of the green world, its plot being assimilated to the ritual theme of the triumph of life and love over the waste land. In *The Two Gentlemen of Verona* the hero Valentine becomes the captain of a band of outlaws in a forest, and all the other characters are gathered into this forest and converted. Thus the action of the comedy begins in a world represented as a normal world, moves into a green world, goes into a metamorphosis there in which the comic resolution is achieved and returns to the normal world.[36]

And this strife between the normal and the green world permeating every stratum of the Elizabethan society was actually a reflection of two different philosophies of life. One, ideologies of the ruling class – i.e. the rising bourgeoisie, two, protest wrung out from the hearts of the repressed commoners while renouncing material comforts for appeasing their rulers. But for Shakespeare an anguished soul like Lysander could not be allowed to fall a prey to any class conflict hence society perforce sends him to the green world till his problem is sorted out. Once the real world takes note of this departure and is repentant the playwright deems it right to bring him back and thus the resulting comic resolution.

The Merchant of Venice

Shakespeare's treatment of class consciousness actually culminates in two of his plays, *Othello* and *The Merchant of Venice.* Both these plays have a Venetian setting with a closely-knit society of self-satisfied people. And the characters in both show a marked affinity in their refusal to admit any outsider to the inner circle of their social life. Othello's refusal is the result of a racial discrimination quite rampant in Elizabethan society, while Shylock's usury blacklists him in Venetian society. But in both the plays the Venetian society is not reluctant to accept their assistance when required.[37] Othello, therefore, assists the ruler in providing security to the country while Shylock in spite of having a stigmatized bearing is a major source of finance to the merchants and nobles of Venice. In both cases English society represented by an exclusive body of people relies heavily "for their finances and security on aliens whom they do not admit to their inner circles."[38] Shakespeare's class treatment of the characters, however, differentiates the two plays radically. In *The Merchant of Venice,* the playwright treats the different social classes in relation to money, whereas in *Othello,* the central focus is on the study of racial insecurity in an alien society. But in both the cases the aliens are represented as non-conforming individuals, whose presence questions the social assumptions subverting its values. Hence, the ensuing friction often threatens its continuance and the general response is to do away with them.

Money as mentioned above predominates all social relationships in *The Merchant of Venice,* though the monetary approach as indicated in the play is fundamentally different from that of *The Comedy of Errors* or *The Taming of the Shrew*. Explicating this aspect G.K. Hunter opines:

> What we have here ... is a world of finance, where lovers, Christian gentlemen, friends, enemies, servants, in terms of financial relationship; and where the difference between love and hate, beauty and selfishness, mercy and justice, Christianity and Jewry are all treated in terms of money and how to handle it.[39]

So the opposition here is against the non-Christians and whose commercial practice is considered to be a part of his religious attitude – "legalistic obdurate revengeful."[40] This attitude may be attributed to the general hatred against the infidels who at that point of time often threatened to still the unity of the Christendom. Yet Shakespeare does not directly mention religion here except to present a contrast between the man who is ready to give his life for his friend and the self-justifying legal pundit who can only try to execute the bond. This may again have been provoked by the contemporary hatred of the Christians who considered usury as an anti-Christian practice. Because going by the biblical records it was Judas a remote ancestor of Shylock who had sold Christ for thirty pieces of silver. Explaining this hostility in contemporary context David Palmer thus writes:

> The Elizabethan theatre reflected the life and mind of the nation, and when Shakespeare sat down to write *The Merchant of Venice* in 1594, anti-Semitism was in fashion.[41]

Even though the plot Shakespeare employed was contrived and too horrible to believe yet the public was ready to believe anything about a Jew. There is another set of theory which critics often tend to sight, the execution of Lopez[42] whom the sensitive citizens of London believed to be innocent. Hence the able and convincing arguments of Shylock – don't the Christian themselves condemn their debtors to worst forfeits, binding all the body into a slavery? And didn't the Romans consider it legal to imprison and beat the free citizens having failed to clear their debts?

It went without saying that debtors who failed to keep their contract had to abide the consequence and so it was essential for Antonio to give Shylock his due. Moreover in the given context it was no great a matter to take a pound of flesh from one who by flouting the norms of the bond actually endangered the creditor's reputation and solvency. To a man of business both these aspects were more important than his life. And significantly the Duke has no answer for all these arguments. Presumably Shakespeare in presenting Shylock to his viewers in this light was deliberately appealing to the more human aspects of his comedy.[43]

The play actually suggests two ways of making money, Shylock's and Antonio's in respect to the inherited wealth of Portia. This inherited wealth dominates all relationships throughout the play and determines the social standing of all the characters. Both Antonio and Shylock are basically merchants who lend money to the Venetian citizens at their respective interest rates, but the nobility of the country prefer Antonio to Shylock because Shylock is a wealthy alien. Bassanio, on the other hand, represents the declassed aristocrat, like Falstaff, who is in search of an heiress. Portia's wealth is, therefore, the real incentive for Bassanio to try his luck in the famous casket scene. Though Bassanio does not declare openly to the world, like Petruchio, his intentions too is to retrieve his lost social status and wealth through marriage and hence he assures Antonio that after his marriage he will be able to repay all his outstanding debts. (I i 146-152)[44] His attitude reminds the audience of the "Elizabethan aristocrat's practice of cash-raising through marriage."[45] None of the early comedies of Shakespeare manifest such strong preference for money in determining the relationships of the characters.

The conflict between Antonio and Shylock too is a reflection of this tendency. Since the rising bourgeoisie predominated in the Elizabethan society, their constant perusal for money, capital gains etc, was bound to clash against the interests of the existing money lenders. Antonio representing the former class lends money on gratis while to Shylock usury being his sole sustenance, this lending money on gratis spelt a potential threat. Naturally the thought of money never seems to abandon him. But strangely enough even to Antonio money seems to be the here all and end all business: "at nights they have no rest; they have dreams in plenty and money broke sleep" (I) though he claims otherwise. It is in no way different from Shylock's: "There is some ill-brewing towards my rest/ For I did dream of money-bags tonight. (II v 1) In both their speeches Shakespeare discusses this mysterious movement of money. Shylock's angst is not because Antonio is a Christian but more because of his monetary strategy. "But more for that in low simplicity/He lends out money gratis, and brings down/ The rate of usance" (I iii 38). If there is an inflow of money in the market then the rates of usury is bound to fall leading to a loss for the usurer and this is what troubles Shylock. In fact he even goes to the extent of describing money in biblical terms. (I iii 84) The classic illustration of the shepherd waving colored hankies before the mating sheep, which resulted in their giving birth to multi-colored sheep – which was then a lucrative business. Antonio then raises the pertinent question 'is this how you seek a heavenly sanction to your usury?' Shylock replies "I cannot tell; I make it breed as fast."(I iii 91). The tendency to equate breeding of sheep with growing money indicates Shylock's clarity of thought regarding economics. This in its turn reflects Shakespeare's realization of money as the supreme controller both of trade and commerce and production of the country. It was as if the bourgeoisies knew that by sowing money they would be reaping its bumper harvest hence the popular expressions – 'breed as fast,' 'woolly breeders' etc. Sheep wool then was indeed the source of making ready money for the merchant community of England. Shylock's language seems to be perfectly moulded by his monetary interests. But unlike Antonio even his personal relationships too seems to be constantly influenced by money 'about my moneys and usances' (Antonio) 'all for the use of that which is my own' to Lancelot Gobo at his slow paced profit 'snail-slow in profit' etc. Even Jessica's escape does not stir his paternal feelings rather it pains him that she has escaped with a lot of money (III i 72). Like wise when at the court Portia begs him to be merciful he refuses because Antonio "This is the fool, that lent out money gratis" (III ii 2). Lending money on gratis means declination of the usury market, and in a bourgeois society mercy was both sign of weakness and folly. Antonio being a member of the Rialto did not conform to this rule and hence cannot be pardoned.

Antonio however is aware of Shylock's reaction and so is the Duke – the ruler of a bourgeois society. But neither Antonio nor the Duke can do anything about it. Since, the Elizabethan society was controlled completely by the merchant community even the Duke cannot afford to punish Shylock without a trial. Because punishing Shylock without trial meant a disruption of the free flow of money in the society. Hence even the Duke is unable to pardon Antonio straightaway. Likewise even the demand of a pound of flesh isn't deemed, a criminal act for in bourgeois society where money was the supreme deity capable of buying anything it desired. Therefore, Portia can do nothing about the blasphemous bond except plead with Shylock. "The pound of flesh which I demand of him/ Is dearly bought, 'tis mine" (IV i 99) no argument can prevail upon him and so no one tries to argue on that ground. Portia's pleading is bound to fail in the share market and so she takes recourse to a totally different argument. In this bourgeois society every relationship is based on money – father-daughter (Shylock and Jessica), husband-wife [Bassanio and Portia] servant-master {Shylock and Lancelot}, state and subject [the inability of the Duke to protect Bassanio].

Yet Antonio's condemnation of Shylock out of pretended superiority, "Shylock, albeit I neither lend nor borrow/By taking nor by giving of excess" (I iii 56-57), is born out of the fact that Shylock unlike him does not indulge in any kind of superfluous relationships like friendship etc. (Even though a representative of the bourgeois, Antonio deliberately cultivates Bassanio's friendship for some concealed reason – the intention to gain political ascendancy). There was a section of the feudal lords in the sixteenth century, who observing the growing affluence of the merchant community thought it wise to support them to overcome their own financial crisis. While the bourgeoisie exploring this opportune moment for gaining political supremacy of the land simultaneously extended their hands of friendship. Hence men like Bassanio often pounded by economic paucity sought Antonio's assistance because they knew they could trust the magnanimity of the man. In contrast, Shylock is bereft of friends because he has no such commitments nor is he ready to part with his cash even at the behest of his own daughter. As an alien he can never dream of gaining political ascendancy like Antonio and his only recourse to live independently and with self-respect is the money he is earning from usury. And it is here that Antonio beats him and also hurts him most. Antonio's pretended pragmatic munificence is well known to Shylock but he cannot duplicate it as an alien hence he turns revengeful. Professionally both are equal, but Antonio expresses his superiority over Shylock by calling him a baser creature:

> He hates our sacred nation and rails
> (Even there where merchants most do congregate)
> On me, my bargains, and my well-thrift. (I iii 43-45).

Again Antonio can never be called as innocent as he pretends to be in respect to Shylock. He clearly reflects the existing hostility of the Elizabethan society against the Jews. Shylock is the eyesore to all the English merchants not only because he is an alien but also because he is a successful trader – a non-Christian and yet successful the thought was unbearable to them. English history reveals that the feeling expressed by Shakespeare here is by no means an isolated one. Since Edward I, England officially expelled all the Jews for not conforming to the rules of Christianity and the injustice of expulsion became all the more pronounced because the Jews (because of their sincerity and perseverance) had succeeded in amassing a large fortune. Therefore, Shylock's demand for a pound of flesh though grotesque, cannot be regarded as an evidence of cruelty. His gesture is cruel but his anger is not unjustified. Shakespeare appears to be neutral on this issue, because he gives Shylock ample opening to express his grievances against Antonio and the Christian community in general (I iii 101-124) and (III i 47-86). And, significantly enough, when Shylock pours out his venom against the Christians they hardly find adequate words to oppose him. The basic fact which Shakespeare purports here is, to Shylock usury is sole source of independent income and means of sustenance while to Antonio it is just one of his occupations, merchandise being the main one. Therefore it is certainly not possible for him to forgo his interest purely for charity. If he does condescend to act like Antonio then he will have to starve with his daughter. So when Antonio mocks him for charging interest he cannot help but keep quiet. This indicates the playwright's possible sympathy for Shylock. But being an Elizabethan himself and enjoying the royal patronage Shakespeare could not flout the rule of the land and, therefore, Shylock is ultimately punished for demanding a pound of flesh of a Venetian citizen. The Venetian law pardons Shylock only when the state is convinced of his complete economic liquidation.

Added to it the very idea of Bassanio approaching Antonio for money and Antonio going to Shylock is again a significant practice of the time. Bassanio is a lord while Antonio even though wealthier is not. And as an aristocrat Bassanio is beyond state censure while Antonio even though his friend's guarantor merely, has to bear the brunt. Therefore when Bassanio asks Antonio to be his sponsor Shylock knows that there is chance of his retrieving money whereas had Bassanio directly borrowed from him there would be a remote chance of debt recovery.[46] Neither did the existing society allow such a practice. So in spite of being a pauper Bassanio enjoys the privilege of his inherited title while poor Antonio has to suffer for 'his' extravagance. And when Shylock bounds Antonio he is actually binding the representative of a system where Antonio is nothing but a pawn. This inequality of social status does come into focus when Shakespeare constructs the famous courtroom scene.[47]

Apart from the squabble between Antonio and Shylock another interesting feature of the play is the characterisation of Portia. She seems to have integrated within herself many remarkable qualities of the heroines of the early comedies. Like Julia *(The Two Gentlemen of Verona)*, Portia readily assumes a new identity (disguise) to assist her husband. There is no unnatural bashfulness in her behaviour. The whole world, including her husband, fails to identify her till the end. Again, like the Princess of *Love's Labour's Lost,* Portia is the sole heiress of a large property, yet, economic freedom has not corrupted her normal propriety. The instruction of her deceased father still regulates her marriage and she considers it to be a bond of compulsion. As seen in *A Midsummer Night's Dream* here too the Elizabethan father controls the choice of his daughter's spouse even after his death. And it is obligatory on the part of Portia to remain committed to his wishes. Yet, Shakespeare deliberately portrays her as an intelligent human being no less powerful than all the male characters in respect to her self-determination. At times even Bassanio appears insignificant in contrast to his wife. But Portia never tries to override the Elizabethan conventions. Unlike Kate, she decides to save Antonio. And even when she talks about the strange bindings of her father the tone of complaint is within the limits of decency and decorum (I ii 1-26).[48] Hence when she decides to accept Bassanio as her husband, her acceptance is wholehearted, "Commits itself to yours to be directed,/As from her lord, her governor, her king" (I ii 164-165). And citing this as an example, Karen Newman observes, "Portia's speech figures women as microcosm to man's macrocosm and as subject to his sovereignty."[49] The pledging of her ring is another episode where Portia consciously accepts the well-defined hierarchical relation of man and woman in Elizabethan society. She submits to Bassanio and publicly accepts the Elizabethan marriage system, which demanded total surrender of woman. Her speech observes Karen Newman:

> The governing analogy in Portia's speech in the third scene of the third act...is the Renaissance political commonplace that figures marriage and the family as kingdom in a small, microcosm ruled over by the husband. Portia ratifies this prenuptial contract with Bassanio by pledging her ring, which here represents the codified hierarchical relation of men and women in the Elizabethan sex/gender system in which a woman's

> husband is "her lord her governor, her king." The ring is a visual sign of her vow of love and submission to Bassanio; it is a representation of Portia's acceptance of Elizabethan marriage which was characterized by women's subjection, their loss of legal rights and their status as goods or chattel.[50]

Portia's willing subjugation is thereby easily explicable. If like Adriana she dares to question Bassanio's whereabouts in all likelihood she will have to face similar segregation. All other comic heroines of Shakespeare manifest similar commitments in order to stay harmoniously in the codified world of the patriarchy. And whenever they dare to question the norms of the patriarchy like Kate in *The Taming of the Shrew* they incur the wrath of the entire society. So once married it is expected of a woman to renounce all her claims of inheritance. No wonder Portia's father had devised such an ingenious plan to help Portia to choose the correct husband who would marry her for her sake and not for her inheritance.

The final impact of the play is however a feeling, which the playwright deliberately inculcates in the mind of the reader regarding Antonio's misfortune – it is the handiwork of the newly risen bourgeois class. Historically their constant thirst for money and control over the exchequer of the land often inflicted a lot of suffering upon common men in the Elizabethan society. And as a conscientious artist Shakespeare could not remain impervious to this increasing social malaise. Men at large too were against this class which often both exploited and repressed them in all possible manners. The problem of Antonio was his growing influence over the economy of Venice. Men befriended him not out of love but for their quest for money. But once that power was gone Antonio was completely ineffective and defunct. Bassanio, for instance, was completely oblivious of his plight till Antonio sent him an emissary. And finally when he did arrive to assist him it was too late. So all the professed love and promise to return the loan at the earliest opportunity appear futile in the courtroom scene where Shylock is seen to sharpen his knife. Could we then call the conflict as a conflict of values old and new –

Shylock representing the conventional values, because usury was an ancient practice while Antonio heralding the new bourgeois values where money meant power and bankruptcy meant social segregation? In brief with all its conflicting values *The Merchant of Venice* does leave the reader a bit confused about its generic codification – is it truly a comedy with tragic undertones or is it a tragedy with comic intermission here and there? Like other middle comedies marriage here is the central motivating force but unlike the others here marriage appears to be the actual cause of racial contention. So what did the playwright actual indicate? One is at a loss to state categorically.

As You Like It

As You Like It is a play characterised by largeness rather than by intensity and by diffuseness rather than by concentration. And though Rosalind is as brilliant as Portia, she neither faces an antagonist like Shylock nor establishes her decisive victory in any encounter resembling the trial scene in *The Merchant of Venice*. Her only opponent being her uncle, who ultimately banishes her for being her father's daughter, however does to an extent denigrate her personally. Unlike the other earlier plays of Shakespeare this comedy exhibits a many-sided-world which includes the court as well as the forest, four pairs of lovers, shepherds and courtiers, philosophers and fools, treacherous brothers and faithful servants. The largeness of this world is enhanced by the presence of two vaster forces of Nature, which befit the background of a pastoral romance.

In this multi-coloured world of comedy Shakespeare introduces another declassed aristocrat whose name is Orlando. But unlike Falstaff or Sir Toby Orlando is not a victim of any kind of moral corruption. He is a typical English youth who prefers wrestling to fencing. He is not as fortunate as Bassanio or Orsino and has neither wealth nor adequate learning, but unlike Bassanio, he never aspires to marry for the sake of retrieving his lost social status. A perfect model of a romantic lover (an ideal eulogised by Renaissance humanists), he desires to win Rosalind whose social status is as temporary and uncertain as his, if not worse. Being "rustically" (I i 7)[51] brought up Orlando's position in society is no better than that of a pet animal of his brother and so when he meets Rosalind and receives her undivided attention, he is overjoyed. Their fates run parallel throughout the play, except at the end, when Duke senior is able to retrieve his lost kingdom. But what is significant about their love is the inequality of their social status which, however, does not debar them from being united. Orlando as mentioned previously is the victim of "primogeniture"[52] and as a result he has neither wealth nor a gentleman's education. In sixteenth century England the social analysts[53] point out the prime malaise that affected all families which owned property was due to this unequal distribution of wealth. It went for determining even the behaviour and character of both parents and children, and to govern the relationships of the siblings. Here in this play Oliver's apathy towards Orlando is therefore quite an understandable historical phenomenon.

Rosalind, on the contrary, though not victimized by the above practice is as helpless and insecure as Orlando because she is the only daughter of a Duke who has been exiled to the Forest of Arden. The affinity between her would be lover however ends there. She is intellectually far superior to Orlando because of her upbringing in the palace, where she was allowed to enhance her scholarship. Consequently, she is far more educated than her lover. Yet Rosalind loves the penniless son of Roland de Boys because the playwright is convinced of the fact that an ideal society is one which "not merely permits but in fact guarantees equality between men and women."[54] Renaissance humanism, it may be mentioned, assessed a man's worth by his own potentialities and not by any inherited or conferred title. Shakespeare's Orlando is similarly adjudged to be an ideal match for Rosalind in spite of their social disparities.

As mentioned above the malady that afflicts Orlando is the injustice of primogeniture[55] which leaves him but a poor thousand crowns. For the rest of his requirements he has to look upon the munificence of his elder brother who is not ready to provide him with a single farthing. Oliver denies

Orlando even basic education, though he is ready to bring up the youngest son of Roland de Boys as a proper gentleman. The selective generosity is apparently inexplicable, but if the gesture is the normal reaction to a potential threat from Orlando, the action, though mean, can be somewhat justified. Both physically and morally Orlando is far too superior to Oliver and it is this strength that comes in the way of his respectable means of livelihood. But Oliver's strength lies in his economic solidity[56] and he exploits this strength to make his social status secure. He forces Orlando to flee from his house and live an uncertain life of hardship, whose pressure might ultimately crush his moral power. And Orlando has no other recourse than to comply with the wishes of his brother, because that is the rule of the land. He flees to the Forest of Arden where Duke Senior and his courtiers dwell.

Shakespeare, however, fails to provide a clear definition of the pastoral qualities of Arden. It is clearly not a wilderness, but a parish of scattered sheep cotes and mostly pasture lands with some wood. And what actually matters is the play's ecology. With all its exotic suggestions the Forest of Arden clearly appears to depict a district closer to the rural Warwickshire. Sheep here link up the pastoral world and the real world. As soon as the courtiers come within the boundaries of Arden, they encounter Corin who explains to them his profession of a hired labourer, "But I am shepherd to another man, /And do not sheer the fleeces that I graze" (II iv 76-77). The old story of exploitation seems to have been repeated in this otherwise heavenly setting. Then the talk drifts to real estate and landed property, and Corin appears to be a part-time real estate agent who is happy to oblige Rosalind later in buying a small cottage. Shakespeare here is explicit. The society of Arden is a real society which runs on money, capital, wages, and the means of acquiring desirable property. And the tone of the Duke and his men is consistently sophisticated, contrary to what is expected of their rough rustic exterior (III ii 249-254).

At the very onset of the play Shakespeare introduces the central problem through the words of Orlando. Orlando is found accusing his elder brother Oliver for enforcing both idleness and poverty upon him. Gentility which is his birthright is denied to him "My brother Jaques he keeps at school and report speaks goldenly of his profit" (I i 5-6) but for him the heavens are empty. Orlando is not taught to make anything and even his natural virtue is being marred "with idleness." Adam his 'confidante' advises him to leave the family but that does not strike the right cord in Orlando's mind. He contemplates estrangement with horror for he knows with his intellectual attainments the only recourse left to him for sustenance is either beggary or highway robbery.[57] This is however, Shakespeare's deliberate strategy to plunge the characters along with his audience into the controversy about a structural principle of Elizabethan personal family and social life. The expression and resolution of sibling clash and its social implications[58] are the integral part of the play both forming it and enabling to function. Elucidating Shakespeare's efforts to expose the social hierarchy L. A. Montrose observes:

> His plays explore the difficulty or impossibility or establishing or authenticating a self in a rigorously hierarchical and patriarchal society, a society in which full social identity tends to be limited to propertied adult males who are the heads of households.[59]

Orlando's complaint here is therefore quite comprehensible – barred from genteel education, deprived of proper living and even socially debased as an individual his cry does appeal to the reader and viewer alike at the very inception of the play. Expressing his bitterness to his personal experience of this social contradiction he asks Oliver his elder brother:

> Shall I keep your hogs and eat husks with them?
> What prodigal portion have I spent,
> That I should come to such penury? ....
> The courtesy of nations allows you my better,
> In that you are the first-born; but the same tradition
> Takes not away my blood,
> Were there twenty brothers betwixt us (I i 40- 51).

Since, patriarchal family is the basis of the political unit of patriarchal society, Orlando's protests hint that primogeniture involves disagreement both in the categories of social status and those of kinship. Hence he is not only subordinated to his sibling as a son to Rowland de Boys, but is also subordinated to a fellow gentleman in the society.[60]

Next, at the behest of Adam, Orlando escapes to the Forest of Arden where he encounters Duke Senior with his courtiers who instantly check his advance. It is a different world where he is exposed to, a three functional age of the Elizabethan society – youth, maturity and old age and for the time being not victimized by any form of class consciousness. But contrary to the rest of the inhabitants Orlando is a youth and Duke Senior and his courtiers are years senior to him. And Orlando belongs to the first order about whom Lawrence Stone states that during the Elizabethan age there was "a strong contemporary consciousness of adolescence (then called youth) as a distinct stage of life between sexual maturity at about fifteen and marriage at about twenty six." [61] And since it was the prerogative of an Elizabethan household to keep the youth along with children and servants under strict patriarchal control Orlando could not be allowed to go scot-free, hence this vigilance by Duke Senior. This vigilance observes Stone: "helped to keep in check potentially the most unruly elements in any society, the floating mass of young unmarried males."[62] Orlando though physically powerful, in Arden he is infantilised socially and hence considered weak.

In the Forest of Arden the viewers are introduced to another unique Elizabethan character Jaques. "Shakespeare's contemporaries would hardly ever have had difficulty in recognizing in Jaques a variant of the Elizabethan melancholy man"[63] observes Harold Jenkins. Nonetheless Jaques is an interesting figure. Towards the end of sixteenth century a temperamental hypersensitivity and thoughtfulness often a genuine response to the stresses of an age of transition was high fashion. And melancholy was also classified as a disease condemned as a vice or exalted as the condition and symptom of genius. But all these diverse traditions about melancholy express, implicitly the idea of its social importance – it was a physical and psychological condition that expressed an orientation towards the world and society and this made it particularly susceptible to literary treatment. Such undoubtedly is the use Shakespeare makes of the melancholy Jaques.

The most significant feature of the play however is the stance of Rosalind. It will not be wrong to presume her to be a victim of social demands. Rosalind is the rightful heir of the place because she is the only daughter of the banished Duke. But here, in her uncle's administration she is nothing but a dignified slave. Her redeeming feature is her strong attachment to Celia the daughter of Duke Fredrick that keeps her afloat temporarily. Had Celia not sponsored her, life for Rosalind would have been dangerous. Yet on reaching adulthood, she becomes the cause of anxiety for the existing duke.

> Duke F: You cousin.
> Within ten days if that thou be'st found
> So near our public court as twenty miles,
> Thou diest for it. (I iii 38-41).

Rosalind is accused of being a traitor and hence must depart immediately. Celia tries to break in but her father cuts her short saying that it was at her behest he had tolerated Rosalind all these years but now things need mending. Rosalind's inherent politeness and tolerance is construed by him as vile and cunning: "Her very silence, and her patience/Speak to the people and they pity her" (I iii 74-75); and it is this facet of her disposition that scares him. If the general mandate is for Rosalind then his position is likely to be destabilized. Consequently in spite of her repeated entreaty: "Then good my liege, mistake me not so much/ To think my poverty is treacherous" (I iii 60-61), he does not find it safe to allow her to stay back. Therefore it is clear as long as she stays in the palace her position is nothing more than a hostage in her uncle's house. And it is strange that her father in spite of his bitter enmity with Fredrick thought it judicious to leave behind his daughter under his sponsorship. The resultant outcome of this indiscretion is borne by poor Rosalind. Unlike Celia Rosalind is therefore hesitant at every step. The palpable threat of being eliminated looms large.

From that perspective Rosalind's position is quite akin to that of Orlando. Both face banishment for no fault of theirs. And society at large in spite of being sympathetic towards them cannot help in reinstating them to their rightful social position. It is the all powerful state that decides their destiny, little realizing how that would turn into their favour. So in spite of being in a better social position Rosalind cannot ensure her safety like Orlando. But once in the forest as Ganymede[64] Rosalind manifests a strange kind of anxiety regarding her erroneous identity. She is a girl but here in the forest she is Ganymede dressed in hose and doublet. Transvestism is essential to hide herself in a world where a girl's beauty is more tempting than the prized possession of gold. It's dangerous to tread out to the world without a chaperon. Hence, Rosalind cannot do otherwise even if she wants to. She realizes that even Orlando's presence will not mend matters. On the contrary if Orlando realizes her true identity then there is every possibility of his taking advantage of her weakness as a woman.

The interesting feature about her reaction is her distrust of Orlando. If she really loves Orlando and believes him to be a good man then why can't she confess the truth? Her maidenly anxiety prevents her from doing so. Knowing her identity Orlando might attempt to devastate her virginity. And once ravished the patriarchy will not allow her to live within its fold. So she decides to woo him by proxy. Conventionally wooing is a man's prerogative, but for Rosalind such a proposition does not hold good. "Come woo me" she invites Orlando in perfect abandon when she realizes that without her active labours their relationship will never materialise. It is also a kind of role reversal.[65] Ganymede becomes aggressive to entice Orlando, while conventionally aggressiveness is the domain of man only. And this she does because she believes like any other Elizabethan that love is the final solution to all problems. Once that is achieved the tortures of banishment will appear "heavenly." The situation is distinctly different from a typical Restoration comedy where the husband belongs to a high society and the woman to low society. But Shakespeare does this deliberately to strike at the root of class consciousness. Renaissance humanism preached equality but in practice society did not really accept it that easily as seen in contemporary social history. The plot assuredly assumes a greater complexity because of such contradictory values preached implicitly by the playwright.

Twelfth Night[66]

Twelfth Night is perhaps the most mature of Shakespeare's middle comedies, combining within itself wit, sentiment and entertainment. On a superficial level, the play is just a manifestation of Christmas revelry but a closer scrutiny reveals that festivity is just an apparel to cover up many problematic issues raised within the framework of the comedy. The play begins on an anti-comic note because of an external prohibition upon love and merry-making by Olivia. A complex confusion of roles and identities follow this prohibition when Viola becomes Cesario and Malvolio a cross-gartered lover. And finally with the formation of a new society and after all the characters are happily united by banishing Puritanism for good, a mode of true and natural affection and fellowship begin. The most interesting aspect of *Twelfth Night* is possibly the playwright's unusual concern with the minor characters of the play. Most of them, however, belong to Olivia's household, thus centralizing the attention upon Olivia for a longer period of time. Olivia's household comprises of two classes of members, the unruly kinsman and his associates and the strong reprimanding Puritan Malvolio, Olivia's favourite steward. Sir Toby, a cousin of Olivia's belongs to the first category and the entire household is aware of his notoriety. "That quaffing and drinking will undo you" (I iii 14).[67] His position in Olivia's house strongly reminds the audience of Sir John Falstaff in *The Merry Wives of Windsor*. Both are essentially social parasites, without any steady income to sustain them decently. Falstaff, however, is worse because unlike Sir Toby his misdeeds are not confined to his household only. In order to make out a decent living he tries to allure the innocent country wives and get access to their husbands' purses. Sir Toby on the other hand living under the patronage of Olivia[68] exploits only Sir Andrew to quench his thirst for merry making. Licentiousness is apparently not Sir Toby's forte contrary to Falstaff. Both however are dissatisfied with their humble subsistence reflecting the general dissatisfaction of the declassed aristocrats of Elizabethan England. And it is this frustration that instigates the otherwise fun-loving creatures to steal other people's purses.

Feste and Malvolio are two other interesting characters of Olivia's household. Both of them at times act as the lady's moral guardian (I v) but in reality are her paid servants. Feste's cheerful disposition directs his sympathy towards Sir Toby and his lady assistant Maria, while Malvolio's austerity makes him an alien in the house. Except Olivia there is nobody in the house, who is ready to listen to his Puritanical messages. It will not be a deviance to indicate here the words of Hesketh Pearson about Shakespeare's actual intention in depicting Malvolio thus – as a staunch puritan. Elucidating Shakespeare's standpoint regarding Malvolio Pearson observes:

> Shakespeare probably set out with the intention of ridiculing Puritanism from which he and his fellows had suffered in the character.[69]

Malvolio's self-righteousness, therefore links him with the Puritans who, in Shakespearean England, were not only hostile to the conspicuous consumption of the aristocracy but also representative of an important emergent social group.[70] Therefore, when at the end of the play he threatens to avenge his mistreatment his threat momentarily creates a disruption to the aristocrat control of the final harmony. Feste's role, on the other hand, though suggestive of the poor condition of the court-jester, does not in any way disrupt the social harmony of the play because he is just an extended image of the decayed aristocracy. He merely tries to please Olivia to make a living out of it and she in turn bestows very little favour to help him live a decent life. Maria is possibly the most interesting figure in the entire household. Historically, she reflects the qualities of those gentle women who lacked dowry potential and were sent by their parents to the house of nobility to find proper employment. There the girls would be protected properly and also given enough opportunity to meet suitable young men to marry in future. Maria, therefore, is not a typical uneducated rustic woman and her importance in the household of Lady Olivia is considerable. Maria's imitation of Olivia's handwriting is another indication of her gentle breeding and hence it is hardly surprising to find Olivia confiding in her all her daily problems.

Critics however seem to be more interested in Malvolio than any other characters in the play *Twelfth Night* because he appears to be more complex and formidable than any one else. Analysing this spoil sport steward of Olivia Leo Salinger opines:

> Malvolio is more complex and formidable character. Evidently Maria's 'good practice' on this over weaning steward was the distinctive attraction of *Twelfth Night* to Stuart audiences; but that does not mean... that Malvolio is presented as contemptible butt. An audience is more likely to enjoy and remember the humiliation of some one who in real would be feared than the humiliation of mere imposter like Parolles. Malvolio is neither a puritan nor an upstart, though he has qualities in common with both.[71]

Malvolio's problem is his over officiousness. In Olivia's household the rest of the paid servants never seek to repress the prevailing unruliness except Malvolio. And because he does that out of a sense of commitment he becomes the general eye sore. Yet his principle of degree and order is simply a sluice for his pride. Actually he is sick of self-love and is unable to live spontaneously in the community. His recoil from the sociable side of jester's art is just an indication of his growing social maladjustment. Nonetheless after having humiliated him beyond redemption Shakespeare attributes certain integrity, which makes Malvolio protest – 'I think nobly of the soul' (when Feste talks about the transmigration of souls). Rightfully therefore, even at the end he remains a force to be reckoned with. From that perspective his conflict with Sir Toby too can be accredited to the reaction of two opposed reaction towards changing social and economic conditions. In Malvolio's eyes Sir Toby does nothing but merely wastes the treasures of his time and must be repeatedly censured. He views the aristocrat from the world of law and business, i.e., outside the festive circle of the play and suffers due to a rigid belief in principles. While to Sir Toby Malvolio's unnecessary probing indicates his growing vanity because of Olivia's patronage. This heightens their rift resulting finally to the latter's imprisonment.

As in the other middle comedies, marriage plays an important part in *Twelfth Night.* It not only enhances the carnivalesque atmosphere of the comedy but also assists the ladies to reestablish their social identity. Olivia is introduced to the audience as a lady in mourning, who refuses to meet any stranger or entertain any marriage suit. Her reason is simple— recent death of her father and her brother, her two male protectors. In a patriarchal society to remain protector less was definitely a dangerous proposition and may be this insecurity makes Olivia decide instinctively to shun male company till she meets her proper match (I v). She continues to do the same with the exception to Cesario by whom she has clearly been smitten. And only after marrying Sebastian (IV i) does she renounce her vow and is ready to meet even Orsino her potential suitor right from the beginning of the play.

Viola's transvestism, as mentioned before, is a means to protect her in an alien world and only after she feels secure on seeing Sebastian (V i) she is ready to declare to the world her true identity. Orsino's marriage proposal makes her social security complete; hence she readily accepts it (V i 310-322). The only other female character in the play is Maria, the lady-in-waiting of Olivia. Maria is clearly a well-bred woman whose handwriting is very similar to that of her lady (II v 178). Her possible drawback is her father's incapacity to pay a handsome dowry to get her married to a suitable young man. She is employed by Olivia both to provide her with proper security and to allow her to find ample scope to meet young men of the world so that she can ultimately get married. Maria utilises her situation and finally extracts a promise from Sir Toby to marry her when she befools Malvolia (II v 182).[72] And significantly enough, her active participation in the story ends with that scene itself, because her identity is established in the patriarchy and the playwright no longer needs her presence. But in case of the male characters marriage is just a completion of their life, as seen in cases of both Orsino and Sebastian, while in Malvolio's case marriage results into a comedy. There is, however, no bitterness on the part of any characters when Malvolio attempts to impress Olivia because that was a practice not totally unheard of in the sixteenth century. And as M. C. Bradbrook observes,

> Malvolio's obedient hope was not exactly madness—since the countess does marry one whom she takes to be a serving man; moreover, in real life, as perhaps some of the audience would remember, that formidable royalty, the widowed Duchess of Suffola, had married her youthful Master of the House.[73]

In conclusion, it can be said that though many episodes of *Twelfth Night* often resemble parts of *The Comedy of Errors,* the background of both the plays are very different. Characters in the early comedy belong to the mercantile society of sixteenth century and concern business transactions. But the characters in *Twelfth Night* are mostly aristocrats who have enough leisure to pursue pleasure rather than secure their daily bread. All the characters of the play, in fact, evoke the elegance and refinement of contemporary English society and their pursuits- hunting (I i 16) and participating in masques and revels (I iii 111-112), contribute to the image of a sophisticated society. And, above all, it is a woman (Viola) who stands at the centre of the action, while her relationship with the other female characters of the play forms the principal mechanics of the plot. The change is possibly a reflection of the playwright's own shift of approach to the new Renaissance thinking which tended to treat all human beings, both men and women, as equals.

Shakespeare's social messages of the early comedies seem to have over flown into the middle comedies in a more integrated form. Along with building up the romantic atmosphere of the middle comedies the playwright clearly continues the same line of social criticism through 'round' characters and concrete plots. What is realistically stated in the early comedies is romantically developed in the middle comedies on a more homogeneous manner, showing the amazing development of the dramatic skill of the playwright.

Notes

1. *Shakespeare's Comic Rites*, Cambridge University Press, New York, 1984, p.1.
2. These plays were normally performed and written by professional actors in the Italian troupes famous all over Europe at that point of time. Normally following the Plautine tradition these playwrights introduced in their plays the motifs of mistaking and adventures. And their characters were direct descendents of masks of ancient comedy.
3. Kate in *The Taming of the Shrew*, Adriana in *The Comedy of Errors.*
4. Page in *The Merry Wives of Windsor.*
5. Proteus in *Two Gentlemen of Verona.*
6. Macduff's child in *Macbeth.*
7. *A Midsummer Night's Dream.*
8. The development of Proteus in *The Two Gentlemen* can be cited as an ideal illustration of this process.
9. *As You Like It.*
10. *Twelfth Night.*
11. *The Merchant of Venice.*
12. It was the prerogative both of the boy and the girl to serve their in-laws before marriage and thereby get to know the family more intimately.
13. All textual references to *The Taming of the Shrew* are to the Arden Shakespeare *The Taming of the Shrew, ed.* Brian Morris, Methuen, London, 1981.
14. 'English Marriage and Shakespeare' in *Shakespeare Quarterly*, 1979, p. 69.
15. Petruchio's courtship here is very significant:

    Marry, so I mean, sweet Katherine in thy bed;
    And therefore, setting all the chat aside,
    Thus in plain terms; your father hath consented.
    That you shall be my wife; your dowry' agreed on;
    And will you, kill you, I will marry you (II i 260-4).

    First of all marriage to him is equivalent to killing her. Secondly, his interpretation of the marriage contract in present tense "will." A vow made in present tense signified an agreement to marry immediately. And Petruchio does exactly as he promises.

16. *Ibid.*, p. 41.
17. Quoted in Graham Holderness, *Shakespeare in Performance: The Taming of the Shrew*, Manchester University Press, Manchester, 1989, p. 40.
18. *Ibid.* p. 41.
19. Judith Cook, *Women in Shakespeare*, W.H. Allen & Co, London, 1980, rep.1990, p. 28.
20. *A Preface to Shakespeare's Comedies*, Pearson Education, Singapore, 1996, Indian reprint 2003, p. 139
21. *The Arden Shakespeare The Taming of the Shrew*, ed. Brian Morris, Methuen, London, 1981, p.6.
22. 'Renaissance Family Politics and Shakespeare's *The Taming of the Shrew*' in *Shakespeare's Comedies,* **ed.** Gary Waller, Longman, London, 1991, p. 47.
23. *Shakespeare and Social Class,* Humanities Press, New Jersey, 1989, p. 23.
24. The introduction of the fairies was deliberate because the contemporary audience believed in such extra-terrestrial creatures and their magical qualities. Hence is only natural that Shakespeare should make a special appeal to this faith is some of his comedies.
25. All textual reference to *A Midsummer Night's Dream* are to the Arden Shakespeare, *A Midsummer Night's Dream,* ed. Harold F. Brooks, Methuen, London, 1979.
26. *Patriarcha and Other Political Works*, ed. Peter Laslett, Oxford University Press, Oxford, 1949, p. 63.
27. Ralph Berry, *Shakespeare Social Class,* Humanities Press, New Jersey, 1988 rep. 1989, p. 35.
28. Love being an iexplicable emotion was viewed as an other worldly affair hence Shakespeare was justified in assigning Puck the task of executing the love potion which could work magic.
29. Valerie Traub, 'Behind the Seen: Visibilizing Female Homoeroticism in Shakespeare's Plays,' in *William Shakespeare: Canon and Critique,* ed. Leela Gandhi, An Anthology of Recent Criticism, New Orientation Series, Delhi, Pencraft International, 1998, p.145.
30. There is an indication in Traub's writing about the prevalent homoeroticism in the nunneries, which according to him bound the nuns together. But to the patriarchy homoeroticism, especially among women, proved to be a potential threat to the society, because

homoeroticism always encouraged flouting the patriarchal regulations. In the nunneries on the other hand it proved to be a blessing in disguise, creating an air of sexual self-sufficiency.

31. *Ibid.*, p. 135.
32. *Ibid.*, p. 138.
33. James A.S. McPeek, 'A *Midsummer Night's Dream*' in *Shakespeare Quarterly,* 1972, p. 74.
34. *Op. cit.*, p. 37.
35. *Anatomy of Criticism, Four Essays*, Princeton University Press, New Jersey, 1957.
36. *Ibid.*, p. 23.
37. And this is the inherent hypocrisy of the English society which the playwright decidedly highlights. Shylock is condemned by Antonio for his high rate of interest yet when Bassanio comes to him for money Antonio goes to this contemptible Jew and not to any other Christian usurer.
38. Philip Edwards, *Shakespeare a Writer's Progress*, Oxford University Press, New York, 1986, p. 44.
39. 'Elizabeth and Foreigners' in *Shakespeare Survey* 17 CUP, 1964, p. 47.
40. *Ibid.*, p. 48.
41. *Comic Characters in Shakespeare,* Macmillan, London, 1949, p. 55.
42. In the decade during which the play was written, the only widespread and militant anti-Jewish feeling was occasioned by the trial and execution of Roderigo Lopez for alleged high treason. It was clearly a latent rather than an active feeling and due to inherited suspicion rather than current religious or social thought.
43. As the history of English drama reveals Shakespeare's play was merely reflecting a topical interest in Jews and is thus a part of contemporary literature. And Shakespeare manifesting deepest regard for both public interest and public appreciation thought it wise to represent Shylock in a more humane manner.
44. All textual reference to *The Merchant of Venice* are to the Arden Shakespeare *The Merchant of Venice,* ed. J.R. Brown, B.I. Publications, Delhi, 1964 rep. 1983.
45. Lars Engle, 'Thrift in Blessings in Exchange and Explanation in *The Merchant of Venice*' in *Shakespeare Quarterly,* 1986, p. 20.
46. In mid seventeenth century England a nobleman could not be arrested for debt. Likewise neither was he obliged to repay any debt. So the class distinction between Antonio and Bassanio becomes quite

clear in the given context. Understandably therefore Antonio grows extraordinarily violent while repudiating Shylock's attempts to draw parallels between them (I iii 48-53).

47. It has been established by the social historians that loans at interest though essential was considered perilous and hence much feared in the last two decades of Elizabeth's reign because almost two third of the peerage seem to have been in growing financial difficulties. Hence usury often led to minor scandal in the peerage.

48. Marriage of the elites in Elizabethan England was primarily a commercial transaction determined by the question of dowry (*The Taming of the Shrew*), familial alliances and inheritance. Female wards were often pawns in the political and social maneuvers of their families. Hence commercial language was used to describe even love relationships in Elizabethan poetry. And the marriage of Portia manifests not only the economic determinants of marriage in Elizabethan society but also the country's economic climate. No wonder Shakespeare presents the rising tension between trade and usury in *The Merchant of Venice* with the ultimate triumph of trade that is Antonio who is readily incorporated into the aristocratic world of Belmont.

49. 'Portia's Ring: Unruly Woman and Structures of Exchange in *The Merchant ol Venice*' in *Shakespeare Quarterly*, 1978, p. 25.

50. *Ibid*., p. 25.

51. All textual reference to *As You Like It* are to the Arden Shakespeare As *You Like It,* ed. Agnes Latham, B. I. Publications, Delhi, 1975, rep. 1988.

52. L.A. Montrose, 'Social process in *As You Like It*' in *Shakespeare Quarterly, 1981*, p. 31.

53. Lawerence Stone *Crisis of Aristocracy.*

54. Sarup Singh, 'A note on *As You Like It*' in *The Indian Journal of English Studies* 4, 1963, p. 162.

55. Both in the Sixteenth and Seventeenth centuries primogeniture was both widely and rigorously practiced in England by all the land owners irrespective of their statuesque in the social hierarchy. It was more an English phenomenon because nowhere else in Europe the malaise was that strong. The consequent abuses and hardships primogeniture inflicted on the society generated a literature of protest by and for the younger sons to which Jaques refers in his speech (II v 57-58).

56. The gentry of that period undoubtedly experienced a rise in wealth and status but the rise was restricted only to the inheriting eldest son and at the expense of his younger siblings. So the hatred of the two

brothers in the given play is quite explicable. Added to that the drive of the eldest son to both aggrandise and perpetuate his estate led him to a ruthless application of primogeniture thereby leaving him without the adequate means to provide for his younger siblings. As a result there was a downward social mobility and relative impoverishment in the ability to marry or late marriage and also fewer children.

57. This again was a common practice for the younger siblings of landed gentry who were deprived of a decent living. The entire period was well-known for rampant highway robbery.
58. As a result of primogeniture the younger sons had to either work hard for their living starting from nothing or else led an idle life like Orlando full of boredom, depending on the benevolence of their elder brother. While the eldest son enjoying the privileges of inherited property lived comfortably depriving his younger siblings.
59. 'Social process in *As You Like It*' in *Shakespeare Quarterly,* 1981 no.1 p. 37.
60. There is a saying that in Sixteenth century England it would be vilifying a person by referring to him as the second or youngest son of a nobleman.
61. Stone Lawrence, *The Family Sex and Marriage in England* 1500-1800, Ernest Benn, London, 1970, p. 108.
62. *Ibid.* p. 27.
63. '*As You Like It*' in *Shakespeare Survey* 8, p. 45.
64. Transvestism was extremely popular with the Elizabethan audience and hence Shakespeare opted for it readily to enhance the plays comic value.
65. This gesture is again speculated as the result of Renaissance humanism which gave absolute freedom to woman for spiritual freedom in love.
66. The name *Twelfth Night* itself is very suggestive, because it indicates the culmination of last of great Christmas feast. It reminds the reader of the old English festivity which was celebrated by masques and other fantastic happenings and followed by St. Distaff's Day and Plough Monday to a sunny Mediterranean land where it was always sunny afternoon. In other words it was a way of escape from the harsh realities of everyday mundane life where social contentions are temporarily held in abeyance. The only discord here is the ill-will of Malvolio which kills entertainment of the noisy rapacious court.
67. All textual references to *Twelfth Night* are to the Arden Shakespeare *Twelfth Night,* eds. J.M. Lothian and T.W. Craik, Routledge, London, 1975 rep. 1994.

68. Had Sir Toby been a different sort or person, he would be designated the respected position of Olivia's natural guardian. Old houses often harboured such characters to establish their proof of antiquity and dignity. But here since he belongs to rough countrified society his place is assigned below the stairs with Fabian and hence he often lands into trouble for bear baiting, a common parlance of the time for any kind of mischief.

69. *A life of Shakespeare*, Hamish Hamilton paperback, London, 1987, p. 90.

70. It will not be wrong to presuppose here that Sir Toby's repeated attack against Malvolio is actually a reflection of the old world resisting the new. It is therefore a life of discomfort equivalent to hiccups and melancholy which is trying desperately to ignore the new Puritanism and efficiency. But Olivia proves to be a deviation here who prefers the new order which spells of order and efficiency, hence her sympathy for Malvolio.

71. 'The design of *Twelfth Night*' *Shakespeare Quarterly* 1958, p. 134.

72. The fooling of Sir Toby and Maria cannot be called exactly vindictive because courtiers in the sixteenth century played similar jokes on each other. In fact fools would treat rival fools with even greater violence. Interestingly the cross garter and yellow hose that was recommended to Malvolio on this occasion were actually the dress code of the henpecked husband in a popular song of the time.

73. *Shakespeare the Craftsman,* Chatto and Windus, London, 1969, p. 60.

8

CONCLUSION

Comedy as has been discussed earlier is basically an art form, which does not differ very much from tragedy in its approach. While tragedy tries to portray man in a better light than he actually is, comedy portrays man as a creature worse than he is in reality. Both the art forms, therefore, have a common ground to work upon; man and his behaviour, studied from two different perspectives. And the aim of both these art forms is to provide a release for man's pent-up emotions. Comedy, however, has two distinct approaches to the performance of its function of catharsis, the subversive approach, and the normative approach. But, unfortunately serious thinkers like Plato and at a much later time Rousseau, having overlooked this important function of comedy instructed their audience not to indulge the Lord of Misrule, the corrupter of the human soul. The present day psychological critics have ignored the words of caution of the ancient masters and declared the essential nature of the comic release in human lives. The comic action, they feel, is an invaluable instrument for man to reduce himself periodically and thereby maintain his mental equilibrium. Any serious playwright, therefore, while using this medium of self-expression, cannot overlook its basic social function. And it is but obvious that a genius like Shakespeare would conscientiously use the medium for restoring the mental balance of his viewers.

The themes of comedies have undoubtedly varied from generation to generation, but, strangely enough, there are a few basic themes, which the comic writers have preferred all along, irrespective of their age and country, and they are the themes of love and sex. The probable reason for favouring these two themes is inherent in the form itself, which tends to deal with the most normal and usual departments of human lives. Sex and love, being the two most usual and normal reactions of man in his everyday social interaction, provide the widest field for studying the human behaviour for all the comic playwrights. Moreover, sex is that department of human life where there is more jostling than any other department, and hence it is only in this department that all men and women become quite bizarre. Comedy also celebrates the human capacity to endure the same kind of social pressures and constraints experienced in one's real life. It also portrays man's capacity to overcome his tragic fate with a kind of energy and exuberance and their capacity, which enable them to be joyous survivors in an acceptable and accepting world. The spirit of comedy is thus the spirit of resurrection, which unites the lovers in marriage to regenerate the old decaying society, which at first opposes the union of the lovers. All the Shakespearean comedies convey this message of resurrection, unite the lovers despite their parental opposition, and ultimately breathe a new life into a world of baring and depressing statuesque.

Prior to him, however, both in the Interludes and in the comedies of the University Wits we find the playwrights manifesting in a typified manner the existing depression of the society. Consequently, the comic elements in their plays are often marred by brutal sarcasm. This trend of portraying the social malaise though well perpetrated by Shakespeare however, never manages to take precedence over his comic spirit. On the contrary, the entertaining value of the genre appears much more generous and liberal when contrasted against the works of his predecessors. And this happens because he prefers presenting them for the sake of his audience. Moreover, he has the liberalness to accept men with all their failures. He does not shun them; even when he decidedly mocks at the varied human failures his attitude is that of a gentle creator who takes all the pain to carve out a decent figure out of the most incongruous objects.

This difference of approach becomes enormously pronounced when one compares Shakespearean comedy with that of his predecessors and contemporaries. For instance, when one glances through Robert Greene's *A Looking Glasse for London and England* one grows aware of the playwright's unambiguous intention of satirising bitterly the English nobility in general. Likewise even Ben Jonson arouses the comic spirit in his Comedy of Humour by simply portraying the social maladies, through sharp criticism of human follies. Shakespeare however, remains content purely by laughing with all peccadilloes, foibles and imperfections of man.

The sharp biting satire or the strong censuring of man's moral lapses which was Ben Jonson's forte was totally absent in the works of Shakespeare who definitely appeared to be more tolerant towards all human failures. Therefore, if the tone of *The Merry Wives of Windsor* appears to be unusually ironic for Shakespeare that of *Every Man in His Humour* is surprisingly balanced for Jonson, for here he merely strikes an attitude of amused disapproval of most human failings through the representation of some humour-slanted individuals. A similar dissimilarity of approach is observed when the works of Shakespeare are compared with those of the Restoration playwrights, Etherege, Wycherly and Congreve. The comedy of manners, a typical product of the Restoration shows a marked preference for the Jonsonian humours and hence all the three outstanding playwrights insist on ridiculing the behaviour of the social elite. The comic situations of their plays mainly arise out of people's way of adjusting to social life, reflecting the balance of men's instincts against their moral principles. They are incessantly trying to make fun of the unscrupulous selfishness and obsessive animalistic approach of all men and women of their time. Hence, their works seem to be extremely time-bound in contrast to the works of Shakespeare.

The difference of approach to human failures on the part of Shakespeare has two plausible explanations. First Shakespeare's moral insight being deeper than that of either

Ben Jonson or all the three major Restoration playwrights sought to present life in its totality. Life to him was an admixture of tragedy and comedy, of suffering and happiness. Therefore, to reproduce an authentic picture of human life one cannot avoid the tragic strains even in a comedy or the comic touches in a tragedy. Like the ancient Sanskrit plays[1] of Sudrak and Bhababhuti Shakespeare too readily and gracefully accepts man with all his imperfections, because all men are basically born imperfect and to laugh at the imperfections of others is in reality laughing at one's own self. And these imperfections of man are the real cause of his sufferings, which the artist ought to sympathise with and not scorn. The reason can be attributed to the new school of Renaissance philosophy, which was actually the end product of bourgeois democracy. Man's social status now being redefined, depended more upon his economic conditions, unlike the inherited social status of the feudal hierarchy. This duly stressed both his individuality and his eternal quest for an ideal life partner (the key word of Romantic love), which till then was practically unknown in England. Moreover, Shakespearean women, unlike the earlier female characters of the English stage, were being recognised for the first time as individual beings, who had enough personality like Portia (*The Merchant of Venice)* to air their opinions in public. Shakespearean heroines are, therefore, not only emancipated and self-sufficient but also able to evade the image of the stereotype which society imposes upon them. Though Marston's heroine's at times do manifest these traits, Shakespearean women are more authentic and artistic and hence lauded by modern feminists.

Shakespeare's concept of society is another aspect that distinguishes his comedies from those written by other playwrights. Though Shakespeare was perfectly aware of the existing class-consciousness of his time, he never for once seemed to have been totally influenced by its narrowness. The Elizabethan social structure was to him a mere framework upon which his genius worked. Society he regarded was an idea rather than a particular set of persons, or a small community living together in a small area. The term in fact embraced the entire humanity and at times even the creatures of the woods and wilds (A *Midsummer Night's Dream* and the *The Tempest)*. But even within this apparently incongruous social framework one can detect the corporate structure of the entire Elizabethan society. And thus in his most parochial play *The Merry Wives of Windsor* the entire borough is seen to be somehow involved in the amorous adventures of Sir John Falstaff. And through the unravelling of the plot the histories, the affairs of the state, the high personages of the state, the porters, grooms and other citizens, the common soldiers, gardeners and even common murderers are skillfully introduced.

The social settings of some of Shakespeare's early plays, however, appear to be clearly influenced by their sources, but their presentation is totally Shakespearean. For instance the materialistic, down-to-earth Plautus's society *(Menaechmi* and *Amphitruo)* certainly stimulated the dramatist's imagination to compose the commercial society of *The Comedy of Errors*. Yet, while handling the totally unromantic plot of Plautus the temperamentally romantic Shakespeare infused in it the romantic Elizabethan values. Antipholus of Syracuse arrives at Ephesus, a politically stable international trading center, where men's sole business is business itself and upsets both its social and family setups. And since any sort of social disturbance is detrimental to the functioning of a commercial society Antipholus's freethinking upsets the familial ties. It is treated as the offensive act of an insane man, which the local judicial body instantly punishes. Moreover, the other brother being a hard-core businessman (who readily declines the friendly offers of dinner), Antipholus's (of Syracuse) ready acceptance of life as is offered to him (his ready assent to Adriana's dinner) strikes the local merchant community as something strange and unheard-of. They cannot imagine even in their dreams that here is another totally different individual who, regardless of an external similarity, is temperamentally opposite to the leading merchant of Ephesus. The play can, therefore, be interpreted as a portrayal of the conflicting values- the commercial versus the romantic. Yet, significantly enough the ladies of the comedy are not influenced by the commercial values of Ephesus. On the other hand, they clearly voice their protest against the tyranny of the male folks who generally tend to treat them as their personal property. Adriana, therefore, in spite of being the wife of a wealthy merchant, opposes her husband's waywardness and complains to her sister about the unlicensed liberty of Antipholus of Ephesus. But Shakespeare here takes no risk of preaching the message of the equality of sexes because that would mean a call to anarchy for contemporary audience and hence he is seen to pacify the genuine wrath of the devoted wife through the advice of Luciana, (the subjection to authority is part of the divinely appointed order of Nature).

Like *The Comedy of Errors, The Merry Wives of Windsor* too deals with the merchant community of Elizabethan England. The play in effect prefers to portray the lives of the townspeople with whom the dramatist was extremely familiar. The only noble man of the play is Sir John Falstaff whose presence is deliberately made incongruous by the dramatist himself. He is a titular aristocrat lacking in the basic resources of self-sustenance. But the pride of his noble heritage prevents him from admitting the fact publicly and the only recourse left for him is to pilfer the pockets of the wealthy merchants of Windsor, and this he tries by enticing their wives. Underestimating their common sense and also their moral values he approaches them three times and on all the three occasions they browbeat him and punish him for his infamous conduct. Falstaff and Sir Toby are undoubtedly the familiar declassed aristocrats of Elizabethan England, who only inherited the family title without inheriting the family property. The world of *The Two Gentlemen of Verona* at first appears to be the old medieval world of chivalry and romance but on closer scrutiny the viewers realize that the medieval exterior is just a covering for all the Elizabethan social problems dealt at length in the play. The left shoe with the worse sole, which Launce speaks of for his mother, is nothing but a reflection of the women's true position in the Elizabethan society. Though the Puritans of the age supported women's right for equality and individuality by declaring that God who created man also created women, halving His consciences into two equal parts, the general mass of the Elizabethans refused to acknowledge it. To them women were nothing but the personal properties of men and, therefore had to endure all the whimsicality of their masters – either fathers or husbands.

The other interesting aspect of *The Two Gentlemen of Verona* is its attitude towards the Elizabethan gentlemen. 'Gentlemen', however proves to be a generally illusive term casting the widest net to include men of all social classes. At times, the term indicates not merely a rank but also an ideal of conduct, and hence all Shakespearean heroes including Hamlet, Ferdinand, Malvolio, Proteus and Coriolanus are gentlemen irrespective of their social status. And if the outlawed Valentine is treated from that perspective, his behaviour notwithstanding his banishment is more gentlemanly than his so-called back-stabber friend Proteus. The gentleman Proteus's villainy, in this context can be said to be twofold, betrayal of his friend's faith in him and forsaking his ladylove for better pastures. Valentine in contrast is quite consistent in his behaviour; his love for his friend does not desert him even after he realizes the evil intentions of his friend in the forest. He not only forgives him, but also offers him his precious Silvia. Both young men apparently belong to the same social stratum, but their outlooks are very different. And this difference implies Shakespeare is not born of man's social position, it is congenital. But significantly none seems to be much concerned about Silvia's preferences when Valentine exhibits his munificence. It is after all an all males world where such petty considerations cannot be taken into account.

Though, the setting of *Love's Labour's Lost* appears to be the court of King Ferdinand of Navarre, yet with the development of the plot the viewers become conscious of its strong ties to the rural community of England. Navarre seems to inhabit instead of the royal court a large manor house, belonging to an estate-owner. His close proximity to the village folks increases these suspicions. And this leads us to conclude that though Shakespeare refers to Ferdinand as the king of Navarre actually, he treats him as a wealthy estate owner who had no royal servant to serve him or courtiers to advice him. The three young men whom Shakespeare tries to project as the courtiers of Ferdinand are in reality his friends who instead of guiding him properly dance to his impracticable tunes. Even the picture of the place where the commoners interact resembles a deer park of an English country. The play therefore, can be called a play of domestic reality, where royalty is just a reflection of the English aristocracy. The minor characters however are true representative of their class in all what they do or say. And even Don Armado the alien, faithful to his Spanish birth, mispronounces all the English words he has learnt. The other English learned citizens disapprove this misuse of their mother tongue and repeatedly censure the poor man at every opportune moment, generating a whole complex of comic situations. The women characters of the play, on the other hand represent the world of reason and logic. Unlike their male counterparts they are conscious from the very beginning that the vows of the king and his men are simply unrealistic which they will have to renounce at the earliest opportunity but because the gentlemen refuse to see the irrationality of their vows the ladies decide to teach them a lesson and inflict upon them a year long penance of abstinence. This play is interesting from this perspective because at the end of it all the women characters appear to be at the helm of the action – dictating terms to the king and his courtiers. And the playwright too makes no commitment about their actual intentions – will they return after a year and marry the men of Navarre? It is up to the viewers to presume things.

According to the social historians of England, after the economic and religious unrest of the middle Tudor period, the freedom preached by the humanists rejuvenated in a way the moral of the entire nation. And Shakespeare having chanced upon the best time in which to live had ample opportunity to exercise, with least distraction and most encouragement, the highest faculties of man. His comedies, therefore, register most comprehensively the characteristics of the congenial social atmosphere of his time. The saturnalia presented in his comedies are not inimical to the positive aspects of a new bourgeois social setup, which facilitated the notions of peace and order. But inside the large England, which still retained the remnants of monarchy and aristocracy, society was afflicted by many discordant elements, which Shakespeare never failed to notice and record. As an assiduous comic playwright, he infused in his saturnalia the hints of many social injustices, the oppressive patriarchy (Egeon and his diktats against his daughter for daring to choose her own husband in *A Midsummer Night's Dream*), the crisis of aristocracy (Sir Toby and his like in *Twelfth Night*), the degeneration of moral values leading to an erosion of social values in a mercantile society, and the historical retrospection of the turbulent past.

The infusion though pronounced in his early comedies is not entirely absent in the middle comedies, which contain elements of social realism behind a romantic exterior. The audience would naturally realize that both the early and the middle comedies of Shakespeare were inter-linked in the context of the social realism of the Elizabethan period. The delicate relationship of Oberon and Titania in *A Midsummer Night's Dream*, for instance represent a different version of matrimony throughout causing the reader to question the validity of the institution. Likewise in *The Taming of the Shrew* one is at a loss at the end of the play when Kate appears to be more subservient than either her sister or the widow. Has marriage actually tamed her or has she relinquished her past misdemeanours willingly because she has fallen in love with Petruchio? The world in *Twelfth Night* is also clearly demarcated into two classes – the landowning wealthy aristocrats and the titular aristocrats whom Lawrence classifies as the 'declassed aristocrats.' The historical retrospection of the past is made clearer at this apparently incongruent point, than in all other romantic comedies.

If *The Comedy of Errors* is presumed to be Shakespeare's earliest attempt to write a comedy, it will not be incorrect to say that Shakespeare began his dramatic career with the inscription of the mercantile social values of his time. The society of Ephesus is a money-based society, where the prime business, of its citizens is business alone, and in such a society if a man is economically handicapped like Egeon, he becomes vulnerable to the laws of the land. Therefore, when Antipholus of Ephesus unknowingly plays hide and seek with his creditors, the law keepers are summoned to punish him, though he is one of the most respectable citizens of Ephesus Similarly, in the middle comedy, *The Taming of the Shrew*, Baptista Minola a prosperous merchant, finds money to be the only means to a respectable marriage of his daughter who happens to be the shrew. In *The Two Gentlemen of Verona*, however, Shakespeare uses a different social association to partially recapitulate the unruly middle Tudor period, and to emphasize at the same time a few other contemporary social prejudices. Valentine's life in the forest as the chief of the outlaws possibly alludes to the historical record of both the highway robbery rampant in Tudor times and the unpredictability of the men in authority, to punish innocent gentlemen for no conclusive reasons. Moreover, the Duke's opposition to the match between Silvia and Valentine may be a reflection of the oppressive patriarchy, which debarred girls from marrying men of their choice. Girls in the middle comedies (*A Midsummer Night's Dream* and *The Merchant of Venice*) also suffer the same fate. Both Hermia's and Portia's marriages are completely controlled by the authoritative injunctions of their parents, to decide the marriage of their female wards. Another important feature of *The Two Gentlemen of Verona* is the portrayal of male friendship. Valentine's friendship with Proteus illustrates this friendship, which is temporarily snapped when Proteus decides to possess Silvia by applying physical force, but at the end when Proteus realises his faults and apologizes, Valentine readily forgives him, offering Silvia in lieu of their lost friendship. Antonio's love for Bassanio in *The Merchant of Venice* can be cited as a continuation of the theme of this male bond in the middle comedies. The center of focus in *The Merry Wives of Windsor* appears to be the crisis of aristocracy, a typical social malady of Elizabethan England. The saturnalia of the comedy offer only a feeble camouflage to the depressing poverty of Sir John Falstaff. From the very beginning of the play the audience is aware of Falstaff's incurable lust for money and this disease practically spurs him to seduce the wives of Ford and Page (I iii 8-45). With only ten pounds a week it is but natural that he will be "almost out at heels" (I iii 29) resulting into cony-catching, "I must cony-catch;/ Shift" (I iii 31-32). Therefore, it is hardly surprising that the Windsorites amicably make up with him even after his exposition, and invite him to Anne Page's marriage feast. Sir Toby in *Twelfth Night* an extended image of Sir John Falstaff suffers from similar economic crisis. Paucity of funds brings about the moral degeneration in both of them, but society is aware of their helplessness and hence adopts a benevolent attitude towards them. Moral corruptions do not really afflict Orlando, another declassed aristocrat (*As You Like It*), rather his gentlemanliness assists him in redeeming his lost social status. The theme of male friendship is recurrent in *Love's Labour's Lost*, though in a much subdued form. This is, in fact, the only early comedy, which borders on sarcasm and has a problematic ending. Ferdinand's vow of celibacy is not only an impractical proposition but also a great hindrance to his social amelioration and its fulfillment. Man's social life is never complete without marriage; therefore, when Ferdinand and his courtiers try to contravene the accepted social order, society in the guise of the French Princess sneeringly turns them back to reason.

Note

1. Incidentally Sanskrit plays were never categorically divided into either tragedy or comedy. The cause for such a formulation of dramatic theory by Bharata, maybe because he felt that playwrights ought to present life in its totality and not fragmentize it like their European counterparts.

BIBLIOGRAPHY

Primary Sources

William Shakespeare

All textual references to Shakespeare's plays are to the Arden Shakespeare.

A *Midsummer Night's Dream,* ed. Brooks Harold F., Methuen, London, 1979.

As You Like It, ed. Latham Agnes, B.I. Publications, Delhi, 1988.

Love's Labour's Lost, ed. David R.W., Methuen, London, 1985.

The Comedy of Errors, ed. Foakes R.A., Routledge, London, 1962.

The Merchant of Venice, ed. Brown John Russell, B.I. Publications, Delhi, 1964 rep. 1983.

The Merry Wives of Windsor, ed. Oliver H.J., Methuen, London, 1971 rep. 1985.

The Taming of the Shrew, ed. Morris Brian, Methuen, London, 1981.

The Two Gentlemen of Verona, ed. Leech Clifford, Methuen, London, 1969 rep. 1986.

Twelfth Night, eds. Lothian J.M. and Craik T.W., Methuen, London, 1989.

Shakespeare William, *Shakespeare's Plays in Quarto,* eds. Allen Michael B. and Muir Kenneth, University of California, Berkeley, 1981.

Shakespeare William, *The Complete Works of William Shakespeare,* ed. Craig W.J., Oxford University Press, London, 1945.

Shakespeare William, *The Complete Works of William Shakespeare,* Gramercy Books, Outlet Books, New York, 1990.

Shakespeare William, *The London Shakespeare* I and II, ed. Munro John, Eyre and Spottiswoode, London, 1958.

Shakespeare William, *William Shakespeare Complete Works,* ed. Peter Alexander, E.L.B.S. and Collins, London, 1951 rep. 1961.

Others

Aristophanes, *The Wasps The Poet and the Women The Frog,* ed. Barret David, Penguin, London, 1964.

Bale John, *The Dramatic Writings of John Bale,* Early English Dramatists, ed. Farmer John S., Charles W. Traylen, Guildford, England, 1966.

Congreve William, *William Congreve Letters and Documents,* ed. Hodges John C., Macmillan, London, 1964

Dekker Thomas, *The Dramatic Works of Thomas Dekker,* Cambridge University Press, Cambridge, 1953.

Fielding Henry, *Joseph Andrews and Shamela,* ed. Davis Douglas Brooks, Oxford University Press, Delhi, 1968 rep. 1987.

Goldsmith Oliver, *The Collected Works of Oliver Goldsmith* III, ed. Friedman Arthur, Clarendon Press, Oxford, 1966.

Greene Robert, *Friar Bacon and Friar Bungay,* The Fortune Play Books, ed. Harrison G.B., Robert Holden and Co. Ltd., London, 1927.

Greene Robert, *The Plays and Poems of Robert Greene* I, ed. Collins J. Churton, Oxford University Press, Oxford, 1905 (MDCCCCV).

Heywood John, *The Dramatic Writings of John Heywood,* The Early English Dramatists, ed. Farmer John S., Traylen Charles W., England, 1966.

Homer, *Odyssey,* ed. Rieu E.W., Penguin, London, 1945.

Jonson Ben, *Volpone,* ed. Cook David, Methuen, London, 1962 rep. 1982.

Lyly John, *The Complete Works of John Lyly* III, ed. Bond R. Warwick, Clarendon Press, London, 1902 rep. 1973.

Medwall Henry, *Fulgens and Lucres,* eds. Boas F.S. and Reed A.W., Oxford University Press, London, 1926 (MCMXXVI).

Peele George, *The Old Wives' Tale* in *Elizabethan and Jacobean Comedies,* eds. Witworth Charles W. Jr. and Gibbon Brian, Ernest Benn Ltd., Gt. Britain, 1984.

Plautus, *The Rope and Other Plays,* tr. and ed. Waiting E.F., Penguin, Gt. Britain, 1964 rep 1979.

Sheridan R.B., *The Rivals,* ed. Herring Robert, Macmillan, London, 1929 rep. 1952*e Bible,* National Bible Press, Philadelphia, 1978.

The Complete Roman Drama I, ed. Duckwarth G.E., Random House, New York, 1942.

Udall Nicholas, *The Dramatic Writings of Nicholas Udall,* Early English Dramatists, ed. Farmer John S., Charles W. Traylen, England, 1966.

Secondary Sources

Abrams M.H., *A Glossary of Literary Terms,* Macmillan, Delhi, 1957 rep. 1989.

Allen John A., 'Bottom and Titania' in *Shakespeare Quarterly,* 1967.

Anderson J.J., 'The Morality of *Love's Labour's Lost*' in *Shakespeare Quarterly,* 1967.

Anderson T.H., 'Shakespeare and Nature of Women' in *Shakespeare Studies* II, 1973.

Aristotle, *Aristotle Theory of Poetry and Fine Arts,* ed. Butcher S. Kalyani Publishers, New Delhi, 1951 rep. 1987.

Aristotle, *Aristotle on the Art of Poetry,* ed. Bywaters Ingram, Oxford University Press, Delhi, 1977 rep. 1992.

Arnott Peter D., *An Introduction to Greek Theater,* Macmillan, London, 1959 rep. 1962.

Arthos John, *Shakespeare The Early Writings*, Bowes and Bowes London, 1972.

Arthos John, *Shakespeare's Use of Dream and Vision,* Bowes and Bowes London, 1977.

Barber C.L., *Shakespeare's Festive Comedies,* Princeton University Press, New Jersey, 1959 rep. 1972.

Bennell Margaret, *Shakespeare's Flowering of the Spirit,* Lanthorn Press, London, 1971.

Bereton Geoffrey, *A Short History of French Literature,* Belle Sauvaj Library Cassell, London, 1954.

Berry Edward, *Shakespeare's Comic Rites,* Cambridge University Press, Cambridge, 1984.

Berry Ralph, *Shakespeare and the Awareness of the Audience.* Macmillan, London, 1985.

Berry Ralph, *Shakespeare and Social Class,* Humanities Press International, New Jersey, 1988 rep. 1989.

Berry Ralph, *Shakespearean Structures,* Macmillan, London, 1981.

Biswas D.C., Shakespeare's Transmutation in *'Measure for Measure'* in *Essays and Studies I,* Jadavpur University Press, Calcutta, 1968.

Biswas D.C., 'Some Shakespearean themes in the dark comedies' in *Essays and Studies* II, Jadavpur University Press, Calcutta, 1972.

Biswas D.C., *Shakespeare's Treatment of his Sources in the Comedies,* Jadavpur University Press, Calcutta, 1971.

Boas F.S., *Shakespeare and his Predecessors,* Mr. John Murry Pub. Ltd., London, 1896 Indian rep. 1963.

Bose Amalendu, 'A Preface to Shakespearean Comedy' in *Essays on Shakespeare Quarter Centenary Memorial Volume* Burdwan University, Orient Longman, Bombay 1965.

Boulton Marjorie, *The Anatomy of Drama,* Kalyani Publishers, New Delhi, 1966 rep 1992.

Bradbrook M.C., *Shakespeare the Craftsman,* Chatto and Windus, London, 1969.

Bradbrook M.C., *Shakespeare the Poet in his World,* Methuen, Gt. Britain, 1978 rep. 1980.

Bradbrook M.C., *The Collected Papers Vol. 4 Shakespeare in his context,*Harvester, New York, 1989.

Bradbrook M.C., *The Growth and Structure of Elizabethan Comedy,* Cambridge University Press, Cambridge, 1955 rep. 1973.

Bradbrook M.C., *The Living Monument Shakespeare and the Theatre of his time,* Cambridge University Press, Cambridge, 1979.

Bradbrook M.C., *The Rise of Common Player,* Chatto and Windus, London, 1979.

Brennan Anthony, *Shakespeare's Dramatic Structure,* Routledge and Kegan Paul, London, 1986.

Brockbank J.P., *On Shakespeare Versus Shakespeare and Karl Marx and Other Essays,* Basil Blackwell, Oxford 1989.

Bronstein Herbert, 'Shakespeare the Jew and *The Merchant of Venice*' in *Shakespeare Quarterly* 1969.

Brooke Stopford A., *On Ten Plays of Shakespeare,* Kalyani Publishers, Delhi, 1937 rep. 1988.

Brown J.R., *Shakespeare and his Comedies,* Methuen, London, 1957.

Brown J.R., 'The Presentation of Comedy: The First Ten Plays' in *Startford-Upon-Avon Shakesperian Comedy* 14, eds. Bradbury Malcolm and Palmer David, Edward Arnold, London, 1972.

Brown J.R., 'The interpretation of Shakespeare's Comedies' in *Shakespeare Survey* 8.

Bullough G., *Narrative and Dramatic Sources of Shakespeare I,* Routledge and Kegan Paul, London, 1957.

Calderwood James L., *Shakespeare Metadrama,* University of Minnesota Press, Minneapolis, 1971.

Charlton H.B., *Shakespearian Comedy,* Methuen, London, 1938 rep. 1960.

Chute Marchette, *Shakespeare of London,* Condor Book, Sovenir Press, Gt. Britain, 1977.

Cicero, *De Oratore* I and II, The Loeb Classical Library, tr. Sutton E.K., ed. Rackham H., William Heinman Ltd., London, 1942.

Coghill Nevill, *Shakespeare's Professional Skills,* Cambridge University Press, Cambridge, 1965.

Coghill Nevill, 'The basis of Shakespearean Comedy' in *Shakespeare Criticism* 1935-60, ed. Riddler Anne, London, 1963.

Colman E.A.M., *The Dramatic Use of Bawdy,* Longman, London, 1974.

Cook Judith, *Shakespeare's Players,* Harper and Row, London, 1983.

Cooper Lane, *An Aristotlean theory of Comedy,* Harcourt and Brace and Co., New York, 1922.

Corrigan R.W., *Comedy Meaning and Form,* Harper and Row, New York, 1981.

Cotton Nancy, 'Castrating Witches: Impotence and Magic in *The Merry Wives of Windsor*' in *Shakespeare Quarterly,* 1987.

Cox John, *Shakespeare and the Dramaturgy of Power,* Princeton University Press, New Jersey, 1989.

Crane Milton, *Shakespeare's Prose,* The University of Chicago Press, Chicago, 1953 rep. 1968.

Curtis M.H., 'Education and Apprenticeship' in *Shakespeare Survey* 17.

Daley Stuart, 'The Dispraise of the Country in *As You Like It*' in *Shakespeare Quarterly,* 1985.

Dante Alighieri, 'Epistle to Can Grande' in *Literary Criticism,* tr. and ed. Haller Robert S., Lincoln University Press, Nebraska, 1973.

Dean L.F., *Shakespeare Modern Essays in Criticism,* Oxford University Press, New York, 1957 rep. 1967.

Dent Allan, *World of Shakespeare Animals and Monsters,* Osprey, England, 1972.

Dollimore Jonathan and **Sinfield Alan,** *Political Shakespeare New Essays in Cultural Materialism,* Manchester University Press, Manchester, 1985.

Donaldson Ian, *The World Up-Side-Down,* Clarendon Press, Oxford, 1970.

Dover K.J., *Aristophanic Comedy,* B.T. Batsford Ltd., London, 1972.

Dowden Edward, *Shakespeare A Critical Study of His Mind and Art,* Routledge and Kegan Paul Ltd., London, 1875 rep. 1967.

Duckwarth George E., *The Nature of Roman Comedy,* Princeton University Press, New Jersey, 1952.

Dusinberre J., *Shakespeare and the Nature of Women,* Macmillan, Hong Kong, 1975.

Dutton Richard, *William Shakespeare,* Macmillan, London, 1989.

Eagleton Terry, *William Shakespeare,* Basil Blackwell Ltd., Oxford, 1986.

Echeruo Michael J.C., 'Shylock and Conditional Imagination' in *Shakespeare Quarterly,* 1971.

Edwards Philip, *Shakespeare a Writer's Progress,* Oxford University Press, Oxford, 1986.

Edwards Philip, *Shakespeare's Style Essays in honour of Kenneth Muir,* Cambridge University Press, Cambridge, 1980.

Eliot T.S., 'Four Elizabethan Dramatist' in *Selected Essays,* Faber, London, 2nd edn. 1934.

Engle Lars, 'Thrift in Blessing Exchange and Explanation in *The Merchant of Venice*' in *Shakespeare Quarterly*, 1986.

Enright D.J. and **Chickera E.D.,** *English Critical Text,* Oxford University Press, Delhi, 1962.

Erickson Peter, *Patriarchal Structures in Shakespeare's Drama,* University Press, Berkeley, 1985.

Erickson Peter and **Kahn Coppelia,** *Shakespeare's Rough Magic, Renaissance Essays in Honor of C. L. Barber,* University of Delaware Press, New York, 1985.

Evans Bertrand, *Shakespeare's Comedies,* Clarendon Press, Oxford, 1960.

Evans Malcolm, 'Deconstructing Shakespeare's Comedies' in *Alternative Shakespeare,* New Accents, ed. Drakakis John, Methuen, London, 1985.

Evans Malcolm, 'Mercury Versus Apollo A reading of *Love's Labour's Lost*' in *Shakespeare Quarterly,* 1975.

Evanthius, 'De Tragaedia et Comedia' in *European Theories of Drama,* tr. Rogers Mildred ed. Clarke Barrett H., Appleton, New York, 1918.

Everett B., 'Two Damned Cruces *Othello* and *Twelfth Night*' in *The Review of English Studies* 38 No. 146, May 1986.

Ford Boris, *The Age of Shakespeare,* The New Pelican Guide to English Literature, Penguin, London, 1982.

Fraser Antonia, *The Weaker Vessel Womans Lot in Seventeenth Century England,* Widenfield and Nicolson, London, 1984.

Frazer James George, *The Golden Bough A Study in Magic and Religion,* Macmillan, Gt. Britain, 1922 rep. 1983.

French Marilyn, *Shakespeare's Division of Experience,* Cape, London, 1982.

Frye Northrop, 'Old and New Comedy' in *Shakespeare Survey* 22.

Garber Marjorie, *Coming of Age in Shakespeare,* Methuen, London, 1981.

Gordon George, *Shakespearian Comedy and Other Studies,* Oxford University Press, Gt. Britain, 1944 rep. 1945.

Goldstein N.L., *Love's Labour's Lost* and the Renaissance Vision of Love in *Shakespeare Quarterly,* 1974.

Granville-Barker H. and **Harrison G.B.,** *A Companion to Shakespeare,* Cambridge University Press, Cambridge, 1962.

Granville-Barker H., *Prefaces to Shakespeare* 2, Princeton University Press, New Jersey, 1946-47.

Greenblatt Stephen, *Shakespearean Negotiations The Circulation of Social Energy in Renaissance England,* Clarendon Press, Oxford, 1988 rep. 1990.

Greene Thomas M., *'Love's Labour's Lost* The Grace of Society' in *Shakespeare Quarterly,* 1971.

Grivelet Michael, 'Shakespeare as Corrupter of Words' in *Shakespeare Quarterly,* 1971.

Hankins John Erskine, *Background of Shakespeare's Thought,* The Harvester Press, Gt. Britain, 1978.

Hapgood Robert, 'Shakespeare and the Rivalists' in *Shakespeare Survey* 15.

Harbage Alfred, *Shakespeare Without Words,* Harvard University Press, Massachusetts, 1972.

Hassel R.C. Jr., *Faith and Folly in Shakespeare's Romantic Comedies,* University of Georgia Press, Athens, 1980.

Hattaway Michael, 'Drama and Society' in *The Cambridge Companion to English Renaissance Drama,* eds. Braunmuller A.R. and Hattaway Michael, Cambridge University Press, Cambridge, 1980.

Hayles Nancy K., 'Disguise in *As You Like It* and *Twelfth Night*' in *Shakespeare Survey,* 32.

Hey Cyrus, *'Love's Labour's Lost'* in *Shakespeare Quarterly,* 1962.

Hochman Stanley, *McGraw Hill Encyclopedia of World Drama* 5, McGraw Hill, U.S.A., 1984.

Holderness Graham, *The Shakespeare Myth,* Manchester University Press, New York, 1988.

Holmes Martin, *Shakespeare and Burbage,* Philimore and Co. Ltd., London, 1978.

Honneyman David, *Closer to Shakespeare,* Merlin Books Ltd., Braunton Devon, Gt. Britain, 1990.

Horace, *Ars Poetics* in *A History of Literary Criticism,* eds. Wimsatt W.K. and Brooks Cleanth, Oxford and I.B.H. Pvt. Co. Ltd., Delhi, 1957.

Hubler Edward, 'The Range of Shakespeare's Comedy' in *Shakespeare Quarterly,* 1964.

Hunter R.G., *Shakespeare and the Comedy of Forgiveness,* Columbia University Press, New York, 1965.

Jenkins Harold, *As You Like It* in *Shakespeare Survey* 8.

Kahn Coppelia, *Man's Estate Masculine Identity in Shakespeare,* University of California Press, Berkeley, 1981.

Knight G.W., *Shakespeare and Religion,* Routledge and Kegan Paul Ltd., London, 1967.

Knight G.W., *The Golden Labyrinth,* Phoenix House Ltd., London, 1962.

Knight W.N., 'Equity *The Merchant of Venice* and William Lambarde' in *Shakespeare Survey* 27.

Kott Jan, *Shakespeare Our Contemporary,* Routledge Chapman and Hall, London, 1965 rep. 1988.

Kronenfield Judy K., 'Pastoral Ideas and *As You Like It*' in *Shakespeare Quarterly,* 1978.

Legatt Alexander, *Ben Jonson His Vision and His Art,* Methuen, London, 1981.

Legatt Alexander, *Shakespeare's Comedy of Love,* Methuen, London, 1974.

Lenz Carolyn R.S., Greene Gayle, Neely C.T., *The Woman's Part,* University of Illinois Press, Urbana, 1980.

Levin Harry, *Shakespeare and the Revolution of Times,* Oxford University Press, New York, 1976.

Loomba Ania, *Gender Race Renaissance Drama,* Oxford University Press, Delhi, 1992.

Luce T. James, *Ancient Writers Greece and Rome* II, Charles Scribner's Sons, New York, 1982.

Lynch Kathleen, *The Social Mode of Restoration Comedy,* Macmillan, London, 1926.

Mac Carey W.T., '*The Comedy of Errors* A Different Kind of Comedy' in *New Literary History* XI no. 3, 1978.

Mackay Maxim, '*The Merchant of Venice* a reflection of the early conflict between courts of law and courts of equity' in *Shakespeare Quarterly,* 1964.

Maitra Sitanghshu, *Shakespeare's Comic Idea,* Firma K.L. Mukhopadhyay, Calcutta, 1960.

Matus Irvin Leigh, *Shakespeare The Living Record,* Macmillan, Hong Kong, 1991.

Mc Donald Russ, *Shakespeare and Jonson Jonson and Shakespeare,* The Harvester Press, Gt. Britain, 1988.

Mac Farland Thomas, *Shakespeare's Pastoral Comedy,* The University of North Carolina Press, Chapel Hill, 1972.

Mc Peek James A.S., *A Midsummer Night's Dream* in *Shakespeare Quarterly,* 1972.

Meredith George, 'An Essay on Comedy and Uses of Comic Spirit' in *Meredith and Bergson Comedy,* ed. Sypher Wylie, The John Hopkins University Press, London. 1956 rep. 1983.

Milward Peter, *Religious Background,* Sidwick and Jackson, London, 1973.

Mincoff Marco, 'Shakespeare and Lyly' in *Shakespeare Survey* 14.

Montrose Louis Adrian, 'Social Process in *As You like It*' in *Shakespeare Quarterly,* 1981.

More Thomas, *Complete Works of St Thomas More,* eds. Surtz Edward and Hunter J. H., Yale University Press, New Haven, 1965.

Muir Kenneth, *Interpretations of Shakespeare British Academy Shakespeare Lectures,* Clarendon Press, Oxford, 1986.

Muir Kenneth, Halio Jay L., Palmer D.J., *Shakespeare Man of the Theater Proceedings of the Second Congress of the International Shakespeare Association 1981,* University of Delaware Press, New York, 1983.

Muir Kenneth, *The Singularity of Shakespeare,* English Texts and Studies, Liverpool University Press, Liverpool, 1977.

Neely C.T., *Broken Nuptials in Shakespeare's Plays,* Yale University Press, New Haven, 1985.

Nelson T.G.A., *Comedy The Theory of Comedy in Literature Drama and Cinema,* Oxford University Press, London. 1990.

Nevo Ruth, *Comic Transformations in Shakespeare,* Methuen, London, 1980.

Newman Karen, 'Portia's Ring' in *Shakespeare, Quarterly,* 1980.

Nicoll Allardyce, *British Drama,* George C Harrap & Co. Ltd. London, 1925 rep. 1962.

Nicoll Allardyce, *World Drama,* George C. Harrap & Co. Ltd., London, 1949 rep. 1951.

Nutall A.D., *A New Mimesis,* Methuen, London, 1983.

Palmer D.J., *Comic Characters' of Shakespeare,* Macmillan, London, 1949.

Palmer D.J., *Comedy,* A Case Book, Macmillan, London, 1984.

Parker G.F., *Johnson's Shakespeare,* Clarendon Press, Oxford, 1989.

Patterson Annabel, *Shakespeare and Popular Voice,* Basil Blackwell, Cambridge, 1989.

Philips O'Hood, *Shakespeare and the Lawyers,* Methuen, London, 1972.

Pisan Christine–de, *The Book of the City of Ladies,* tr. and ed. Richards Early Jeffrey, Pan, London, 1983.

Plato, *Philebus and Epinomis,* tr. Taylor A.E., ed. Klibansky Raymond, Dawsons and Pall Mall, London, 1956 rep. 1972.

Potts L.J., *Comedy,* Hutchinson University Library, London, 1948 rep. 1960.

Priestly J.B., *The English Comic Characters,* Bodley Head, London, 1963.

Raddadi Mongi, *Davenant's Adaptations of Shakespeare Ada* Universitatis Upasaliensis, Studiaca Anglistica Upasaliensia, Uppasala, 1979.

Razzell Peter, *William Shakespeare the Anatomy of Enigma,* Caliban Books, London, 1990.

Reese M.M., *Shakespeare His World and His Work,* Edward Arnold Publishers Ltd., London, 1953 rep. 1980.

Rees R.J., *English Literature An Introduction to Foreign Readers,* Macmillan India, Madras, 1973 rep. 1992.

Roberts Jeanne Addison, '*Merry Wives* as a Hallow 'en play' in *Shakespeare Survey* 25.

Ronald Margaret Loftus, 'English Marriage and Shakespeare' in *Shakespeare Quarterly,* 1979.

Rowse A.L., *Discovering Shakespeare,* Weidenfield and Nicolson, London, 1989.

Rowse A.L., *Shakespeare's Globe His Intellectual and Moral Outlook,* Wiedenfield and Nicolson, London, 1981.

Rowse A.L., *Shakespeare's Self Portrait Passages from his Works,* Macmillan, London, 1966.

Salgado Gamini, *English Drama A Critical Introduction,* Edward Arnold, London, 1980.

Salinger Leo, *Shakespeare and the Traditions of Comedy,* Cambridge University Press, Cambridge, 1974.

Salinger L.G., 'The Design of *Twelfth Night*' in *Shakespeare Quarterly,* 1958.

Sandbach F.H., *The Comic Theatre of Greece and Rome,* Chatto and Windus, London, 1977.

Sargent R.M., 'Sir Thomas Elyot and the Integrity of *The Two Gentlemen of Verona*' in *PMLA* 65 no. 6, 1950.

Schanzer Ernest, 'The Marriage Contracts in *Measure for Measure*' in *Shakespeare Survey* 13.

Schwartz Murray M. and Kahn Coppelia, *Representing Shakespeare,* John Hopkins University Press, Baltimore, 1980.

Scragg Leah, *Shakespeare's Mouldy Tales,* Longman, London, 1992.

Sen Gupta S.C., *A Shakespeare Manual,* Oxford University Press, Delhi, 1977 rep. 1987.

Sen Gupta S.C., *Shakespearian Comedy,* Oxford University Press, Delhi, 1950 rep. 1961.

Sen Gupta S.C., *The Whirligig of Time,* Orient Longman, Delhi, 1961.

Shirley Frances A., *Swearing and Perjury in Shakespeare's Plays,* George Allen and Unwin, London, 1979.

Singh Sarup, 'A Note on *As You Like It*' in *The Indian Journal of English Studies* 4 no.11, 1963.

Smidt Kristian, *Unconformities in Shakespeare's Early Comedies,* Macmillan, London, 1986.

Smidt Warren D., Shakespeare's Shylock' in *Shakespeare Quarterly,* 1964.

Speaight Robert, *Shakespeare The Man and His Achievement,* J.M. Dent, London, 1977.

Stanbury Joan, 'The Four Young Lovers In *A Midsummer Night's Dream*' in *Shakespeare Survey* 35.

Steadman John M., 'Falstaff as Actaeon A Dramatic Emblem in *Shakespeare Survey* 35.

Stone Lawrence, *The Crisis of Aristocracy* 1558-1641, Clarendon Press, Oxford, 1965.

Stone Lawrence, *The Family Sex and Marriage in England* 1500-1800, Ernest Benn, London, 1970.

Swinden Patrick, *An Introduction to Shakespeare's Comedies,* Macmillan, London, 1973.

Thakur D., 'A new look at *Midsummer Night's Dream*' in *The Indian Journal of English Studies* 7, 1966.

Tillyard E.M.W., *Essays Literary and Educational* Chatto and Windus, London, 1962

Tillyard E.M.W., *Shakespeare's Early Comedies* Chatto and Windus, London, 1966 rep. 1983.

Tillyard E.M.W., *The Elizabethan World Picture,* Chatto and Windus, London, 1960.

Traversi Derek, *William Shakespeare the Early Comedies,* Longman and Green Co. Britain, 1960.

Tennenhouse Leonard, *Power on Display the Politics of Shakespeare's Genres,* Methuen, London, 1986.

Ungerer Gustav, 'Two Items of Spanish Pronunciation in *Love's Labour's Lost*' in *Shakespeare Quarterly*, 1963.

Van Loan Thomas F., *Role Playing in Shakespeare*, University of Toronto Press, Toronto, 1978.

Waller Gary, *Shakespeare's Comedy*, Longman, London, 1991.

Weiss Theodore, *The Breath of Clowns and Kings*, Chatto and Windus, London, 1971.

Williams Penry, *The Tudor Regime*, Clarendon Press, Oxford, 1979.

Wilson John Dover, *Shakespeare's Happy Comedies their Origin and Special Quality*, Cambridge University Press, Cambridge, 1938.

Womack Peter, *Ben Jonson Re-reading Literature*, Basil Blackwell Ltd., New York, 1987.

INDEX